OF DOUBT AND PROOF

Of Doubt and Proof *highlights issues of considerable importance for the social sciences, not least for lawyers and others such as anthropologists concerned with what Bourdieu called the 'juridical field'. Its comparative scope, with studies of ritual and judicial processes in Africa, Asia and Europe, is especially impressive and enhances its originality.*

Ralph Grillo, University of Sussex, UK

Doubt is not the opposite of belief, as anthropologists have recently shown, but depends upon belief and in turn helps to constitute it. This book, in writing that is both precise and wonderfully imaginative, explores this apparent paradox in relation to the legal terrain, where doubt is routinely cast and then dispelled through compelling public performances. In the process, the book – showing how law and ritual may have much more in common than formerly supposed – innovatively ranges across settings from asylum courts in France, Denmark and the UK, through Indian temple consultations, to Chinese divination. It ambitiously challenges us to think beyond the level of the obvious, while also making a thoughtful and rigorous contribution to the novel field of the anthropology of doubt and evidence.

Deborah James, London School of Economics, UK

This volume represents a crucial intervention into the question of what happens in institutional settings where doubt must be exercised, not as a presumed internal or affective state, but as a technique of knowledge formation. The cases presented here show that doubt is such a successful technique that it must be managed through a host of other social forms. These cases also show that it is often divinatory practices, and not courtroom judgements, in which doubt is more rigorously exercised in arriving at a decision. This is a collection that shows through felicitous juxtaposition of the legal and the ritual how the former shares far more sociological elements with the latter than is often acknowledged.

Melissa Demian, The Australian National University

Juris Diversitas

Rooted in comparative law, the *Juris Diversitas* series focuses on the interdisciplinary study of legal and normative mixtures and movements. Our interest is in comparison broadly conceived, extending beyond law narrowly understood to related fields. Titles might be geographical or temporal comparisons. They could focus on theory and methodology, substantive law, or legal cultures. They could investigate official or unofficial 'legalities', past and present and around the world. And, to effectively cross spatial, temporal, and normative boundaries, inter- and multi-disciplinary research is particularly welcome.

Forthcoming title in the series

Stateless Law
Evolving Boundaries of a Discipline
Edited by Helge Dedek and Shauna Van Praagh
ISBN 978 1 4724 2784 7

Of Doubt and Proof
Ritual and Legal Practices of Judgment

Edited by

DANIELA BERTI
CNRS/Centre for Himalayan Studies, Villejuif, France

ANTHONY GOOD
Edinburgh University, UK

GILLES TARABOUT
Laboratoire d'Ethnologie et de Sociologie Comparative
CNRS/Nanterre University, France

ASHGATE

Published by
Ashgate Publishing Limited
Wey Court East
Union Road
Farnham
Surrey, GU9 7PT
England

Ashgate Publishing Company
110 Cherry Street
Suite 3-1
Burlington, VT 05401-3818
USA

www.ashgate.com

British Library Cataloguing in Publication Data
A catalogue record for this book is available from the British Library

The Library of Congress has cataloged the printed edition as follows:
Of doubt and proof : ritual and legal practices of judgment / by Daniela Berti, Anthony Good and Gilles Tarabout.
pages cm. – (Juris diversitas)
Includes bibliographical references and index.
ISBN 978-1-4724-3451-7 (hardback) – ISBN 978-1-4724-3452-4 (ebook) – ISBN 978-1-4724-3453-1 (epub) 1. Law and anthropology. 2. Belief and doubt. 3. Law and religion. I. Berti, Daniela, editor. II. Good, Anthony, editor. III. Tarabout, Gilles, editor.
K487.A57O33 2015
340/.115–dc23

2014030875

ISBN 9781472434517 (hbk)
ISBN 9781472434524 (ebk – PDF)
ISBN 9781472434531 (ebk – ePUB)

MIX
Paper from responsible sources
FSC® C013985
www.fsc.org

Printed in the United Kingdom by Henry Ling Limited, at the Dorset Press, Dorchester, DT1 1HD

Contents

List of Figures

Notes on Contributors

Daniela Berti is a research fellow at the National Centre for Scientific Research (CNRS) in Paris, and a member of the Centre for Himalayan Studies at Villejuif. Her research in North India focuses on ritual interactions, politico-ritual roles and practices formerly associated with kingship, on 'Hindutva' entrenchment in local society, and on the Indian judicial system. She recently coordinated with Gilles Tarabout an international team project entitled 'Just-India: A Joint Programme on Justice and Governance in India and South Asia' (2009–2013).

Véronique Bouillier is directrice de recherche at CNRS, and a member of the Centre d'Etudes de l'Inde et de l'Asie du Sud, Paris. She has studied religious communities in Nepal and India and written extensively on sociological aspects of Hindu asceticism. She is presently studying French judicial processes, focusing on cases involving people of South Asian origin living in France. Her published work includes 'French law courts and South Asian litigants' in *Cultural Expertise and Litigation: Patterns, Conflicts, Narratives*, edited by Livia Holden (Routledge, 2011).

Jan Budniok is a lecturer at the Department of Anthropology and African Studies at the University of Hamburg (Germany). His research interests cover judges and the judiciary in Ghana, the anthropology of the state, political anthropology, anthropology of law, the legal profession, and elite and middle-class formation in Africa.

Antoine Garapon, PhD, is a former juvenile court judge, Chevalier de la Légion d'Honneur and Secretary-General of the Institut des Hautes Etudes sur la Justice (IHEJ), and is on the editorial committee of the journal *Esprit*. His publications include *Le Gardien des promesses, le juge et la démocratie* (Odile Jacob, 1996), *Bien juger. Essai sur le rituel judiciaire* (Odile Jacob, 1997), *Des crimes qu'on ne peut ni punir, ni pardonner* (Odile Jacob, 2002), *Juger en Amérique et en France. Culture juridique française et common law* (with Ioannis Papadopoulos, Odile Jacob, 2003), *Peut-on réparer l'histoire? Colonisation, esclavage, Shoah* (Odile Jacob, 2008) and *La raison du moindre État. Le néolibéralisme et la justice* (Odile Jacob, 2010). In 2013 he was commissioned by the French Minister of Justice to report on the role of judges and prosecutors, producing *La Prudence et l'Autorité* (with Sylie Perdriolle and Boris Bernabé, Odile Jacob, 2014). He also directs the Bien commun collection at Michalon Publishing and hosts a weekly radio programme, 'Le bien commun', on France-culture.

Anthony Good is Emeritus Professor of Social Anthropology at the University of Edinburgh. He was also a one-time reserve wicketkeeper for Peradeniya University staff cricket team, Sri Lanka. His research interests cover Tamil Nadu, South India and Sri Lanka. He frequently acts as an expert witness in asylum appeals involving Sri Lankan Tamils. His recent research concerns uses of expert evidence in British asylum courts and (with Robert Gibb) a comparative study of asylum processes in the UK and France. His publications include *Worship and the Ceremonial Economy of a Royal South Indian Temple* (Edwin Mellen Press, 2004) and *Anthropology and Expertise in the Asylum Courts* (Routledge-Cavendish, 2007).

Stéphanie Homola has a PhD in social anthropology from the École des Hautes Études en Sciences Sociales (EHESS), Paris and is Visiting Fellow at the Internationales Kolleg für Geisteswissenschaftliche Forschung, Erlangen. Her research deals with mantic practices in contemporary China and Taiwan as the crossroads between religious, Confucian and scientific traditions. Her recent publications include 'Pursue good fortune and avoid calamity: the practice and status of divination in contemporary Taiwan', *Journal of Chinese Religions* (2013) and 'La relation de maître à disciple en question: transmission orale et écrite des savoirs divinatoires en Chine et à Taïwan', *Extrême-Orient, Extrême-Occident* (2013).

Tobias Kelly holds a Personal Chair in Social Anthropology at the University of Edinburgh. His research interests include human rights and legal anthropology. He has carried out field research in Israel/Palestine, at the UN in Geneva and in the UK, and he has worked at the Birzeit University Institute of Law, the LSE's Crisis States Programme, and the Centre for Socio-Legal Studies, Oxford. His publications include *Law, Violence and Sovereignty among West Bank Palestinians* (Cambridge University Press, 2006), and *This Side of Silence: Human Rights, Torture and the Recognition of Cruelty* (University of Pennsylvania Press, 2011).

Carolina Kobelinsky is a Research Fellow at the Ecole des Hautes Etudes Hispaniques et Ibériques, Casa de Velázquez, Madrid. Her interests cover migration and asylum policies, ethnography of the everyday and the anthropology of the state. She has worked at EHESS Paris (Postdoctoral ERC Programme), and St Antony's College, Oxford (2012/13 Deakin Fellow). Her publications include *L'accueil des demandeurs d'asile. Une ethnographie de l'attente* (Editions du Cygne, 2010) and *Enfermés dehors. Enquêtes sur le confinement des étrangers* (edited with Chowra Makaremi) (Editions du Croquant, 2009).

Gilles Tarabout is directeur de recherche at CNRS and member of the Centre for Ethnology and Comparative Sociology (LESC) at University of Paris West-Nanterre. His research focuses especially on relationships between society and religion in Kerala (South India). He has recently been coordinating with Daniela Berti an international research programme funded by the Agence Nationale de la Recherche (ANR), entitled 'Just-India: A Joint Programme on Justice and Governance in India and South Asia'.

Zachary Whyte holds a DPhil from the University of Oxford, and recently completed a postdoctoral fellowship at the University of Copenhagen. He works with asylum seekers and refugees in Denmark and is interested in intersections of transnationality, state practices, uncertainty and everyday life. His recent publications include 'Enter the myopticon', *Anthropology Today* (2011) and 'Asyl, insh'allah: Tro og mistro i det danske asylsystem', in *Islam og Muslimer i Danmark*, edited by M. Holm Pedersen and M. Rytter (Museum Tusculanums Press, 2011). His most recent fieldwork is on refugees at Danish language centres.

Foreword[1]

What a good idea to bring together in one volume such varied contributions, covering such different contexts! The table of contents is an anthropological argument in itself. This collection is in fact based on two assumptions: first, that the separation between supposedly rational justice and other forms of procedure should not be seen as absolute; second, that it is more interesting to consider a judge's decision in terms of its opposite, or perhaps its precedent, namely doubt, rather than positively. Both aims are fully achieved.

The approach adopted here is the exact opposite of the perspective from which judgment is usually addressed by lawyers. The latter, in fact, tend to separate the judgment from the event of judging, detaching it from both the circumstances of the case and procedural questions. They disembody the court's decision, in that they consider only its contribution to a normative structure and its role in the incremental construction of law, while neglecting its search for the truth of the facts.

But as this book shows, if one wishes to get to the heart of the act of judging, it is necessary to travel in the opposite direction. Procedural rules are more interesting than substantive rules; how judges rule on questions of fact is more indicative of a culture than the legal solutions they arrive at; tribunals that are usually overlooked, such as asylum courts, are more revealing than higher courts dealing with 'big' cases; issues of credibility are more interesting than great constitutional debates. We must return to the flesh and blood persons who render justice.

Legal orthodoxy automatically opposes so-called scientific evidence to magico-religious evidence: the former is seen as incompatible with the latter and has, moreover, replaced it historically. What is the point, then, of saying any more about that earlier form? Leave it to the anthropologists. But this book proves the opposite: it shows the usefulness of thinking about them together. To understand this, it is illuminating to draw a comparison with economic anthropology. Marcel Hénaff shows that, contrary to widespread belief, the 'commercial currency' on which today's economists work and to which they apply their scientific theorems, has not supplanted the ceremonial currency used to make offerings and communicate with foreign groups, but the two have always coexisted.[2] This leads to two conclusions: there were many economies in traditional societies and, conversely, symbolic meanings continue to exist in today's economy. The same

---

1 Translated from the French by Anthony Good.

2 Marcel Hénaff (2002) *Le Prix de la vérité. Le don, l'argent, la philosophie*, Paris: Seuil, pp. 389ff.

applies to modes of magico-religious evidence or ritual, vis-à-vis the methodical search for truth. The link between them is, precisely, the role of doubt.

It would be mistaken to believe that ritual leads automatically to an irrational form of truth, through a mechanism in which human opinions have no place – as if the oracles were absolutely crucial; as if the transcendent intervened directly in the process. In fact, many studies have demonstrated that ritual is a framework that allows great latitude to its performers. Only fieldwork can tell us that. In all these procedures we encounter a fixed part, corseted by rites or procedure, and a more dynamic and interactive part: these are not mutually exclusive but it is a question of proportion.

That is why the judge's conviction is not fully reducible to reason: it always involves witness credibility on one hand and beliefs regarding 'types of truth' on the other. Doubt, as this book shows us, may take transitive form – that is, between the beliefs *of* the institutions and the belief *in* institutions.

The methods adopted in this book are in line with the perspectives of several authors who have renewed our understanding of the law in recent years, starting with the approach of Michel Foucault, who opposed two stories of truth. There is an *internal* story taking scientific truth as its standard and constantly seeking to correct itself starting from 'its own regulatory principles'. The second, *external*, story is forged not out of a quest for truth, but from observing the different places where truth is formed and where reason, subjectivization and assertions of power combine in particular ways. In so doing, Foucault reverses several assumptions from classical debates on judicial truth. An external account of truth does not address the oppositions between truth and falsehood, reality and illusion, scientific and non-scientific, or rational and irrational, but has regard to the practices that constitute them. 'Of all the social practices for which historical analysis allows us to locate the emergence of new forms of subjectivity, legal practices or, more precisely, judicial practices are the most important.'[3] Foucault comes close to seeing in these practices the matrix of other forms of philosophical, rhetorical and empirical knowledge.

Foucault criticizes philosophy (but we could extend this complaint to legal doctrine or even comparative law) for restricting itself to legal theory, to rules, and for remaining highly impermeable to practice, starting with judicial practice – that is, with the actual organization of discourse in the trial. But the closer you get to actual practice, the more complex does the object become, because a trial – we might say, plagiarizing Marcel Mauss – is a total legal fact. It is at once a social event, a demonstration of power and a legal act, or more accurately a constellation of legal acts (requests, production of documents during the procedure, judgment); at once produced by law and producing law.

---

3 Michel Foucault (2001 [1974]) 'La vérité et les formes juridiques', in *Dits et écrits*, vol. 1: *1954–1975*, ed. François Ewald and Daniel Defert, Paris: Collection Quarto, Gallimard, pp. 1406–1514, at p. 1408.

Doubt is the equivalent of deliberation in the progression towards *intime conviction* – that is to say in the passage from subjectivity to objectivity. A witness is already a secondary judge of a situation which he objectifies through his testimony, and a judge is also a secondary witness, except that the reality he takes into account is that of the hearing rather than external reality. Etymology attests to this ambiguity between witness and judge. Indeed, in Latin *arbiter* means witness as much as judge (*arbiter* has two meanings, a witness and he who decides): however, *arbiter* denotes a witness who sees without being seen, as opposed to *testis* (from *tertis*, third) who is a witness in full view, acting as guarantor of a legal transaction.[4] A witness is always a third party in relation to the action, and in relation to the protagonists in the case.

A judge is a witness of witnesses, an observer of those who have seen. Judges, one might say, are public witnesses. Their third-party judgments are given the power to transform the truth claims of the parties, the investigating judge (*juge d'instruction*) or the prosecutor into recognized truths, based on indications to which they grant the status of 'evidence'. Until the judgment, the provisional truth produced by the investigating judge has no objective value; it remains a subjective claim, in competition with others, demanding to be adopted by the judges, the jury and, more profoundly still, by all those who watch them judge; that is the meaning of 'in open court'. That is why, according to Hannah Arendt, the act of judging should not be confused with an action. The judge, for her, is comparable to the audience of a play. In a theatre, in fact, none of the actors can take a holistic view of the plot insofar as the protagonists are caught up in the 'tragic bias of action'.[5] Whereas investigating judges or prosecutors engage in positive actions to find the truth and prosecute the perpetrators, trial judges do not: they punish the actions of others through the act of judging.

'Judgment', said Jean Carbonnier, 'is a doubt that decides'.[6] But on what should this reflection be brought to bear: on 'doubt' or on 'doubting'? Everything hangs on the transition from noun to verb, from a moral sentiment that permeates a subject or even an attitude towards life (scepticism), to an action – that is, a result of the will or even a professional gesture. Habit, repetitive cases or automatisms must not exhaust the judge's ability to doubt. Doubt for a judge is the equivalent of curiosity for a scientist or surprise for a philosopher – that is to say, a way of preserving a sense of the novelty of life. Doubt is thus not a form of technical knowledge, but a technique of knowledge, a way for judges to ignore what they already know about a case. Doubt is the interior mirror in the presumption of

4 Emile Benveniste (1969) *Le vocabulaire des institutions indo-européennes: 2, Pouvoir, droit, religion*, Paris: Editions de Minuit, p. 120.

5 Myriam Revault d'Allonnes (2002) *Doit-on moraliser la politique?*, Paris: Bayard, p. 78.

6 Jean Carbonnier (1978) *Sociologie juridique* (2nd edn), Paris: Presses Universitaires de France, Collections Thémis, pp. 135–6.

innocence. The latter requires him to act 'as if' the accused was not guilty, and therefore as if the accusation might be unfair.

The action of doubting can be decomposed into three mental operations. The first operation of judgment is to organize the 'putting in doubt'. To do so, the judge must suspend any judgment already made, and of which he is often himself unaware; he must resist any implicit prejudgments – that is to say, presuppositions of which he is not aware but which result from unconscious identifications (what psychoanalysts call counter-transference). The first act of doubting is thus working on oneself to conjure up determinism. The judge must cultivate an open-minded disposition. This task is all the more difficult for French judges because the procedure puts them in a position where the matter has already been examined by other judges, hence by colleagues.

The second step consists of putting the evidence to the proof. He must test the hypotheses. The French expressions *intime conviction* and *for interieur* ('inner self') show the relationship between the external work of the hearing and the inner work of the judge. The judge must identify with the position of each protagonist in turn and consider it literally; in other words, he must take at face value stories that, by definition, are not directly accessible to him through the senses. Hence the role of imagination is essential to judgment. When judging, says Hannah Arendt, you must close your eyes; the judge is a 'blind poet'.[7]

The third operation is in symmetry with the first: the judge must emerge from doubt. This is by no means easy: the ending of doubt is also a deliberate operation, perhaps even more delicate. In effect, it is necessary to put an end to indecision so as not to sink into unending procrastination. If the doubt remains too strong, the judge has a rule at his disposal: *in dubio pro reo*, the doubt should benefit the accused. But what level of doubt? Common law distinguishes several standards of proof, according to which one must convince a jury 'beyond reasonable doubt'. The expression has some piquancy: could there be an unreasonable doubt? A professionalized doubt? Judges experience this every day. Academic lawyers should undergo the experience more often.

Antoine Garapon
Institut des hautes études sur la Justice, Paris

7 Hannah Arendt (1991) *Juger. Sur la philosophie politique de Kant*, trans. M. Revault d'Allonnes, Paris: Editions du Seuil, p. 105.

Introduction
Technologies of Doubt in Law and Ritual

Anthony Good, Daniela Berti and Gilles Tarabout

This book is based on a panel of the same title, which took place during the 12th European Association for Social Anthropology (EASA) Biennial Conference at Université Paris Ouest, Nanterre, in July 2012.[1] The panel directly addressed the theme of the conference as a whole, which was 'Uncertainty and Disquiet', and the fact that this major conference, the principal social anthropology event in the European conference calendar, was organized around this theme in itself indicates the importance and centrality of the topic, as does the roughly contemporary appearance of another edited volume arising from an entirely separate, and somewhat earlier workshop, also on the broad theme of doubt (Pelkmans 2013). This introduction explains the ideas behind the EASA panel and summarizes the issues raised by the chapters that follow. First, however, it examines ways in which notions of doubt and states of doubting have hitherto been understood in various academic disciplines, including, of course, law and social science. This necessarily involves also a consideration of the related notions of (un)certainty and the state or states of being (un)certain.

The distinctive approach underlying this volume – differentiating it from, for example, the monumental recent study by Hecht (2003) – is its focus on doubting as a technical matter. It seeks to show how judgments in both rituals and legal proceedings, in order to be accepted as valid and legitimate, must be backed up by an authority that arises partly from the judges' displayed mastery of techniques of doubting, and of dispelling doubt, and partly from their social and political position.[2] The individual contributions reveal and illustrate the range of techniques employed for generating and dispelling doubt in ritual contexts – broadly understood – and formal legal procedures. They aim thereby to deepen theoretical understandings of the social role of doubt, both in social science and in law.

---

1 The panel was an off-shoot of the Just-India programme on 'Justice and Governance in India and South Asia' (http://just-india.net) funded by the French National Research Agency (ANR-08-GOUV-064) and convened by Gilles Tarabout and Daniela Berti.

2 This link may, however, operate differently in law and ritual. The validity and legitimacy of legal judgments increase as one moves up the hierarchy of courts (from High Court to Supreme Court, for example). In ritual contexts, however, the authority accorded to a judgment may not relate to social hierarchy in this simple way; for example, the judgment of a medium drawn from a marginal or low status background may sometimes carry more legitimacy than that of a medium of high social status.

In all the legal or ritual contexts discussed below, doubt appears first and foremost as a technique controlled by ritual or legal professionals rather than as a question of belief. The forms such techniques take, and the contexts in which they are applied, vary widely however. The extent to which these techniques succeed in promoting or dispelling doubt also depend partly on the degrees of moral authority asserted by and awarded to those claiming the capacity to judge. Himalayan mediums must convince petitioners that they are voicing the views of the deity rather than pursuing agendas of their own (Berti, this volume), while Ghanaian judges must constantly regulate their social interactions, even with strangers, so as to evade suspicions of corruption (Budniok, this volume). In short, while there are many valid approaches that could be and have been taken towards notions of doubt – in theology and philosophy, for example – the approach taken here is a technical one, focusing on the techniques for creating and removing doubt employed by professional practitioners, be they lawyers in French Assize Courts, international cricket umpires or Taiwanese diviners (see, respectively, Bouillier, Good and Homola, this volume).

Law and Ritual

According to Pierre Bourdieu (1987), the 'rigorous' study of law requires us to take an external view of the juridical field. This involves transcending the internal debates of jurisprudence, where the key theoretical division separates *formalists*, such as Kelsen (1967) and Dworkin (1986), who see law as functioning as a wholly autonomous entity independent of any social influence whatever, from *legal realists*, also known as *instrumentalists*, like Holmes (1963) and Llewellyn (2000), who see law as directly reflecting the judge's own experience and the existing power relations within which the law is embedded, and hence as being a tool at the service of hegemonic groups. While the formalist approach – in effect, 'the professional ideology of legal scholars' (Bourdieu 1987: 814) – is clearly unlikely to win adherents among social anthropologists, the instrumentalist approach might seem more attractive in view of its attention to the socio-political context. In Bourdieu's view, however, both these rival discourses are equally guilty of ignoring the 'juridical field' within which the social practices of law are embedded, and which he defines as

> a 'field' whose specific logic is determined by two factors: on the one hand, by the specific power relations which give it its structure and which order the competitive struggles (or, more precisely, the conflicts over competence) that occur within it; and on the other hand, by the internal logic of juridical functioning which constantly constrains the range of possible actions and, thereby, limits the realm of specifically juridical solutions. (1987: 816)

The 'juridical field' connotes a different kind of social space from that connoted by the notion of 'legal system', which 'confuses the symbolic structure, the law properly so called, with the social system which produces it', and hence risks lapsing back into a new version of formalism. We must therefore distinguish the 'symbolic order of norms and doctrines' making up the legal system from the 'order of objective relations between actors' (Bourdieu 1987: 816).

Only a small minority of legal scholars take a perspective compatible with that of Bourdieu, by taking seriously not only issues arising outwith the field of law itself, but also the internal socio-structural features of law as a profession. Notably, William Twining, in a series of papers on evidence – now collected in Twining (2006) – has argued that, whereas lawyers are trained in detailed analysis of questions of law, the analysis of facts is largely neglected in legal pedagogy and hence highly underdeveloped in legal practice. The presentation of factual evidence by advocates, and its analysis by judges, therefore tends to reflect 'a tradition of relatively complacent commonsense empiricism' that devotes relatively little attention to problems and issues involved in processing, presenting and weighing factual information (Twining 2006: 28).[3] More recently, Chase (2005: 127) cites Bourdieu (1987) in support of his view that law is best seen simply as one among the various forms of dispute settlement available in any particular cultural context, albeit a rather specialized form in that it derives its coercive power from the state. While this is hardly an earth-shaking conclusion from an anthropological perspective, it is a relatively radical approach for a legal scholar to adopt because it runs counter to the dominant formalist approach.

While developing his position, Bourdieu (1987: 832) draws upon the theory of speech acts put forward by the linguistic philosopher J.L. Austin (1962). In Austin's terms, the language of legal advocates can be seen as above all perlocutionary in character. Rather than comprising mere locutionary statements aimed at *describing* 'what currently is', their pleadings are attempts to *persuade* judges and juries regarding 'what should be'. As for those judges and juries, their verdicts, once delivered – 'guilty', 'innocent, 'appeal dismissed' and so on – are illocutionary in that by being uttered they bring into being the state to which they refer, 'what from now on is'. The force of such illocutionary utterances is not usually intrinsic to the language used in itself, though it may be, as in the case of spells or mantras for example. Generally, however, it derives also from the social authority bestowed on a particular speaker, which may, according to context, derive ultimately from the coercive power of the state or some non-state institution such as a caste council

---

3 In an earlier paper, Twining compared legal and anthropological approaches, taking as a paradigm case Llewellyn and Hoebbel's study of Cheyenne dispute mechanisms (1941). He concluded that in such collaborations lawyers may need to make more adjustments than are required of anthropologists, but that whereas anthropologists find legal approaches too narrow and too unconcerned with the broader context, lawyers often find anthropological writing too generalized and lacking in technical detail (Twining 1973: 577–9).

or religious body, from the inherited or achieved position of the speaker, or from local tradition and custom.

While Bourdieu used Austin's ideas to develop his approach to the juridical field, anthropologists like Finnegan (1969) and Tambiah (1968, 1973) drew upon them in their analyses of ritual. Tambiah's position is especially relevant here, because he extended Austin's analysis beyond arguing that certain ritualized forms of language have illocutionary force, to contend that ritual *actions* can be interpreted in the same way. That is, non-verbal aspects of ritual can also be seen as 'perlocutionary' attempts to persuade others of the validity of some view or other, or 'illocutionary' attempts to bring about direct changes in the world.

Consider Evans-Pritchard's classic analysis of Zande magic, the case study also chosen by Chase (2005). The Zande word for ringworm means 'chicken-house sickness', and Zande explicitly comment on the resemblance between the scabby patches that this disease produces in children and lumps of chicken excrement. They go on to say that the disease may be caused by small children entering chicken-houses, which they frequently do, and eating the excrement, which they are believed to do. Moreover, they treat the disease by applying the ashes of chicken excrement to the child's skin at the infected places. Evans-Pritchard's explanation of this (1937: 487), if it can be so called, is simply to point out that the disease, its putative cause and its treatment are all known by the same term.

This Zande case would once have been explained (by Frazer 1955 for example) in terms of so-called 'sympathetic magic', as a mistaken assumption of affinity based upon similarities of appearance and/or physical contiguity. So, the argument runs from this perspective, Zande use the ashes of chicken excrement as a prophylactic, in the mistaken belief that it will have a therapeutic effect. Put another way, the assumption is that the Zande use analogy in a scientific – that is, a locutionary way – that their analogies are intended as statements about the world. Tambiah (1973: 216) offers an alternative to this notion of ritual as 'mistaken science'. He suggests that the process is more convincingly explicable as follows. There is a practical contiguity, in Zande daily life, between children and chicken-houses (and so chickens), and a perceived similarity between ringworm and chicken excrement. This is then elaborated as follows. Chicken excrement is an unwanted bodily product which the chicken eliminates from its metabolism. Ringworm is an unwanted bodily product which it is *desired* to eliminate from the child. Hence the desired analogy between chicken and ringworm may be stated as follows:

fowl: excretes bodily waste :: child: sheds scabs

The healing ritual which the Zande perform can then be seen as an attempt to transform the patient's condition so that the relationship applies to the second set of paired terms as well as to the first. It aspires to be an illocutionary, analogical act; an attempt to bring about, by its performance, the state of affairs to which it refers.

This approach has also been used in contexts relating to the creation or dispelling of doubt. Ahern (1979) extended Tambiah's analysis by suggesting that there are several forms of illocutionary ritual act: *strong* illocutionary acts where performers firmly believe that through proper performance of the rite it is possible to achieve the desired result and *weak* illocutionary acts where performers wish for a particular outcome, but do not believe this to be possible. This insight can be extended further than even Ahern attempted to do. Thus one might also imagine slightly less weak illocutionary acts where the result is desired but believed to be highly unlikely. For example, healing rituals may express the wish that a terminally ill person should have a long life or a sterile woman has children (Ahern 1979: 10). All rituals can then be seen as lying somewhere on a continuum between weak and strong, since the outcome – however properly performed and felicitous the rituals may be – is always uncertain, always open to doubt.[4] The uncertainness of the ritual outcome also serves to contrast ritual acts or speeches from legal decisions where the verdict, once pronounced, has a coercive effect for the people involved (a point also noted by Homola and Tarabout, in this volume).

Another way of addressing Austin's theory of speech acts in ritual studies has been developed by authors working on the idea of 'reflexivity', a concept used by Højbjerg (2002) as a way of studying how doubt relates to ritual action. Severi, for example, refers to Kuna shamans who, during ritual performances, are thought to cumulate within themselves contradictory yet non-exclusive and simultaneous identities. He notes how the perlocutionary effect of this formal difference is that the image of the shaman 'entertains a doubt about the always possible assimilation of his ordinary identity into a supernatural one' (Severi 2002: 38).

The relationship between law and ritual has always been a central theme in disciplines such as history, theology and anthropology because these two forms of social practice correspond in several ways. First, both are rule-bound, in that both rituals and legal proceedings risk being invalidated if improperly performed; both words and actions must be appropriate for their purpose. Second, both are commonly employed in processes of dispute settlement (see, for example, Gluckman 1965; Chase 2005). Third, as we have just seen, in both contexts language itself has power, either intrinsically or by virtue of the authority held by or delegated to the speaker. Finally, law is itself ritualized, in its actions, costumes and languages. This is in part designed to increase the authority of the decision reached but it also reminds us of the historical link between some key modern legal norms and procedures, such as the notion of 'reasonable doubt' and the role of the jury, and medieval ritual procedures such as ordeal (see Whitman 2008).

---

4 Ahern also notes that some ritual actions may be emotionally illocutionary; they are not expected to affect the outside world, but we feel better for having performed them. 'Kissing the picture of a loved one … is obviously not based on a belief that it will have a definite effect on the object which the picture represents. It … does not aim at anything; we act in this way and then feel satisfied' (Wittgenstein 1971: 31, quoted in Ahern 1979: 16).

Like Bourdieu, the contributors to this volume treat ritual or legal *practitioners* themselves as objects of study, rather than looking only at their decisions or at the contexts in which those decisions are made. They do so in several different ways, however, going beyond Bourdieu's perhaps rather narrow focus on personal interests and rivalries. In Tarabout's case, for example, it is a matter of the same issues of dispute being handled both by ritual and in strictly legal ways; here, the ritualized processes of dispute settlement generally come first, to be followed by resort to 'formal' legal procedures in situations where those ritual processes fail to produce a resolution acceptable to all parties. In other chapters (Berti, Good) different kinds of dispute are investigated, with a view to pointing out more generalizable similarities and differences between ritualized and legal processes of dispute within, broadly speaking, the same cultural context. In a number of other chapters (Bouillier, Whyte, Kobelinsky) the ritualization of the legal context itself – rituals employed, in large part, in the service of legitimacy and removal of doubt – is at issue. This is most directly evident in the chapter by Budniok, which describes how – through strict adherence to formal, ritualized legal procedures as well as scrupulous regulation of private lives that they believe are under intense scrutiny – Ghanaian judges resist suspicions of partiality and corruption. While formal legal procedures themselves are not directly under discussion in Homola's chapter, she notes that some European astrologers from the Middle Ages onwards have explicitly regarded their practices as 'judicial' both in the sense that they claim a similar degree of rigour for their procedures, and in the sense that, like formal law, they are potentially available to everyone. Rather than ritual serving to bolster the legitimacy of law, it is here rather the other way round.

Doubt, Uncertainty and Disbelief

We do not propose any essentialist definition of 'doubt', preferring the term to take on different but, we would argue, related senses in the various ethnographic contexts described below. Even so, it is worth considering briefly the relationship between 'doubt' and two (or four) other concepts with which it is often associated, '(un)certainty' and '(dis)belief'. Though 'doubt', 'uncertainty' and 'disbelief' have related meanings, they are not synonyms. Anderson (2006) for example, seems to assume a causal link whereby 'Uncertainty … can give rise to feelings of doubt'. For his part Pelkmans sees doubt as 'an active state of mind' which is 'unstable in the sense that it pushes for a resolution', whereas uncertainty merely provides 'the context in which doubt is activated' (2013: 3). In short, doubt implies agency ('triggering a need for resolution') whereas uncertainty does not. Nor is doubt equivalent to scepticism, which rejects *all* explanations on principle, because doubt implies the existence of a less doubted alternative. Indeed, the etymology of the word, in various European languages, implies the existence of two rival possibilities: doubt is, as Pelkmans neatly puts it, the state of 'being of two minds'.[5] Moreover, doubt is not the opposite of belief; indeed, belief implies the existence of doubt, without which it would not be 'belief' but 'knowledge' (Toren 2007: 308).[6] These two notions are not only mutually co-constitutive; they may also be temporally related (Pelkmans 2013: 4–5). Through the course of a ritual performance or legal hearing, for instance, one's initial beliefs may become clouded by doubt, which may in turn give way to fresh beliefs or even new certainties. Examples in the present volume include the emergence of an *intime conviction* in the minds of a French judge or jury (Bouillier, Kobelinsky) or granting 'the benefit of the doubt' in a British asylum claim (Good).

Uncertainty arises in two distinct forms: a phenomenon or event itself may be inherently uncertain ('objective uncertainty') or we may be uncertain about it in our own minds ('subjective uncertainty'). Writing in the field of molecular biology, Tannert, Elvers and Jandrig (2007) argue that objective uncertainty may be either epistemological or ontological in character (see also Van Asselt and Rotmans 2002) – that is, it may be caused by gaps in knowledge, or by the stochastic features of the situation itself. Epistemological uncertainty can in principle be overcome by acquiring more knowledge, through research, but decisions on ontological uncertainties can only be 'quasi-rational' because complete knowledge will, by definition, never be available. For example, no amount of prior research can fully remove uncertainty over how a proposed industrial development will affect a complex local ecosystem. Subjective uncertainty can also be sub-divided into what has been called 'moral uncertainty' (there are no clear moral rules for dealing with this precise situation, so decisions must be based on broader, more generic principles) and 'intuitional' uncertainty (where one can only decide on an appropriate course of action by drawing on general moral convictions and past experience). Thus these two forms of uncertainty are, respectively, rule-guided and intuition-guided.

Anderson (2006), taking an information science perspective, points out that when we begin to perform, or to play a part in performing, a complex task (drawing on the examples in this book, it might be a court hearing, a cricket match, a divination) we cannot determine in advance what information we will need in order to accomplish it. As we proceed through the performance, however, it becomes increasingly clear what information will be required, what processes are needed, and even – eventually – what the range of likely outcomes is going to be. This 'move from uncertainty to understanding' (Anderson 2006), which also involves transition from *problem formulation* to *problem-solving* (Byström and

5 'Although often equated with skepticism, doubt has more focus due to the implied presence of an alternative. At least, that is what the presence of the number two in *dubitare* – the Latin origin of the word – suggests, echoed in the German *zweifel* and the French *doter* [sic; *douter*]. Doubt, in this sense, is about 'being of two minds', about wavering between one possibility and another' (Pelkmans 2013: 4).

6 For a discussion of the relationship between knowledge and doubt as viewed from philosophy, see Rasmussen (1974).

Järvelin 1995), seems likely to characterize many ritual and legal procedures. Most relevantly for the present volume, Anderson (2006) explores the operation of doubt and uncertainty among skilled practitioners in the workplace. Her study suggests, for example, that among academic researchers doubt is associated with questions of relevance ('is this particular information or article relevant to the problem being investigated?') and with the limits to their current understanding, but also that uncertainty must be and is tolerated within quite wide limits, not least because it helps generate the excitement that drives researchers to explore new territory.

Kuhlthau's cognitive and affective approach to information seeking sees it as a process whereby uncertainty decreases as understanding increases. She identifies six stages in this process, though presumably these are best thought of as merging into one another rather than as wholly discrete. She labels these six stages *initiation*, when one becomes aware of one's lack of knowledge or understanding; *selection*, when the general issue or topic is identified; *exploration*, during which the information gathered initially appears inconsistent or incompatible; *formulation*, when the issue begins to be more precisely specified; *collection* of more relevant and better-focused information; and *presentation*, when one is able to explain one's new understanding to others (Kuhlthau 1993). These epistemological stages have corresponding affective states: thus, the anxieties associated with uncertainty and doubt at the initiation stage may increase during the exploration stage, but diminish during formulation and collection, and fade away almost completely by the end of the process (Kuhlthau and Tama 2001: 27).

In his brief eulogy of the positive role doubt should play in anthropology, Handelman argued that the discipline initially had an holistic and positivistic vision; it was assumed that 'the world of humankind could be known in its entirely if only one worked diligently enough at this' (1987: 310). Later, this unitary vision fragmented into numerous sub-disciplines which, nonetheless, produced specialists who saw themselves as 'experts in the creation of certainty about the validity of the knowledge they are expert in' (Handelman 1987: 310). What anthropologists finally learned as a result of this progression, Handelman argues, was that 'the phenomena of our social world are too complex to be grasped fully' (1987: 311). What is more, the most useful explanations are not necessarily the most complete (a theory that 'explains' everything is merely a tautology), but those which, by breaking down when pushed beyond a certain point, demonstrate clearly what they can explain and what they cannot. Clearly, the first two stages both corresponded, though on different scales, to the epistemological view of uncertainty just discussed, whereas the third and final stage represents a form of ontological uncertainty. There is, however, a peculiar methodological difficulty inherent in the ethnographic study of doubt, namely that it is extremely hard to express the nature of one's doubts until they have been partially resolved, at least to the extent that it has become possible to identify and articulate them. As Pelkmans notes, ethnographic approaches 'tend to register only *articulated* thought and *performed* action, and catching doubt in midair is therefore far from a straightforward task' (2013: 5; emphasis in the original).

Any discussion of doubt and uncertainty is likely also to conjure up, for a contemporary audience, apparently related notions regarding risk (Anderson 2006, 2008). That notion does not figure largely in the studies collected here, however, and indeed Boholm (2003: 166–7) suggests that 'risk' is a different, alternative, approach to such matters. Using the case of taboo beliefs among the Hima of Uganda, as discussed by Douglas and Wildavsky (1982), he notes that if, for example, a cow dies, Hima respond by asking what taboo has been broken. Respecting a taboo, he argues:

> has little in common with risk management as a set of strategies to reduce uncertainty. Taboo in traditional societies expresses *fate*, that is to say, certainty, while risk in modern societies deals with (more or less) calculated uncertainty ... Rather than belonging to the same generic category, then, risk and taboo are analytical counterparts. The certainty of a taboo spelling out that a cow dies if a woman comes into contact with it is essentially different from a scientific statement that women are bearers of a contagious infection and that there is a five per cent probability that the cow will catch the infection and die.

In Boholm's examples, 'uncertainty is a fundamental dimension of risk and without uncertainty there is no risk' (2003: 167), but that is not necessarily quite what is at stake in all the following chapters. Risk has to do above all with uncertainty of *outcomes*, and while that is also true of some of the examples here (especially the asylum contexts analysed by Good, Whyte and Kobelinsky, where the ultimate question, in view of the absolute ban on *refoulement*, concerns the risks asylum seekers would face if forcibly returned to their lands of origin), in many other cases the focus is rather upon uncertainty regarding *causes* (the dispelling of which may of course in turn suggest appropriate actions to be undertaken in future). In other words, the range of uncertainties considered here appears broader than that generated by notions of risk alone. A further difference is that risk is an actuarial notion arising out of nineteenth-century developments in insurance. Risk calculations therefore apply meaningfully only to defined populations or sub-populations; they depend on 'statistically-grounded conception[s] of social causality' (Gordon 1991: 39), and it can even be argued that 'strictly speaking, there is no such thing as an individual risk' (Ewald 1991: 203; see also Good 2007: 257). Moreover, *pace* Boholm, it can also be plausibly argued that actuarial 'risk' is fundamentally different from uncertainty: the fact that risk can be measured means it is not a form of uncertainty at all (Knight 1921: 19).

Judging

Institutions that deal with the process of judging, in both ritual and legal contexts, are directly concerned with the question of doubt. Procedures aimed at eliciting and dispelling doubt are used with the intention of exploring or clarifying the facts that need to be judged, or as a way of legitimating or validating the final verdict or decision. Depending on the situation, doubt may come from the person in charge of passing judgment, from the one requesting or receiving judgment, or from spectators witnessing these events. All institutions concerned with the process of judging – whether it be deciding between alternative courses of action, determining a judge's professional integrity, assigning culpability for an alleged crime, or ruling on the credibility of an asylum claimant – are necessarily directly concerned with the question of doubt. By putting ritual and judicial settings into comparative perspective, in contexts as diverse as Indian and Taiwanese divination (Berti, Tarabout, Homola) and international cricket (Good), as well as legal processes in France, the UK, India, Denmark and Ghana (Bouillier and Kobelinsky, Good, Berti and Tarabout, Whyte, Budniok, respectively), contributors to this book seek to offer a broad perspective on techniques for casting and dispelling doubt, and the roles they play in achieving verdicts or decisions that appear both valid and just.

To take a few illustrations from this volume, mediums and astrologers in India (Berti) and Taiwan (Homola) are regularly consulted to arbitrate local conflicts. In both cases, these consultations provide for specific techniques of interrogation and proof whereby petitioners' doubts may be formulated and dissipated during the ritual interaction. This may be compared with judicial settings, such as French Assize Courts (Bouillier), where dispelling or creating doubt over the validity and status of evidence are key strategies pursued by both prosecution and defence lawyers. In asylum decision-making processes in France, Denmark or the UK, on the other hand, where the burden of proof is borne by the applicant, creating doubt over the validity of evidence is a strategy pursued almost solely by the representatives of the state (Kobelinsky, Whyte, Good).

In all these legal contexts, distinctive techniques of interrogation are used to cast doubt on the credibility of accused persons and asylum applicants. But whereas the judicial management of doubt is underwritten in common-law systems by legally-defined standards of proof – and, more generally, the legal notion of 'reasonable doubt' is historically linked to the anxiety that the role of judging and punishing may produce (Whitman 2008) – in French law, by contrast, the resolution of doubt depends in the end on appeals to the judge's and jury's 'intimate conviction' (Bouillier) and hence also, potentially, to their emotions (Kobelinsky). As this example illustrates, some contributors to this book are drawn from, or carried out research within, countries whose legal systems are based on common-law principles, while others belong to, or researched in, countries employing 'continental', code-based systems. This allows several authors (Berti, Bouillier) to introduce a fruitful extra dimension of comparison; not only are formal legal techniques compared with those found in ritual contexts, but the strategies and technologies for articulating or dismissing doubts provided for in the two formal legal systems are also explicitly compared.

In Chapter 1, by Berti, the act of doubting is analysed in relation to two contexts of interaction and judgment in contemporary India. The first comprises temple consultations during which village deities, through their institutional mediums, are asked to elucidate individual problems or arbitrate local conflicts. During such consultations, the possibility that people doubt what the deity tells them is fully accepted and the ritual procedure includes specific techniques of contestation and verification. Analysis shows that doubting has little to do here with the question of belief, but is a way for people to become involved in the interpretative process and for the medium to reinforce the authority of his verdict. Doubting in this context is in fact a creative aspect of the interaction, a communicative technique which leaves room for discussion or contestation. This interactional form of doubting is compared to the principle of 'reasonable doubt' in Indian criminal trials, particularly in judges' rulings. Ethnographic material and court records show how Indian judges may be guided by the notion of 'reasonable doubt' – even when this leads them to go against their personal, more intuitive opinion (their *intime conviction*) about the case – simply because of the lack of admissible evidence submitted to the court. In both cases, then, though in quite different ways, doubting appears to be much less related to conscience, belief or cognition than to the technicalities of evidence and procedure.

Homola then explains in Chapter 2 how Taiwanese divination techniques help petitioners make decisions in a fast-moving and uncertain environment, showing how the structures of these rituals and the ways they cope with doubts can be used as a model of decision-making under uncertainty. She focuses on the process of judging in Taiwanese divination rituals, seen from the viewpoints of both clients and practitioners. A common pattern can be identified, which aims at dealing with doubts arising at two levels. First, regardless of the issue at stake, petitioners must be sure that the answers to their queries are given by a reliable, fully qualified and benevolent authority. Thus, procedures aimed at eliciting and dispelling doubt, or 'techniques of doubting', are designed to dispel petitioners' doubts about the diviner's ability or to assure them that the god is paying attention to their case. Here, techniques of doubting aim at building the authority that will legitimate the subsequent verdict. Second, analysis of the petitioner's case itself is a complex process that can lead to many misinterpretations or mistakes. For example, Taiwanese diviners of a so-called 'modern trend' rely partly on a rigorous formal pattern which combines theoretical concepts (such as fate), technical devices (such as horoscope grids) and open debate during the consultation, to investigate the petitioner's situation, but also rely on their own experience to build their opinion and convince the petitioner. Here, techniques of doubting aim at exploring and clarifying the ins and outs of a decision, as well as the context in which it takes place. Homola shows how, as a consequence of this process, faced with a set of uncertain events, facts and arguments, one particular arrangement of reality comes to take on a 'sense of truth' in the petitioner's mind.

Chapter 3, by Tarabout, studies temple astrology in Kerala (South India) and its occasional judicial aftermath. Hindu devotees proposing to improve a temple or wishing to resolve difficulties arising in its management must first ascertain the will of the presiding deity through an astrological consultation. In this public event, every aspect of temple life is scrutinized, a process full of uncertainties and doubts in which the astrologers harness various techniques in order to try to reach a diagnosis and to recommend solutions. These rituals are often costly and their findings are not always implemented, as devotees may disagree about the next course of action. In some rare cases their disagreement becomes an open conflict leading to a judicial case. A trial, however, is also full of new uncertainties. Judges are anxious to respect religious rights guaranteed by the Constitution while at the same time preserving public order. They may be keen to follow local 'tradition', and so may take account of the results of the astrological consultation, or, on the contrary, may examine accusations of fraud against a particular astrologer. One key difference between the astrological and the judicial contexts (whatever their differences in other respects) is that unlike an astrological consultation a trial ends up with a ruling to be enforced. Tarabout suggests that, while both processes are fraught with uncertainties, astrology leaves open spaces for further doubting and religious negotiation, whereas courts render doubt irrelevant because judges' decisions become legally binding.

Budniok, in Chapter 4, focuses on a setting in which it is the integrity of presiding judges that is potentially in doubt, rather than the testimonies of witnesses. In Ghana judicial corruption is seen as ubiquitous, and the public often perceives judgments as dependent on litigants' corrupt relationships with judges or court officers. The chapter describes how Ghanaian judges deal with such doubts which, as they see it, generally have hardly any factual basis but once raised cannot easily be dispelled. Their everyday behaviour and social interactions come under fierce scrutiny, prompting them to draw rather rigid boundaries to inhibit doubt. In many different spaces of action, such as use of public transport, dining out, or attending weddings, judges try to anticipate possible disruptions to their purported integrity and strive to operate within spatial, social and moral boundaries which they work constantly to create and maintain. The chapter shows how, so as to counter doubt, the professional culture of Ghanaian judges is predicated on a complex interplay between self-regulated public appearances and retreats into self-imposed seclusion.

Chapter 5 stems from Bouillier's research into the complex procedures of French Assize Courts, which she sees as offering an exemplary display of the ideas and ideals governing French notions of Justice, and the ways in which actors and proceedings are supposed to implement these ideals (see also, for example, Bouillier 2011). Assize hearings are processes in which judicial truth, grounded on evidence and reasoning, comes to be contested, constructed and established during the trial. This process is supposed to progress step by step throughout the hearings and thus necessarily implies the presence of doubt, right up until the taking of the final decision. The discussion focuses particularly on the jurors, or lay assessors, who bear the principal burden of doubt in that they remain in a situation of uncertainty throughout the hearing but then, at the end of the trial, have the duty to reach a decision on culpability based on their *intime conviction*, and must – in line with Whitman's analysis mentioned earlier – bear the moral personal consequences of an often difficult choice. This process is wittily contrasted with the very different procedural understandings manifest in common-law systems.

The remaining chapters are all concerned with systems of asylum decision-making, in three different European countries. Here the configurations are crucially different from those in the formal legal procedures considered by Berti, Tarabout, Budniok and Bouillier, for whereas such procedures are generally concerned with events in the past, asylum decisions are predictions about the future: does this person face a 'real risk' of persecution if returned to their country of origin? Here, past events serve at best as proxy indicators of what is likely to happen in the future. If it is accepted that an asylum applicant was tortured in the past, for example, that may make it seem more likely that they will again be tortured in the future, unless it is clear that the political situation back home has improved significantly.

Good, in Chapter 6, examines how 'the benefit of the doubt' is applied or withheld during asylum decision-making in the UK. Most asylum applicants cannot supply documentary proof or eye-witness testimony so decisions depend largely on assessments, by government officials or immigration judges, of the credibility of their narratives of persecution. A claimant whose story *does* appear credible should be given 'the benefit of the doubt' regarding matters that cannot be independently corroborated. In this sense, therefore, doubt and credibility represent opposite sides of the same coin. The dispelling or confirming of doubt is sought to be achieved through various interrogative techniques, whereby asylum applicants' stories are elicited and their credibility tested against 'objective evidence' such as country of origin information, and also, inevitably, against questioners' implicit or explicit assumptions about what constitutes normal behaviour. The process of awarding 'the benefit of the doubt' is familiar in other contexts too, such as the quasi-ritualistic practices of professional sport. The chapter examines the role of doubt in international cricket, with a particular focus on changes brought about by its recent adoption of new technologies. Whereas umpiring decisions in cricket are reached through a sequential process whereby technological evidence is considered step by step, benefit of the doubt decisions on asylum claims should supposedly be reached by considering all the evidence holistically. In reality, however, thanks to failings on the part of decision-makers themselves, and contradictions in the legislative and procedural instructions that they are required to follow, doubts in asylum claims too are most often resolved sequentially rather than holistically.

Whyte then shows in Chapter 7 how doubt, mistrust and uncertainty connect and structure understandings of the asylum system on the part of residents in a Danish asylum centre, as well as their strategies in navigating it. The determination of asylum cases in Denmark ostensibly rests on the authoritative rationalities of law, country of origin information, and medical and linguistic examinations; the standard bureaucratic practices of the state. Yet the production and management of doubt play key roles in caseworkers' resolution of asylum claims, as many decisions hinge on judgments about applicants' credibility. In this transitive sense, doubt is shown to be at once a property and product of the asylum system, and shades into mistrust. To the asylum seekers, however, the asylum process appears a haphazard and uncertain enterprise, feeding doubt in its intransitive sense. For them, uncertainty inflects every part of their experience – not least their meetings with the authorities making judgments on them, whose mistrust they are keenly aware of. Anxiety also arises from the sense that their everyday experiences, and the anecdotes circulating at the asylum centre, jar with the system's self-presentation as rational and impersonal. Here, asylum seekers' doubts feed back into the judicial resolution of their cases, and sometimes become self-defeating, as when their attempts to make their narratives more convincing instead make them seem less credible to caseworkers. For their part, asylum seekers' efforts to overcome their uncertainty, to make sense of a system whose logic and procedures they find hard to understand, may focus on the documents produced for or by their encounters with the Danish immigration system, The 'ordering power' of these documents in regulating their relationships with the state and determining the outcomes of their claims is shown to bear strong likenesses to the role of fetishes in regulating similar cross-cultural encounters between European merchants and West Africans in the pre-colonial period.

Finally, in Chapter 8 Kobelinsky examines the emotions at stake in the French National Asylum Court, which reviews appeals against refusals or withdrawals of refugee status or subsidiary protection by the state. She argues that exploring the role of emotions in asylum proceedings, more precisely 'benign' emotions sometimes felt by judicial decision-makers, helps explain the success of some applicants in obtaining refugee status in contemporary France. Her chapter deals first with public discourses surrounding asylum and the central role that suspicion and doubt play, both in contemporary representations regarding refugees and in routine appeal hearings themselves. It then analyses the role of emotions in the courtroom itself by examining several cases in which the emotional impact of asylum applicants' performances in court – evoking compassion, admiration and even esteem on the part of the judges – led to favourable decisions seemingly at odds with 'objective' assessments of the material in their dossiers. It points out the ambivalent role of these benign emotions and concludes that although positive emotions are not very frequently displayed in the everyday practices of the Court, they are crucial to an understanding how the *intime conviction* of French judges is constructed and how it operates.

Overall, these contributions lay the groundwork for a comparison between processes of judging and techniques for creating or dissolving doubt in both ritual and judicial settings. As explained above, it is this focus upon doubt as a technique or technology that distinguishes the approach taken here. The individual chapters further our understanding of what legal techniques for doubting and judging have in common with, and how they depart from, accepted techniques for reaching judgments and expressing doubts in ritual and other non-legal contexts.

Tobias Kelly's Afterword points out that in many of the contexts described here, these techniques involve doubt being 'made manifest in material form', whether this be the fetished documents described by Whyte and characteristic of Western legal systems generally, or the stones used by Berti's mediums. Doubt therefore has a sensory as well as a technical aspect. Its materialization helps us reach decisions that are, necessarily, in part aesthetically and emotionally grounded rather than being arrived at by purely rational means. This must be so, because the varied doubts discussed in these pages all concern matters of great concern and importance to those directly involved, and often to society as a whole. This affective aspect characterizes the resolution of doubts in legal processes, for all their purported intellectual rigour, every bit as much as in ritual ones. While Kobelinsky's chapter brings this out most clearly, and while – as Bouillier also underlines – French judicial processes make this still more explicit in terms of the centrality accorded to the decision-maker's *intime conviction*, common-law systems too, as Whitman (2008) convincingly shows, derive their notions of 'reasonable doubt' from what are ultimately moral and spiritual, rather than rational concerns. In this respect above all, doubt in law and ritual are essentially similar.

In his Foreword to this volume Antoine Garapon quotes an aphorism by the eminent French jurist Jean Carbonnier: 'Le jugement est un doute qui décide' (judgment is a doubt that decides). Equally appositely, Carbonnier completes that sentence as follows: 'le procès, l'institution d'une mise en doute avec une décision au bout' (a trial is an institutionalized putting into doubt, with a decision at the end) (1978: 136). Whether they deal with formal law or not, that is precisely what happens in the examples that follow.

References

Ahern, Emily M. (1979) 'The problem of efficacy: strong and weak illocutionary acts', *Man* (N.S.) 14(1): 1–17.

Anderson, Theresa D. (2006) 'Uncertainty in action: observing information seeking within the creative processes of scholarly research', *Information Research* 12(1) paper 283, available at http://InformationR.net/ir/12-1/paper283.html (accessed 30 November 2013).

Anderson, Theresa D. (2008) 'The many faces of uncertainty: getting at the anthropology of uncertainty', *The Creativity and Uncertainty Papers: The Refereed Proceedings of the 13th Conference of the Australian Association of Writing Programs, 2008*, available at http://www.aawp.org.au/files/Anderson.pdf (accessed 19 December 2013).

Austin, J.L. (1962) *How to Do Things with Words*, Oxford: Clarendon Press.

Boholm, Åsa (2003) 'The cultural nature of risk: can there be an anthropology of uncertainty?', *Ethnos: Journal of Anthropology* 68(2): 159–78.

Bouillier, Véronique (2011) 'French law courts and South Asian litigants', in *Cultural Expertise and Litigation: Patterns, Conflicts, Narratives*, ed. Livia Holden, Abingdon and New York: Routledge, pp. 53–70.

Bourdieu, Pierre (1987) 'The force of law: toward a sociology of the juridical field', *Hastings Law Journal* 38(5): 814–53.

Byström, Katrina and Järvelin, Kalervo (1995) 'Task complexity affects information seeking and use', *Information Processing & Management* 31(2): 191–213.
Carbonnier, Jean (1978) *Sociologie juridique* (2nd edn), Paris: Presses Universitaires de France, Collections Thémis.
Chase, Oscar G. (2005) *Law, Culture, and Ritual: Disputing Systems in Cross-cultural Context*, New York and London: New York University Press.
Douglas, Mary and Wildavsky, Aaron (1982) *Risk and Culture*, Berkeley: University of California Press.
Dworkin, Ronald (1986) *Law's Empire*, Cambridge, MA: Harvard University Press.
Evans-Pritchard, E.E. (1937) *Witchcraft, Oracles and Magic Among the Azande*, Oxford: Clarendon Press.
Ewald, François (1991) 'Insurance and risks', in *The Foucault Effect: Studies in Governmentality*, ed. Graham Burchell, Colin Gordon and Peter Miller, Chicago: University of Chicago Press, pp. 197–210.
Finnegan, Ruth (1969) 'How to do things with words: performative utterances among the Limba of Sierra Leone', *Man* (N.S.) 4(4): 537–52.
Frazer, Sir James G. (1955) *The Golden Bough* (3rd edn), London: Macmillan.
Gluckman, Max (1965) *Politics, Law and Ritual in Tribal Society*, Oxford: Basil Blackwell.
Good, Anthony (2007) *Anthropology and Expertise in the Asylum Courts*, Abingdon and New York: Routledge-Cavendish.
Gordon, Colin (1991) 'Governmental rationality: an introduction', in *The Foucault Effect: Studies in Governmentality*, ed. Graham Burchell, Colin Gordon and Peter Miller, Chicago: University of Chicago Press, pp. 1–51
Handelman, Don (1987) 'For an uncertain anthropology', in *Cultural Anthropology: A Perspective on the Human Condition* (1st edn), ed. Emily Schultz and Robert Lavenda, St Paul, MN: West, pp. 310–11.
Hecht, Jennifer M. (2003) *Doubt: A History*, San Francisco: Harper.
Højbjerg, Christian K. (2002) 'Religious reflexivity. Essays on attitudes to religious ideas and practice', *Social Anthropology* 10(1): 1–10.
Holmes, Oliver Wendell, Jr. (1963 [1881]) *The Common Law*, Boston: Little, Brown.
Kelsen, Hans (1967) *The Pure Theory of Law* (trans. Max Knight), Berkeley and Los Angeles: University of California Press.
Knight, Frank H. (1921) *Risk, Uncertainty, and Profit*, Boston: Hart, Schaffner & Marx.
Kuhlthau, Carol C. (1993) *Seeking Meaning: A Process Approach to Library and Information Services*, Norwood, NJ: Ablex.
Kuhlthau, Carol C. and Tama, S.L. (2001) 'Information search process of lawyers, a call for "just for me" information services', *Journal of Documentation* 57(1): 25–43.
Llewellyn, Karl N. (2000) *Jurisprudence: Realism in Theory and Practice*, Union, NJ: Lawbook Exchange.

Llewellyn, Karl N. and Hoebbel, E. Adamson (1941) *The Cheyenne Way: Conflict and Case Law in Primitive Jurisprudence*, Norman: University of Oklahoma Press.
Pelkmans, Mathijs (2013) 'Outline for an ethnography of doubt', in *Ethnographies of Doubt: Faith and Uncertainty in Contemporary Societies*, ed. Mathijs Pelkmans, London: I.B. Tauris, pp. 1–44.
Rasmussen, Douglas B. (1974) 'Austin and Wittgenstein on "doubt" and "knowledge", *Reason Papers* (Fredonia, NY) 1: 51–60.
Severi, Carlo (2002) 'Memory, reflexivity and belief. Reflections on the ritual use of language', *Social Anthropology* 10(1): 23-40.
Tambiah, S.J. (1968) 'The magical power of words', *Man* (N.S.) 3(2): 175–208.
Tambiah, S.J. (1973) 'Form and meaning of magical acts: a point of view', in *Modes of Thought: Essays on Thinking in Western and Non-western Societies*, ed. Robin Horton and Ruth Finnegan, London: Faber and Faber, pp. 199–230.
Tannert, Christof, Elvers, Horst-Dietrich and Jandrig, Burkhard (2007) 'The ethics of uncertainty', *EMBO Reports* 8(10): 892–96.
Toren, Christina (2007) 'How do we know what is true?', in *Questions of Anthropology*, ed. Rita Astuti, Jonathan Parry and Charles Stafford, Oxford: Berg, pp. 307–35.
Twining, William (1973) 'Law and anthropology: a case study in interdisciplinary collaboration', *Law and Society Review* 7(4): 561–83.
Twining, William (2006) *Rethinking Evidence: Exploratory Essays* (2nd edn) Cambridge: Cambridge University Press.
Van Asselt, Marjolein and Rotmans, Jan (2002) 'Uncertainty in integrated assessment modelling: from positivism to pluralism', *Climatic Change* 54(1,2): 75–105.
Whitman, James Q. (2008), *The Origins of Reasonable Doubt: Theological Roots of the Criminal Trial*, New Haven and London: Yale University Press.
Wittgenstein, Ludwig (1971) 'Remarks on Frazer's "Golden Bough"', *The Human World* 3: 18–41.

Chapter 1

Technicalities of Doubting: Temple Consultations and Criminal Trials in India

Daniela Berti

The notion of doubt has often been addressed in anthropology in relation to the question of belief. Anthropologists started to question the relevance of using the Western category of 'belief' to describe the practices and attitudes of the people they studied, notably after the publication of the critical approach developed by Needham (1972). By underlining the association generally made between belief and conscience, some authors preferred to replace the notion with other terms less linked to the idea of individual conviction, such as representation (Lenclud 1990; Pouillon 1993; Hamayon 2006; Schlemmer 2009); others started to consider doubt and scepticism as crucial aspects of ritual practices that had erroneously been underreported in fieldwork accounts (Boyer 1990; Beatty 1999; Rappaport 1999).[1]

A debate parallel to that about belief then developed around the notion of reflexivity. In his introduction to a journal special issue, Højbjerg (2002) focuses on 'reflexive attitudes' such as doubt, incertitude or the 'do as if' adopted by people taking part in religious practices. Here reflexivity is intended not only in the sense that ritual actions are submitted to public debate among the audience or to diverging comments from the ritual specialists themselves. It is also considered as being the result of the organizational form of ritual action, including ritual language and the modes of transmission of religious ideas (Severi 2002). In other words, reflexive attitudes are not only part of a discursive register. They may also be devices completely integrated into the rules used in a specific institutional context of interaction.

In line with this perspective, I deal in this chapter with practices of doubting in two institutional settings found in the Himachal Pradesh region of the Indian Himalayas, which are both concerned with the process of judging.[2] My aim is not to investigate personal or cognitive experiences of doubting. By taking doubt as a matter of practice and technique, my aim is to see how doubting is managed and resolved in reference to decision-making processes. First of all I talk about temple

1 A similar debate has developed in the field of history. Veyne (1992), for example, dealt with the question of belief in terms of '*programme de vérité*'.

2 Research leading to this chapter was funded by the French National Research Agency (ANR) as part of the programme 'Just-India: A Joint Programme on Justice and Governance in India and South Asia' (http://just-india.net) (ANR-08-GOUV-064).

consultations during which village deities, through their institutional mediums, are asked to arbitrate local conflicts and to give their verdict on people's misconduct. These ritual procedures are then compared to the ways in which the techniques of doubting and proving are used in Indian criminal trials as well as in judges' rulings.

Although temple mediums and judges may not appear to have anything in common, they do in fact share some similarities: both arbitrate cases, interpret or establish 'facts' and 'truth', and pronounce judgments and verdicts. In one case the arbitrator is a god's medium who speaks on behalf of a village deity; in the other he is a professional judge who speaks in the name of the law.

In both contexts – ritual and judicial – the verdict is preceded by processes to either quell or develop any doubt, but in ways that are almost totally opposite in the two cases. With regard to the deity's medium, the doubt that must be expressed or removed is, above all, the doubt that the person consulting the deity may have about the way the deity interprets their problem – because this interpretation may clash with their perception of the facts. However, given that the deity is considered to already 'know the truth', the doubt in question concerns whether the medium is really speaking on behalf of the deity and not on his own behalf.

By contrast, in the case of a judicial trial, it is the judge's doubt that has to be disproved or confirmed, and during the trial the lawyer for the accused and the prosecutor have to produce a set of evidence and arguments in order to either sow or remove any doubt in the judge's mind. Moreover, in his final ruling, the judge's personal opinion about the facts has to comply with the way the notions of doubt and proof are used in legal codes and judicial procedures.

Consulting the Village God

I will first present this practice of doubting and proving in the context of medium consultations. At the time of ritual consultations (*deopuchna*) a village deity is made part of an interactional setting within which its presence is enacted by its human medium (*gur* or *chela*).[3] The medium's authority comes from the deity by whom he is supposed to have been chosen, although this divine selection has to be officially and publicly recognized during a special village ceremony. Once initiated, a medium has the duty to 'presentify' (Vernant 1985) the deity in all ritual festivals and also to hold regular consultations at people's request.[4] In exchange for his service as a medium he may be granted some tenancy rights over

3 The fieldwork material analysed here has been collected in different villages situated in Kullu district. The official language of the area is Hindi even though in rural areas, especially in the context of temple consultations, people often used Pahari, a local dialect.

4 The expression refers to the French word 'présentifier' used by J.P. Vernant (1985) to indicate the action or process by which an entity that belongs to the invisible world takes form in the human word.

the deity's property or he may receive part of the offerings made by those who come for a consultation.

Consulting a god is thus a highly institutionalized ritual context where the deity's manifestation in the medium's body, as well as the interaction which takes place between the deity and the people, is regulated by a series of procedures and formalized ritual techniques.

Moreover, many of those who attend these consultations also feel that they have institutional links with the deity, either because they have received some of the god's land in exchange for their services at the temple (such as musicians, priests or administrators) or simply because they live within the area (*har*) over which the deity is considered to exercise its power. The multiple names people use to address the deity during a consultation – *Maharaj* (king), *Bhagvan/Bhagvati* (god/goddess) *Mata* (mother) or even *Malik* (landowner) – indicate the multiple registers on which the relationship between people and the deity is constructed. These ritual links and obligations have historical roots in the royal past as many of these deities received land donations from various kings of the region and were somehow considered as local rulers (Berti 2009). Their public role was recognized during the colonial period by the British administrators, who officially declared many village deities of the region owners of the land by recognizing the deity's juristic 'personality' (Sontheimer 1964). The legal existence of a deity continues to be recognized in the post-colonial state to the point that a god may become the main petitioner in a court case (Malik 2010; Berti 2012b; Clémentin-Ojha 2012).

Interestingly, in a bureaucratic setting – for example before a judge or Deputy Commissioner – a deity is represented by the temple administrator since the medium plays no part in it. On the contrary, at village level the medium is the main means of accessing the deity.[5] Through the medium the deity is directly questioned not only about settling personal or family problems but about its opinion on any major decision to be taken at village level.

Disputes among villagers are regularly brought before the deity who is asked to pronounce judgment and to propose a compromise between the parties. The deity's verdict may sometimes even take a form of competition with the court of law when those consulting the deity are involved in an ongoing court case. This judicial role of the deity is specified during the ritual when the medium, when speaking on behalf of the deity, may say 'The court is mine, justice is mine' (Berti 2012a).[6]

During the consultation, the medium, who often belongs to a low-status caste, is addressed as if he were the deity, and what he says is considered to come directly from the deity. This is true in principle, at least. In practice, consulting a deity always involves undertaking a process of doubting, which is induced by the ritual procedure. As I will show in the next section, mediums have recourse to various

5 In Tamil Nadu it is the temple trustee rather than the administrator who represents the deity in court (Anthony Good, personal communication).

6 For the region of Garhwal, see also Malik (2010).

techniques to deal with doubt, some of which are commonly used by all the mediums in the region, while others are specific to a particular deity.

The Presumption of Doubt: 'Distributing Rice'

In ritual consultation, the possibility that people doubt what the medium[7] tells them is fully acknowledged and the ritual procedure includes specific techniques of contestation and verification. Some of these techniques are codified in the gestures that the medium performs at each consultation. For example, at the very beginning of the séance, immediately after the deity has been ritually embodied in the medium, the latter takes out a lock of hair from his forehead. This gesture is described as a kind of promise he makes to speak 'the truth', which means that he will not speak for himself; he will talk only if and when the deity, as people say, 'comes' (*ata he*) into his body.

The general discourse is, in fact, that the deity's presence in the medium is intermittent; it comes and goes – an idea that in itself leaves room for possibly doubting what the medium is saying. The gesture is presented as a sort of oath that the medium has to take before speaking: just like the judge who asks the witnesses to swear that they will speak the truth before the court, here the deity itself is said to ask its own medium to swear that he will not speak for himself, that he will be merely a vehicle for the deity's speech.

At the very beginning, before the individual consultation begins, the medium starts by distributing a small handful of rice to each of those taking part in the consultation. This is another systematic, codified procedure that is followed every time a consultation is held. The one who receives the grains must count them and see if there is an odd or even number. If it is an odd number, it means that the person is 'of one mind', that he does not have any doubts, at least at this stage. On the other hand, if it is an even number it means that he has some doubt. For example, the expression '*char vichar*' may be used among the audience, which means that if one has four grains this shows that the person has some thoughts. The person, or the other attendants, may then react by addressing the deity, for example with the following words: 'O Maharaj! Why these thoughts? We don't want any thoughts. We honour you'. In order to get rid of these thoughts, the person who is supposed to doubt has to throw away the grains and ask the medium to give him or her another handful of rice for as long as it takes to obtain an odd number.

This kind of interaction shows, on the one hand, how the person who is consulting the deity is considered to be somehow unaware of the fact that he doubts

7 Here we enter an area of linguistic fluidity for the anthropological description. If we use the term 'medium' we adopt an analytical point of view; if we use the word 'deity' we take the point of view of those who consult, though we omit the fact that the people themselves may think that it is the medium who is speaking, not the deity. Here I will use the word deity or medium according to which point of view I want to stress.

because the 'thoughts' (*vichar*) are presented as being independent of the person's will. In fact it is the deity, not the person, who is asked by the audience to eliminate these *vichar*. An even number of grains of rice is in fact treated by people as a bad omen or as a negative presence rather than as indicative of the person's mental attitude. On the other hand, the fact that the person has to throw the grains until he gets an odd number shows that the procedure of taking the grains of rice is meant not only 'to check' whether the person harbours some doubts, but 'to make' him not have any.[8]

Interactional Doubt: 'Giving Rice' and '*Ore Pogre*'

Once this collective process of eliminating the *vichar* is complete, interactions take place at a more individual level. The first person to be heard by the deity is again given a handful of rice and they again check the number. This giving rice and counting the grains may be repeated throughout the consultation, which may last some time, especially if the case proves to be serious.

In some cases, during the verbal interactions, the person consulting the deity appears to challenge what the deity says or to propose a different explanation of the problem from the one proposed by the deity. In one particular case, for example, a woman, who was well-known to the medium,[9] did not agree with what the deity was saying about her situation. She was given rice many times but it was always an odd number – which meant that the woman had no doubts. She eventually counted an even number and threw away the rice because that meant that she did have some doubts. The medium then stopped giving her rice and started reproaching her for questioning what he (the deity) said. This case shows how, although the rice is meant to check whether the person has some doubts, it may be used by the medium to somehow accuse the person of not telling the truth and of challenging the deity's verdict.

Another interactional form of doubting is the so-called *ore pogre* which literally means 'round stones' and refers to a procedure by which the person consulting the deity has to arrange three stones in the shape of a triangle on the floor. They have to mentally associate each stone with a possible cause of the problem. One stone may be associated, for example, with the idea that the person's problem is due to an act of witchcraft; the second stone with the idea that what has happened to them is due to some punishment inflicted by a deity; and the third stone with the idea that the problem is due to some planetary movement. Once the person has made this mental association, the medium has to choose the stone to indicate the exact cause.

8 On this topic, see Hamayon (2006) for shamanic procedures of divination.

9 The medium usually knows the person who is consulting the deity, especially when the person is from the same village.

During the consultation, the medium may ask the person 'to put *ore pogre*' in different situations. He may do this when he considers that the person is – as the medium says – 'in two minds', meaning that he has some doubt. The request to put *ore pogre* appears to come from the deity itself and not from the medium. This is made explicit in ritual interactions as the person doing *ore pogre* continues to address the deity. In fact, up until the end of the consultation the possibility that the 'medium' is acting on his own behalf is never openly evoked by the audience. By contrast, it may be paradoxically suggested by the medium himself who, speaking on behalf of the deity, may say to the person 'If you don't believe my *patru* ('recipient', that is the medium), put *ore pogre* and I will tell you myself'. Although in *ore pogre* the medium has to select the stone, the procedure is presented as being somehow less dependent on the medium-as-a-man than the reply that he gives verbally during the consultation. The fact that a reply has been given through *ore pogre* is in fact referred to by people as 'proof' that the reply is 'true'.

Sometimes *ore pogre* is recommended by the medium as a reaction to a person's behaviour. For example, when the deity starts to say that a person's problem is not due to any punishment, that it is simply due to difficult times, or to some inauspicious planets, the person may say 'O Bhagvan, why don't you want to tell me what has happened?' The medium then asks the person to put *ore pogre*. To start with, the person usually refuses to do this because they do not want to challenge the deity. Thus, they may begin to say 'No, deity, I don't want to defy you, I don't want any confrontation with you. Tell me in your own words [that is, through the medium]'. In such cases, people nearby may start asking the person to put *ore pogre* as though they want to convince them to accept – which the person eventually does.

> Man: We don't want to put *ore pogre*.
>
> Medium: First of all you must put *ore pogre* and then I will explain to you and I will fulfil your request.
>
> Man: Eh deity, tell us with your own words, we don't want to put *ore pogre*.
>
> Medium: You put *ore pogre* and I will tell you the outcome! Put *ore pogre*!
>
> Other people: You must say it like that [verbally]! (field notes, Jagatsukh, 1995)

In some cases, the test with the three stones is a way for the person to check what the medium has already said to them verbally; at the same time it may be used by the medium to negotiate the person's reply, and even to adjust or to change his initial reply as a consequence of the interaction he has had with the person. For example, in one case the medium told a woman that she was under a bad planetary influence (*din dasha*) but the woman did not like the idea of simply being affected by a bad planet as this was not regarded as a real explanation for the problem. She began to cry, showing that she was not satisfied with the reply, so the medium told her: 'Put *ore pogre* and satisfy your own mind. [See] if there are some bad planets or if there is a *bhut* [ghost] sent by someone to harm you. Put *ore pogre* and then I will tell you myself!'[10]

The woman then put *ore pogre* and when the medium selected a stone, she let out a cry of joy, which implicitly indicated that the stone chosen was not the one with which she associated bad planets. The medium, speaking on behalf of the deity, then told her, 'There is a *bhut*. Do you see now?', and thus he changed his interpretation of the woman's problem. The woman's satisfaction was clearly evident: having an enemy to fight is more reassuring than believing that one's problems are due to inauspicious planets where it is more difficult to ritually intervene.

The fact that the interpretation of the problem may change during the dialogue is generally accepted. One formula frequently used by the medium during the consultation is 'you're in two minds [you doubt], I have seven speeches'. In other cases, however, the formula used by the medium is 'one word, one weight, one balance', by which the medium confirms what he – that is the deity – had previously said.

In cases where the medium selects a stone that corresponds to a reply that is not what the person would have liked to hear, the reaction may vary: the person may think that the medium is speaking for himself or that the deity does not want to tell them the truth; or they are no longer certain about the association they had made and they want to repeat the procedure; or they may just say that they don't want to find out through *ore pogre* but they want the deity to speak to them directly (that is, through his medium).

It must also be said that the way in which the medium selects the stone may be more or less ambiguous: sometimes he touches the stone with the ritual bell, throwing aside the selected stone; sometimes he pushes away two stones with the bell, which may suggest that he has chosen the third stone. Finally, even if the medium selects what the person thinks is a good reply, the person may carry on having some doubts. They then have to repeat *ore pogre* two or three more times.

Like other ritual contexts reported in the literature, the case of medium consultations analysed here shows how the expression of doubt is internal to the ritual logic. We have seen how, for example, it is by *speaking as* the deity that the medium requests the person to express or to solve his or her doubt. In some cases this even creates a sort of linguistic paradox with the medium speaking as the deity who explicitly says to the people 'If you do not believe my medium [*patru*, that is, recipient] then put *ore pogre* and I will tell you myself'. This shows how the ritual action not only presumes the manifestation of the deity, but may

10 *Bhut* (here ghosts, or minor deities) are often considered to be sent by a witch who takes the *bhut* under their control and orders them to harm the person physically or to upset their family relations.

also challenge it or be performed in order to test the effectiveness of the deity's power (Severi 2002). In the context of the deity consultations analysed here this may even end up creating a kind of short circuit as, for example, when the deity, somehow challenging its own existence, says during the séance 'If you honour me, I am a god, otherwise I am a piece of stone'.

On the other hand, the analysis of the procedure shows how in the context of ritual consultations doubting does not appear to be related only to the question of belief. Instead, it is a way for people to become involved in the interpretative process and for the medium to reinforce his verdict or, on the contrary, to change it. It enables the medium as well as the person consulting the deity to adjust their respective interpretation and comprehension of the situation submitted to the consultation. Doubting in this context is in fact a creative aspect of the interaction, a communicative technique that leaves room for discussion or contestation.

Law Courts and Criminal Proceedings

I will now compare this practice of doubting in this institutionalized ritual setting with the one used in judicial settings (in the same region) and especially with the way doubt is expressed and formulated during a trial as well as in judges' rulings. Unlike in ritual consultations, where doubt expressed during the procedure comes mostly from the person consulting the deity, in the case of a trial, the doubt that must be refuted or confirmed is doubt in the judge's mind about the guilt of the accused.

In his work on the theological roots of the criminal trial, Whitman (2008) argues that 'reasonable doubt' is to be seen as a vestige of a very widespread pre-modern anxiety about judging and punishing. The author shows how the original function of reasonable doubt was not, as it is today, to protect the accused, but to protect jurors against the potential mortal sin of convicting an innocent defendant. The rule of 'reasonable doubt' was, he argues, a 'technique of moral comfort', aimed at protecting the judge from damnation (Whitman 2008: 6). Although in India the religious dangers attendant upon judging were mentioned in Sanskrit texts in the early centuries of the Common Era (Granoff 2010), by the time Western criminal procedures were introduced during the colonial period, they were in no way associated with these medieval religious concerns and were perceived as completely secularized techniques. Some of the practices adopted during colonial times, such as the jury trial, were even abolished soon after Independence, and the absence of the jury trial does not seem to have generated any particular religious anxiety about the judge's salvation in the next life. The procedure followed in India during a trial therefore no longer has any obvious link with Christian or Brahmanical religious concerns, and violations of rules or offences are not sanctioned according to religious precepts but according to sections of the Civil or Penal Code (Berti 2012a).

As in other adversarial systems, here again the criminal trial takes the form of a battle between two (supposedly) equal parties: the prosecution, which attempts to prove its case beyond reasonable doubt, and the defence, which seeks to undermine the prosecution's case and to create reasonable doubt. As Lea (2006) notes regarding the English procedure, the task of the defence is not to prove the innocence of the defendant but to prevent the prosecution from proving their guilt.

Unlike in the British criminal system, the trial judge in India is completely alone in deciding the case. The absence of a jury often leads the judge, the prosecutor and the lawyers to discuss technical points such as procedural constraints of the investigations, legal sections and contradictions between witnesses' versions. The witnesses, especially when they are from rural areas and with no knowledge of English, are unable to follow interactions of this kind, which constantly shift from the vernacular to English. These may also turn out to be rather animated discussions between the judge and the attorneys, with one constantly interrupting the other.

The absence of a popular jury does indeed influence the way a trial is performed. All interactions take place very close to the judge, who follows the verbal exchanges with the file in front of him. Judges often take an active part in the interactions by putting many questions to witnesses, especially when they think that the prosecutor is not asking them the relevant questions. It is also through the judge that witnesses' replies are put into official writing. After each interaction in Hindi the judge translates and dictates to the stenographer the content of the corresponding question-reply, and formulates the sentences in the first person as if the witness were actually dictating.

This process of official transcription, which in cross-examination is sometimes taken over by the defence lawyer, includes conventional formulas which allow doubt to be expressed and, even more importantly, to be somehow suggested in the record. We will now see how, during the different stages in the case, doubt is expressed and solved.

Adversarial Doubting: Hostile Witnesses and Cross-examination

In Indian judicial procedures many verbal and oral techniques are available in order to express doubt in a codified way. One of these techniques is linked to the practice of declaring a witness 'hostile'. This especially happens in relation to prosecution witnesses, who are called by the prosecutor to back the accusations. At the time of the trial, prosecution witnesses are asked to repeat before the judge what they previously stated to the police during the investigations. These witnesses are first questioned by the prosecutor (as well as by the judge) according to the rules that apply to the examination-in-chief, where questions are left open. However, it very often happens that the witnesses' replies contradict their previous statement, the written version of which is included in the police report. When this happens, the witness is accused of not telling the truth. This follows an extremely codified procedure which consists in dictating in English to the stenographer a sentence of the following kind:

> At this stage Learned Public Prosecutor has stated that witness is trying to suppress the truth. As such request is made to cross examine the witness, which is considered and allowed.[11]

Since the sentence is dictated in English, it is not usually understood by the witness who is therefore not aware that he has just been 'officially' accused of telling a lie. However, from a procedural point of view, after this sentence has been dictated, the questions are put to the witness according to the rules that apply to cross-examination. He will be systematically confronted with his previous statement which is referred to after every question. To each question the witness has to reply yes or no. The content of the question is then transcribed and translated by adding the formula 'It is incorrect that …' or 'I have not stated that …' in the event where he replies no and 'It is correct that …' in the case where he replies affirmatively.

When he replies in the negative, the English transcription of the reply is followed by the sentence 'Confronted with portion [reference to the paragraphs] of the statement … in which it is so recorded'. Long paragraphs of the police report may therefore be referred to in court records by using the negative formula 'it is incorrect that …' when quoting from it, which aims at underlining that the witness has changed his previous version and he is thus lying before the court.

Let us look at an example where, during the trial, a father who had previously accused his daughter's in-laws of being responsible for his daughter's suicide denied ever having made this accusation:

> Judge: Look, her mother-in-law and her husband mistreated her. This is all you told the police … Did you tell the police that the accused was beating her?
>
> Man: No, I didn't tell the police. (field notes, Shimla, 2009)

The judge then dictated in English to the stenographer:

> It is incorrect that I stated to the police that the accused were beating Anjana [the witness's daughter] or that they had ever maltreated her (confronted with portion A to A of mark A in which it is recorded). (Court file, *Himachal Pradesh v. Neelam Safri & Susheel Kumar*, 2009)
>
> It is incorrect that my daughter complained to me that the accused had started treating her with cruelty nor did I make such a statement to the police (confronted

11 In fact, as in the example below, this sentence is often dictated on the initiative of the judge but on behalf of the prosecutor.

> with portion B to B of statement ex pw 1-A in which it is so recorded). (Court file, *Himachal Pradesh State* v. *Neelam Safri & Susheel Kumar*, 2009)

Using a negative form of transcription 'it is incorrect that my daughter complained to me', emphasizes the fact that the witness is contradicting the story he had previously given to the police or that he is contradicting what the lawyer wants to suggest. In some cases lawyers make use of a double negation as in the sentence 'It is incorrect to say that I was not present in the spot' – which may sometimes prove rather confusing, even for the judge.

The prosecutor's witnesses are also cross-examined by the defence lawyer. In cases where they have turned hostile, the lawyer will simply ask them some complementary questions. This is not the case, however, for police witnesses, as lawyers will try to undermine their credibility by asking each of them very detailed questions aimed at getting them to make contradictions with their previous report or with each other's replies. Contradiction is in fact essentially used as a way of casting doubt on the credibility of the witness's story.

As soon as the defence lawyer succeeds in throwing light on some discrepancies between the police replies and their past account, the lawyer directly dictates to the stenographer a standardized sentence which enables him to highlight the discrepancy. For example, in a narcotics case, the defence lawyer wanted to put on record that the time a police officer gave during the trial regarding the call he had received from a secret informant did not match the time he had written in his report. After asking the police officer to confirm that the time given in his reply was correct the lawyer dictated to the stenographer the following sentence as if the witness was speaking in the first person; 'My today's testimony is correct, whereas the time of receipt of secret information written in seizure memo [in the report] is incorrect' (Court file, *Himachal Pradesh State* v. *Kanshi Ram*, 2010).

This sentence is the equivalent of the formula 'Confronted with' used in the case of hostile witnesses mentioned above. By emphasizing the discrepancy between the current and the previous account the defence lawyer aims to discredit the police officer's credibility in the eyes of the judge. Here, too, expressing doubt is a written procedure which is not even completely understood by the person concerned, especially those who do not speak English, who do not realize that their credibility has been challenged in the evidence report.

Another codified procedure aimed at introducing doubt about a witness's credibility is used at the end of the cross-examination and serves to elicit the reason why the witness would choose to support the accused, and thus to deny his previous statement. This is done by using another written formula whose effect is to affirm the very opposite of what is being denied. These conclusive sentences are dictated by the lawyer in English to the stenographer on behalf of the witness. The aim is to allow the reason why the witness may be telling lies before the court to emerge. For example, in the case where an offence is committed in a village, the village president is always included among the prosecutor's witnesses at the trial.

In all the narcotic cases I followed, both in Shimla and Mandi Session Courts, the village president started to contradict what he or she was supposed to have said during the investigation. They were therefore declared hostile witnesses and subjected to cross-examination. In one case, for example, the judge, at the end of the cross-examination, told the village president in Hindi:

> Judge: Look, you are protecting them because they are your supporters and you are doing this to win their votes.
>
> *Pradhan*: No, they are not my supporters and I am telling the truth. (field notes, Shimla, 2010)

The judge then dictated in English to the stenographer:

> It is incorrect that I [the village president] am suppressing the truth because the accused backed me in the elections (Court file, *Himachal Pradesh State* v. *Kanshi Ram*, 2010)

As in the other case mentioned above, the negative form is used here to suggest what is apparently being denied, that the village president *is* suppressing the truth.

Reference to the electoral link between the accused and the witness is a very typical way of concluding a hearing with a village president. It is a standard formula added at the end of the court interaction to implicitly suggest that the witness is telling a lie and to give the reason for this. In fact, most of the time the judge and the prosecutor know that as well as winning the votes of the accused the village president has received money from them. Yet, the 'electoral reason' is a conventional form of recording the fact that a village president has turned hostile.

Another common formula used when a fellow villager of the accused turns hostile to the prosecutor points to the links which supposedly exist between those belonging to the same village. For example, in a rape case (*Himachal Pradesh State* v. *Devinder Sharma*, 2010), the formula dictated at the end of the cross-examination was 'It is incorrect to say that I belong to the same village of the accused and that for this reason I am telling a lie' (Court file). In fact, this sentence *does* indeed suggest that the witness is telling a lie and that he is supporting the accused because he belongs to the same village. In another similar case the formula used was 'It is incorrect that I have received consideration from the accused and that for that reason I am telling a lie' (Court file), which suggests that the witness may have received some money or some compensation from the party of the accused in return for testifying in his favour.

This kind of conclusive sentence is also used by the defence lawyer, especially at the end of the cross-examination of police witnesses.[12] For example, in the

12 In fact, as independent witnesses frequently turn hostile the defence lawyer has no reason to contradict them. By contrast, police officers are often submitted to long

narcotics case mentioned above the defence lawyer wanted to put on record that the police officers had invented a false story against the accused and that the case had not been registered in the way they described in their report. At the end of the cross-examination he dictated to the stenographer the following sentence directly in English:

> It is wrong to suggest that the case has been planted upon the accused by the police. It is incorrect that I am deposing falsely (Court file, *Himachal Pradesh State* v. *Devinder Sharma*, 2010)

This final sentence is frequently added at the end of the police's cross-examination by the defence lawyer, to infer that the police officer is in fact telling a lie.

These sentences are aimed at providing the lawyer's version of the story through the witness's denial of what he appears to be stating. This is a conventional form of recording cross-examination: it enables the lawyer to suggest his version without leaving the accused the chance to react in any way. In fact this kind of sentence may even be dictated by the judge or the lawyer even though the witness has not actually been questioned.

As the examples above show, the content of these counter-stories is quite vague and points to some standardized idea such as village corporatism or, on the contrary, the existence of a personal enmity between the accused and the witness. Though conventional, these strategic counterarguments are expected to be found in the file. While in strong cases they may be completely ignored by the judge and considered to be merely the defence's discourse, in cases that are not entirely proven they will be used by the judge as additional arguments to conclude that the case has not been proven beyond reasonable doubt (that the doubt has not been lifted).

Although this procedure of recording slows down the trial, it provides a written transcription of witnesses' testimonies which will be referred to in the successive phases of the trial. Passages from these transcriptions will be read aloud by the lawyer or prosecutor during the arguments and will be quoted by the judge in his written order. They will also be used much later, when the case is examined at the Appeal Court many years after the verdict. Here the appeal judge will rely entirely on these transcriptions to evaluate the case. However, unlike in the trial situation, where the witnesses' appearance, their attitudes and their replies enable the judge to evaluate the truthfulness of their words, the Appeal Court can only rely on the information recorded in the file by the trial judge.

The Percentage of Doubt: The Notion of 'Beyond Reasonable Doubt'

Contrary to these interactional and strategic techniques for introducing doubt into the court file, reference to the notion of doubt is explicitly made by judges in the

---

cross-examination by the lawyer.

judgments they have to write up after a hearing. Here the legal notion of 'beyond reasonable doubt' is often used by the judge to argue his final decision. Although often presented as the highest 'standard of proof' the notion of 'reasonable doubt' is not explicitly defined in legal codes of procedure (Whitman 2008) and judges often use it by making reference to a rather general meaning (or discourse) as found in other judgments, especially from appeal courts.

High Court judges in Shimla were also puzzled when I asked them to tell me the meaning of this notion. They found the question very pertinent and started not only to discuss it with their colleagues but also to raise the question in court. The way in which the notion of 'reasonable doubt' is used in judgments may in fact vary from one judge to another. Let us compare, for example, two judgments passed by two session judges.

The following passage is taken from a judgment concerning a narcotics case. The judge, who was known in the Shimla court milieu as an open-minded and non-convicting judge, addressed this issue as follows:

> The prosecution is bound to stand on its own legs and to prove the case beyond reasonable doubt. In view of the nature of the punishment provided for by the commission of alleged offences, standard of proof is also required to be much higher and case set-up is required to be proved in a mathematical manner and beyond any reasonable doubt. (*State of Himachal Pradesh* v. *Sanjay and others*, 2007)

This may be compared to the judgment of another judge of the Mandi Session Court, who was a close friend of the previous judge, but had more traditional views and was known as a 'convicting judge'.

> It is now fairly settled that there can hardly be a case with cast iron perfections in all respects … The court should not extend exaggerated devotion to the rule of benefit of doubt or lingering suspicion. Justice cannot be made sterile on the plea that it is better to let a hundred guilty persons escape than punish an innocent person. Proof beyond reasonable doubt constitutes a guideline and vague hunches cannot take the place of judicial evaluation. (*State of Himachal Pradesh* v. *Setu Devi*, 2004)

A High Court judge from Himachal Pradesh, who was well known for being very progressive and open-minded, considered the first passage as a 'regressive' kind of reasoning. 'This is what the law was twenty years back', he told me, 'but the law evolves … we cannot forget that witnesses in India can be bought. If independent witnesses turn hostile or if there are minor contradictions, this is not a reason to acquit the accused'. He noted how the notion of 'beyond reasonable doubt' has been subjected to historical transformations of the perception of proof. According to him, whereas twenty years ago the general attitude of judges was to make a ruling only if they were 100 per cent sure that the accused had committed the offence, today most judges 'pass judgment even if they are only 90 per cent or 80 per cent sure', depending on the judge. He also noted how the percentage of doubt that leads a judge to decide one way or another may sometimes depend on the time that has passed since the first sentence, especially when they have to return a verdict to acquit the accused. He gave me as an example a rape case where the accused had been acquitted twenty years earlier by the trial court and for which he now had to examine the appeal. The judge thought that the decision to acquit the accused was wrong and he strongly reproached most of his colleagues for not taking the rape case seriously. However, in the case in question, he finally decided to dismiss the appeal. He explained: 'The accused has now married and has a daughter who is almost my daughter's age. If after twenty years I put him behind bars his wife would be miserable and his daughter too'. He added, however, that he would no doubt have convicted the man if it had been a case of murder.

The experience and the consequence of doubting are probably not the same for a Session judge (who conducts the trial) and an Appeal Court judge. Unlike the appeal judge, who can merely rely on the court file or on the lawyer's statements, the doubt the trial judge has may increase or diminish after the judge has directly interacted with the witnesses and the accused. However, the kind of personal or intuitive opinion the judge has during the trial may sometimes be different from what he decides in his verdict because his decision must be based on the evidence that has been put on record during the hearings.[13] For example, in a rape case tried in Shimla court, during out-of-court discussions the judge appeared to be convinced that the victim, a nine-year-old girl from a Scheduled caste, had been raped by the accused, a Brahman boy, son of the girl's landlord. This could also be deduced during the hearings when, on behalf of the prosecutor, the judge on many occasions dictated the formula suggesting that the prosecution witnesses, who had turned hostile in favour of the accused, were telling a lie because they had received compensation from the party of the accused. In spite of this personal opinion and of the fact that other witnesses, including the schoolteacher, supported the prosecutor, he decided to acquit the accused. He wrote in the judgment:

> Confronted with the evidence discussed, finding recorded and law cited supra, this court is left with no option except to hold and conclude that the prosecution has miserably failed to prove its case beyond reasonable doubt. (Court file, *Himachal Pradesh State* v. *Devinder Sharma*, 2010)

He explained to me that, even when he thinks that the accused is guilty, he is strictly bound by the evidence required by state law. In this case, for example, even if important prosecution witnesses, such as the girl's teacher, had testified against

13 In such cases, the judgment of acquittal recorded by the trial judge sometimes appears to be in contradiction to the attitude he may have towards the prosecution witnesses at the time of the trial (accusing them of not telling the truth and of turning hostile).

the accused, the fact that the victim and her mother denied the offence transformed the other versions into 'hearsay'.

In cases like this where the judge considers that there are obstacles to convicting the accused, the notion of 'beyond reasonable doubt' might be used by the judge in a rhetorical way, as a catch-all notion automatically invoked to justify the decision of an acquittal. Here the presence of doubt is often associated with the 'chain of evidence theory' frequently used by judges in their written decisions. What follows is a short passage of a Supreme Court judgment referring to this idea of 'chain of evidence' in a High Court decision:

> There must be a chain of evidence so complete as not to leave any reasonable grounds for the conclusion consistent with the innocence of the accused and must show that in all human probability that the act must have been done by the accused. (*Sharad Birdhi Chand Sarda* v. *State of Maharashtra*, 17 July 1984)

As in the case of the mathematical certainty mentioned above by the Shimla judge, the 'chain of evidence theory' is played down by some judges who consider it possible to convict the accused even if some minor links in the chain are missing. The reasonable doubt that may prevent the judge from convicting a man may therefore vary depending on a multiplicity of factors which lead judges to present this notion as a 'doctrine' rather than as a personal or cognitive experience.

As A.C. Dogra, a former session judge who at the time of my fieldwork was Law Secretary in the Himachal government, told me:

> Each judge has his own approach to evaluating the evidence; that's why in a given case you find that the trial court will acquit the accused and then the High Court will convict the person. People may say that the trial judge has not assessed the evidence properly, that he overplayed the contradictions in the evidence. Now, the appreciation of circumstantial evidence depends on the judge's mindset. (Interview, Shimla 2011)

The technical rather than cognitive nature of doubting emerges in the way a judge may try to elude – at least partly – an element of doubt in order to convict the accused. Let us take an example. In 2012 during a criminal appeal at Himachal Pradesh High Court, a two-judge bench overturned a ruling to acquit the accused that had been pronounced by a trial court in 2004 concerning a case where the two accused, a man and his mother, had been charged simultaneously under section 372 (murder) and section 498a (harassment). They were accused of having harassed their respective wife and daughter-in-law by insisting that she bring a larger dowry, of having finally killed the woman and of staging the murder as a suicide. This theory was backed by the medical report according to which the cause of death was ante-mortem internal injuries, not hanging. It was also backed by the victim's family who had testified before the court regarding the dowry demands. However, a suicide note had allegedly been found by the husband, which said that none of her family should be held responsible for her suicide. This note, which a laboratory had certified as having been written by the victim, had led the trial judge to acquit the accused by giving them the benefit of the doubt. However, the appeal judges who, as one of them told me, were 'convinced that it was a case of murder' thought up a way of getting around what they admitted to be an element of doubt – the suicide note – by affirming that the woman had committed suicide as a result of the harassment inflicted on her by her husband and mother-in-law. They thus convicted the accused not of murder but of harassment and abetment to suicide. The way one of the judges on the bench explained their decision to me shows the reasoning process behind their decision:

> To be honest, if the suicide note was not there we would have sent them down for murder. Both of us were convinced in our minds that it was murder but what was standing in our way was the suicide note she had written. In fact, it may also be that the doctor had not done his job properly ... Now when there is a doubt, when a suicide note exists ... If there is a suicide note it cannot be murder. My brother (the other judge of his bench) and I, we kept discussing this matter. We discussed it many times. It took us two weeks to deliver the judgment, which is unusual in my court. So I said, OK [let it be murder], but we won't let them both get off scot-free. In the ruling we have come to the conclusion that it was not murder but suicide, and that the note was written under coercion. As there was also a case about dowry demands, we got them for a dowry death, which is seven years whatever the provision ... You see, these are cases where we have to think a lot. We thought that if we sentenced them for murder and then the suicide note worked at the Supreme Court [that is if the suicide note was again taken as an element of doubt] then they would be acquitted even for dowry death because no one will raise that issue there, so we thought it better to opt for a lesser crime. This is the way we work.[14]

The example shows how in this case the element of doubt, far from being a state of mind, was a technical obstacle for the judges which had to be strategically overcome. It also shows how judges may, in difficult cases, twist the case away from what they personally understand, when they are uncertain about how their decision is going to be received at the next level.

This kind of strategy that aims to find an alternative solution in order to convict the accused, even when there are technical obstacles to proving the offence, is not specific only to the court. The conversations I had with various state legal officers reveal a system that shows a similar attempt to sidestep the question of proof. According to this system, all serious criminal cases punishable by more than seven or ten years' imprisonment and which result in an acquittal by the

14 For information, the judge told me that both the accused were eventually acquitted by the Supreme Court.

Session Court are almost systematically sent to the Appeal Court. As one senior Advocate General in Shimla explained to me:

> When I worked at the Law Department we received from the prosecutor's office so many files that we didn't have time to examine them in detail. So we used to simply say that a file had not been properly examined by the court … In a criminal appeal it is very easy to prepare one or two pages on these grounds to file an appeal to the High Court instead of examining the case in detail. (Interview, Shimla, 2011)

This routinization of the appeal process seems to have less to do, here again, with a mental attitude than with a form of 'procedural doubt' where doubting appears to be integrated into the procedure itself.[15]

Concluding Remarks

In both contexts of judgment, doubt not only has to be resolved through the (ritual or judicial) procedure: it first has to be produced and made explicit. In both cases, the process of doubting appears less as a cognitive attitude than as a technical device completely integrated into the procedural rules which may be used both as a communication strategy and as a space for producing or imposing contrasting points of view. Although in ritual consultations doubting is presented as coming from the person who has to be judged (not from the judge, as in the case of a trial), in both cases doubt is first and foremost a technique controlled by ritual or legal professionals.

In ritual consultations, management of the 'verification techniques' (rice distribution, *ore pogre*) is a way for the person to become involved in the interpretative process and for the medium to reinforce the authority of his verdict. The technical character of doubt appears even more clearly in the context of criminal trials where casting doubt on the witnesses' credibility is part of the fighting spirit common to the adversarial procedure. Here the techniques of doubting (cross-examination, strategic use of the negative/affirmative in dictation) are very much aimed at casting doubt on what the witness is saying and on their credibility. Most of these techniques are not even understood by the person on whom doubt is cast

15 Behind this systematic recourse to appeal, there is also a problem of accountability, with every officer leaving the decision to the next officer. In fact, when a criminal case ends in an acquittal, the file of the case starts its journey through various offices where people have to give their opinion on whether the case should be sent for appeal. For serious offences, where the sentence is more than seven or ten years' imprisonment, the file is sent from the Home Department to the Law Secretary and then to the office that deals with criminal cases. In the event that an appeal is recommended, the file is sent to the Advocate General who represents the state at the High Court.

because they are pronounced in English and dictated directly to the stenographer. This therefore constitutes codified doubt, which is recorded in the file and is likely to be effective later on – when the (trial or appeal) judge has to write his decision.

Compared to these strategic and interactional techniques of doubting, the notion of 'beyond reasonable doubt' referred to by judges in their decisions may appear to rely on the judge's personal conscience. However, even this notion which is common to all adversarial systems seems rather far from the idea of an 'emotionally disrupting experience of doubting' as is often described in relation to the French idea of '*intime conviction*', which allows the judge (and the jurors) to pronounce a person 'guilty' or 'innocent' (Bouillier, this volume). As the expression may somehow suggest, 'reasonable' doubt lays emphasis on a more weighted, rational attitude which appears to be far from the 'disquiet and uncertainty' experienced by French jurors who, in a 'contemplative silence' and 'searching for the truth deep down within themselves', are eventually and suddenly 'invaded by an *intime conviction*' (Cuer 2011). In comparison, 'beyond reasonable doubt', at least in the way it is used in India, appears to be the consequence of an application of formal rules, which the judge may use independently from and even in contradiction with his '*intime conviction*'.

References

Beatty, Andrew (1999) *Varieties of Javanese Religion: An Anthropological Account,* Cambridge: Cambridge University Press.

Berti, Daniela (2009) 'Kings, gods and political leaders in contemporary India', in *Bards and Mediums in the Khas Kingdoms*, ed. Marie Lecomte-Tilouine, Almora: Himalayan Book Depot, pp. 107–36.

Berti, Daniela (2012a) 'Ritual faults, sins, and legal offences: a discussion about two patterns of justice in contemporary India', in *Sins and Sinners: Perspectives from Asian Religions*, ed. Phyllis Granoff and Koichi Shinohara, Leiden: Brill, pp. 153–72.

Berti, Daniela (2012b) 'Filing religion: the judicialisation of a religious conflict in Himachal Pradesh', Just-India Workshop, *Religion and the Court (India, Nepal)*, Paris, 18–19 June 2012.

Boyer, Pascal (1990) *Tradition as Truth and Communication: A Cognitive Description of Traditional Discourse*, Cambridge: Cambridge University Press.

Clémentin-Ojha, Catherine (2012) 'Claiming religious rights from a secular power: a judgment on the rules of succession to the charge of shebait in a North Indian temple', Just-India Workshop, *Religion and the Court (India, Nepal)*, Paris, 18–19 June 2012.

Cuer, Roland (2011) 'Doute et subjectivité du juge' [Le Bien Commun, with Antoine Garapon, originally broadcast 2 July 2011], available at http://ww.franceculture.fr/player/reecouter?play=4270827 (accessed 24 December 2013).

Granoff, Phyllis (2010) 'Justice and anxiety: false accusations in Indian Literature', *Rivista di Studi Orientali* 83(1–4): 377–98.
Hamayon, Roberte (2006) 'L'anthropologue et la dualité paradoxale du "croire" occidental', *Revue du MAUSS* 28(2): 427–48.
Højbjerg, Christian K. (2002) 'Religious reflexivity: essays on attitudes to religious ideas and practice', *Social Anthropology* 10(1): 1–10.
Lea, John (2006) 'The criminal court trial', available at http://www.bunker8.pwp.blueyonder.co.uk/cjs/26905.htm (accessed 24 December 2013).
Lenclud, Gérard (1990) 'Vues de l'esprit, art de l'autre. L'ethnologie et les croyances en pays de savoir', *Terrain* 14: 5–19.
Malik, Aditya (2010) 'In the divine court of appeals: vows before the god of justice', in *Hinduism and Law: An Introduction*, ed. Timothy Lubin, Donald R. Davis, Jr. and Jayanth K. Krishnan, Cambridge: Cambridge University Press, pp. 207–14.
Needham, Rodney (1972) *Belief, Language and Experience*, Oxford: Blackwell.
Pouillon, Jean (1993) *Le Cru et le su*, Paris: Seuil.
Rappaport, Roy (1999) *Ritual and Religion in the Making of Humanity, Cambridge: Cambridge University Press.*
Schlemmer, Grégoire (2009) 'Jeux d'esprits. *Ce* que sont les esprits pour les Kulung', *Archives des sciences sociales des religions* 145: 93–108.
Severi, Carlo (2002) 'Memory, reflexivity and belief: reflections on the ritual use of language', *Social Anthropology* 10(1): 23–40.
Sontheimer, Gunther-Dientz (1964) 'Religious endowments in India: the juristic personality of Hindu deities', *Zeitschrift für Vergleichende Rechtswissenschaft* 67: 45–100.
Vernant, Jean-Pierre (1985) 'De la présentification de l'invisible à l'imitation de l'apparence', in *Mythe et pensée chez les Grecs: Étude de psychologie historique*, Paris: La Découverte, pp. 339–51.
Veyne, Paul (1992) *Les Grecs ont-ils cru à leurs mythes?*, Paris: Seuil.
Whitman, James Q. (2008) *The Origins of Reasonable Doubt: Theological Roots of the Criminal Trial*, New Haven and London: Yale University Press.

Chapter 2

Judging Destiny: Doubt and Certainty in Chinese Divinatory Rituals

Stéphanie Homola

Taiwanese divination techniques help petitioners to make decisions in a moving and widely unknown environment. In this chapter, I analyse how the structure of these rituals and the techniques that are used to cope with doubts can be used as a model of decision-making under uncertainty. I focus on the processes of judging in various divination rituals that are widespread in today's Taiwan[1] and assess them from the point of view of both clients and practitioners. A common pattern can be identified, which aims at dealing with doubts that can arise at two levels.

First, regardless of the issue at stake in the divination ritual, the petitioner must be sure that the answer to his query is given by a reliable, fully qualified and benevolent authority. Thus, procedures aimed at eliciting and dispelling doubt, or 'techniques of doubting', are designed to dispel the petitioner's doubts about the diviner's ability or to assure them that the god is paying attention to their case.

Second, the analysis of the petitioner's case is itself a complex process that can lead to many misinterpretations or mistakes. I focus on the example of horoscopy to show how Taiwanese diviners of a so-called 'modern trend' have developed a rational method to give an accurate diagnosis of a complex and multi-dimensional reality. Indeed, diviners are torn between the need to be efficient (to predict something, somehow) and the risk of going beyond their competence (making a wrong prediction). To dispel the doubts of petitioners who often put their efficacy to the test, and to distinguish themselves from 'charlatans' who pretend that they can predict anything, modernist diviners are careful to make a fair use of their authority and advocate a scientific method whose scope is precisely defined and limited.

Focusing on the actual process of judging reveals that the concept of truth is a very unstable one. When drawing a parallel with the 'search for truth' that takes place during legal trials, this also reminds us that, as lawyers well know, the verdicts of judges and juries are often unpredictable. As petitioners and practitioners are faced with various options and interpretations, on what grounds

1 I conducted various periods of fieldwork in Taipei between 2007 and 2011 among fortune-tellers and their clients, most of whom were of Hoklo origin. Often referred to as 'Taiwanese', Hoklo are the largest ethnic group in Taiwan. Their Han Chinese ancestors migrated to Taiwan from Fujian in the seventeenth and eighteenth centuries.

do they admit some elements and reject others? I will thus try to analyse how a 'sense of truth' can arise in their mind.

Chinese[2] divinatory practices include a great a variety of techniques. One of the ways to classify them is to distinguish 'inductive' (or 'intuitive') divination which implies a communication with a non-human entity and 'deductive' divination which does not imply any such interaction.

Chinese 'deductive' divinatory methods are called *shushu* (divinatory arts) and aim at understanding the powers and processes that rule the world. In this category, the most widespread technique in contemporary Taiwan is calendar horoscopy (*mingli*). Horoscopy (also known as natal genethliacal astrology) is based on the construction and interpretation of a birth chart. The horoscope records and models the position of planetary and stellar bodies at the person's time of birth, and provides a frame to analyse their influence on his or her personality and destiny. Chinese horoscopy is known as 'astro-calendric' as it does not interpret the stellar positions but the calendar components of the birth date, through the *yin/yang* and five elements cosmological theories. The most popular horoscopy methods in today's Taiwan are the 'eight characters' (*bazi*) or 'four pillars' (*sizhu*) method[3] and the *ziwei doushu* method ('Numbers According to *Ziwei* [Star] and the Plough', also known as 'Purple Star Astrology'), which has strong Babylonian and Indian influences.

Given the focus on comparing ritual and legal practices of judgment, it is interesting to note that, in the European tradition, horoscopy is considered as a branch of 'judicial astrology'. Horoscopy developed in Europe during the Middle Ages and Renaissance and in Tang (618–907) and Song (960–1279) China, when astrology, which used to be performed by scholars for the benefit of rulers, was popularized among commoners, as personal horoscopes could be cast to judge the destiny of individuals. Thus, the word 'judicial' underlines both the process of judging which takes place in mantic rituals and the fact that this process can be applied to individuals and personal matters, and thus be shared by anyone in society.

Shushu also include name analysis (*xingmingxue*), physiognomony, palmistry, divination through the examination of bones (*mogu*), analysis of Chinese characters (*cezi*), geomancy (*fengshui*) and the *zhanbu* method. *Zhanbu*, which literally means 'to practise divination', is a method based on the *Book of Changes* and aims at answering specific queries.

---

2 I use the term 'Chinese' to designate divination practices that, despite local variations, are similar and widespread in Mainland China, Taiwan and the Chinese world in general. In the Taiwanese context, the use of 'Taiwanese' as opposed to 'Chinese' stresses the claim on the historical, social and cultural specificities of Taiwan, but such is not my point in this study.

3 The four pillars represent the four temporal coordinates of the birth date: year, month, day and hour. As each of them is represented by two signs in the Chinese luni-solar calendar system, the birth date is thus expressed by eight characters.

Divinatory arts differ from 'intuitive' divination practices which are explicit efforts to communicate with divinities or ancestors using divination blocks (*jiao*), divination sticks (*qian*) or by means of a medium. They also differ from the selection of auspicious days (*zeri*) which consists of consulting almanacs to determine the most suitable time for various actions (such as moving or getting married).

I first take the example of various divination rituals – horoscopy consultations, wandering fortune-tellers' devices and temple divination – to examine the techniques of doubting that aim to prove to petitioners that they are getting reliable answers. I then focus on the process of judging that takes place during horoscopy consultations and analyse the rational method through which modernist horoscopists investigate petitioners' cases and build their diagnoses.

Assessing Divination Reliability

The first kind of doubt a petitioner has to face concerns the practitioner's integrity, his ability and the accuracy of his interpretation. As we shall see, such doubts are not limited to 'human' relations and specific procedures aim at proving that divinities' answers are authentic. Indeed, it seems that in ritual practices of judgment in general, a large part of the process of judging consists in ensuring the quality of the relationship that is established between the petitioner and the human or non-human respondent, for the quality of this relation determines the quality of the answer. In this case, procedures for creating and then dispelling doubts aim at building the authority of the person or deity who will judge the case, and legitimating their subsequent verdict. This step generally precedes and is independent from the particular case which drew the petitioner to ask the help of a diviner or a divinity.

Testing Diviners' Skills

In the case of horoscopy consultations, the fortune-teller wins the client's trust and provides evidence of his expertise by commenting on the past and present situation of the petitioner (see also Tarabout, this volume). Indeed, scepticism is widespread among petitioners and may concern both the ability of the diviner and divination practices in general (Homola 2013).

Thus, Meifang, a postgraduate student, was very suspicious the first time she went to see a fortune-teller and the practitioner totally failed to dispel her doubts:

> First, she said that I was in a very difficult situation and that I had problems with my family. Then, as I didn't react, she looked at me with an air of mystery, and said 'Isn't it?' (*Shibushi?*) She wanted to see my reaction. Then she said that I had no problem with my family and that she had rarely seen such a beautiful fate. When she asked me in which branch I was working, I said, 'What do you think?' In fact, I wanted to test her, to see what she would say. Because one says

> that if a person is good at predicting the future, what she says about the past is particularly accurate (*zhun*).

Similarly, a young woman I interviewed went with a friend to consult a blind fortune-teller specializing in the examination of bones (*mogu*) but they did not disclose to the practitioner that the friend had to walk with a crutch because of a car accident:

> He did not see that she could not walk. He said that everything was fine and when we asked if she had to be careful about car accidents, he said no. It was so wrong (*bu zhun*) that we left. Normally, someone who really masters the *mogu* method can guess the number of brothers and sisters of the petitioner, his occupation or his parents' health.

Interestingly, blind diviners are usually said to be more reliable than sighted fortune-tellers because they cannot rely on handbooks and have to memorize the knowledge, and also because they cannot 'cheat' by inferring the petitioner's situation from their appearance.

Far from believing them unquestioningly, clients frequently test (*kaoyan*) diviners' skills. Such was the case of Zongyan, a postgraduate student, who experienced a psychological shock when he consulted a particularly insightful fortune-teller:

> I really believe in the *ziwei doushu* method because of a very special experience. One day, a fortune-teller who was using this method told me that I had a very 'weak' relationship with my parents. In fact, when I was little, I did not live with my parents. When I was born, my parents already had a daughter and a son and gave me to my father's elder brother who had no child. When I heard the explanation of the fortune-teller, I thought that it was really close to my situation.

Later on, the question of his adoption became a test issue when he consulted other fortune-tellers: he waited to see if the fortune-teller was able to read this information in the horoscope by himself. And as none of them had been able to see it, he decided to study the *ziwei doushu* method himself to understand if this element was really present in his horoscope and what interpretation could be made of it. Indeed, it is quite common that, faced with the incompetence of fortune-tellers, petitioners study divination techniques for themselves and through this process may gradually become practitioners.

Petitioners' fascination for powerful diviners and the accuracy of their predictions goes hand in hand with a strong scepticism. They are eager to believe that fortune-tellers can give them access to higher truths, but are constantly in search of evidence. Some practitioners anticipate clients' suspicions and implement their own test procedures so that they can turn them to their advantage.

'Don't Tell Anything, I Can Guess Your Name'

Here I briefly leave the Taiwanese fieldwork to present a case from Mainland China. Mr Yao, a wandering fortune-teller who performs palmistry and physiognomy in the streets of Beijing, has designed a special device to attract clients. Passers-by linger to look at a large poster he has spread on the floor featuring a table of Chinese surnames framed with the maxims: 'Don't need to tell anything, I can guess your name', 'Give me your hand and I know your destiny'. In addition, a small poster describes the services performed by Mr Yao: '*Book of Changes*, marriage, career, wealth, education and exams, promotion, going abroad, children, explaining dreams, solving problems, resolving crisis, geomancy of dwellings and graves, *fengshui*, and so on'. Two small folding stools and a flexible rule complete the fortune-teller's equipment. Mr Yao himself draws attention by his looks: his bright white hair and goatee contrast with his black Chinese style jacket and hat. A cane and a big jade ring give him an air of traditional respectability while fashionable sunglasses add a touch of modernity to this half-scholar, half-gangster style, but his dubious clothes, potbellied silhouette and the mischievous way he addresses passers-by make him look like a vagabond.

How does Mr Yao guess petitioners' names? The poster spread on the floor features a table of Chinese surnames made of 24 cells, each of them containing 25 surnames. Mr Yao first asks the petitioner to show on the poster in which square he can find his name. Then, he takes out of his pocket a set of plastic cards, each of them featuring about thirty surnames, and asks the client to show the card which contains his name. He puts the packet back in his pocket, observes and measures the petitioner's hand with the flexible rule, and finally announces the name of the client. Mr Yao claims he is '90 per cent accurate'. Although Mr Yao pretends he predicts clients' name from their palm, it is easy to understand that each grid cell and game card have only one name in common, which allows Mr Yao to guess the name of the person.[4] Although the names are organized in a logical way, Mr Yao needs a little time for reflection during which he observes the hand of the petitioner without speaking (it is indeed only after he has guessed the name that he starts on a thorough review of the hand).

Does Mr Yao consciously deceive people? Although he denies it, his device to guess petitioners' name can be considered as a fraud. However, from his point of view, this trick is necessary to attract clients. Such a deception is required by the trade but limited to a specific purpose. Once it has baited the client and put him in good psychological condition, Mr Yao can start the proper consultation based on true knowledge and experience. Similarly, some fortune-tellers resort to touts: the fortune-teller can thus impress passers-by by giving particularly accurate answers to a so-called petitioner (Yi 1993: 38). Such tricks are not considered

4 Mr Yao's device is based on the fact that the number of Chinese surnames is limited to a little over 4,000 and that the hundred most common Chinese surnames account for more than 80 per cent of the population in Mainland China.

cheating but rather as the skills of true know-how. As one practitioner puts it: 'With experience, I can guess eighty to ninety percent of people's fate just from their look' (Yi 1993: 16).

In the cases discussed above, both in horoscopy consultations and in Mr Yao's device, the practitioner proves his ability by guessing facts that the petitioner already knows and of which he himself is supposed to be ignorant. Thus, from the point of view of the client, the only purpose of this process is to ensure the ability of the diviner. He does not learn anything new, although in the case of horoscopy, analysis and interpretation of past and present events can lead the client to reflect on his situation or realize things he had been blind to. It is particularly obvious in Mr Yao's device: petitioners do not pay to know their name (one can hope they already know it) but to watch a kind of 'magic trick'. But one is bound to wonder to what extent a magic trick can really gain clients' trust. Magic tricks create a sense of wonder but do not eliminate scepticism. Like spectators of a magic show, petitioners are caught between wonder and the desire to understand the trick. And mostly, instead of winning petitioners' confidence, Mr Yao's device may equally well cast doubt on his subsequent and supposedly more learned performance. Such methods are indeed characteristic of wandering and outdoor fortune-tellers who lie at the bottom of the hierarchy of practitioners. Far from the still atmosphere of a consulting-room where the literate-looking diviner can weigh his words in front of a willing patron who has planned to spend time with him, the street fortune-teller must draw the attention of passers-by with his mere look and speech.

In horoscopy consultations and in Mr Yao's case, the degree of authority of the diviner depends on his ability to master techniques of dispelling doubts. As I shall point out in other cases, the question of authority and the way doubts are dispelled in divination practices is closely related to the social status of the practitioner and his positioning in the hierarchy of the trade. Thus, dispelling doubts by discoursing on the client's past as in the first example is more status-enhancing than guessing the client's name through a trick as in the second example.

Expression of Doubt in Temple Divination

In the case of temple divination using divination blocks and divination sticks, divinities cannot be accused of cheating or swindling. However, ritual procedures still aim at dispelling doubts that can affect the interaction between the petitioner and the god. Has the petitioner correctly formulated his query? Is the god ready to answer it? Does the petitioner understand the answer correctly?

Divination blocks (*jiao*) are two half-moon-shaped wooden blocks which are flat on one side and rounded on the other. Holding their flat sides together in the direction of the god or the ancestral altar, the petitioner makes a request and then throws the blocks on the ground. The answer of the god is positive if one block lands rounded-side-up and the other flat-side-up (*shengjiao*), negative if both fall rounded-side-up (*yinjiao*) and undetermined if both fall flat-side-up (*xiaojiao*, the god is 'laughing' and does not even consider the question).[5] Generally, three consecutive positive answers are required to confirm that the god answered 'yes' to the query. Otherwise, the petitioner can reformulate the question until he gets a suitable answer. This technique is so simple that it can be found in any temple, even in the smallest ones, and at people's homes.

Found only in major temples, the method using divination sticks (*chouqian*) is a sign that the god of the temple is considered to be *ling* (effective). Three elements are required: a pair of *jiao*, a set of one-hundred numbered bamboo sticks (*qian*) and a set of corresponding numbered poems written on small papers. First, the petitioner chooses a topic from a conventional list (marriage, lawsuit and so forth) and throws the *jiao* to see if the god is willing to answer the question. If the answer is positive, he shakes the tub containing the bamboo sticks, takes the one which visibly stands out, throws the *jiao* again and repeats the operation until the chosen stick is approved by the god. Lastly, he reads the corresponding poem and its interpretation which is usually adapted to different topics in the manner of 'marriage: not harmonious' or 'pregnancy: it's a son'. Temple monks can also help explain the message.

In these ritual procedures, doubt is expressed and overcome through repetition (see also Tarabout, this volume): three consecutive positive answers from the divination blocks are required to consider that the god answered 'yes' to the query or approved the selected divination stick. All other configurations are doubtful. Indeed, no consecutive answers are required in the two other cases when the god answers 'no' or refuses to answer the question. In consequence, unless the petitioner asks a query in a negative form, the negative answer is never definitive. Both 'negative answer' and 'the god is laughing' settings mean that the query has to be reformulated or that the problem must be viewed from a different perspective. The ritual process does not only aim at dispelling doubts but also leaves space for doubt (see also Berti, this volume). It provides a way out to the petitioner by leaving his query unanswered.

In his article, 'Taiwanese *poe* divination: statistical awareness and religious belief', David Jordan (1982) explores the statistical properties of *poe* (another pronunciation for *jiao*) divination and suggests that these properties are known and deliberately manipulated by the petitioners even if they claim that the blocks are governed by divine will. When throwing the blocks, petitioners have the same probability (50 per cent) of getting a positive response (two blocks in different positions) or a non-positive response (two blocks in the same position). The probability that the positive answer is confirmed (through three consecutive positive answers) is thus one out of eight. Probability declines if several issues

5 Julian Pas describes the last two settings in these words: 'Both flat sides are up, the curved sides touching the floor tiles. The goddess is laughing. Perhaps the woman did not concentrate enough, but at least, Matsu [the Goddess in this case] is in a good mood. If the blocks fell both on the flat side, they would express the goddess's anger, and one would interpret it as rejection for one's insincere, impure motivation' (Pas 1984: 10).

are linked together. As petitioners put it, it can take a long time before the god is willing to grant something.

Unlike coin tossing, which is determined by chance, divination blocks are said to be governed by divine law. However, petitioners also seem to recognize that *jiao* are subject to other influences than divine will and are aware of their statistical properties. For instance, they know that blocks must be thrown quite high and that it is unreasonable to ask for more than three consecutive positive answers. Jordan (1982: 117) presents the case of an elder in charge of a ritual in a village in South Taiwan. He performed block divination to find out whether the ritual had to be ended but as he himself wished the ritual to continue longer, he asked for more than three consecutive answers. After a while, other elders claimed that he had performed the divination ritual in a way that prevented him from getting a positive answer. Thus, block divination involves a suspension of belief in the statistical characteristics of *jiao* but at the same time, correct use of *jiao* requires action that takes into account its statistical nature. If ritual procedures allow the expression of doubt, it must be closely framed by conventions such as the one that limits the process to three consecutive answers.

Doubts about practitioners or unsettled queries in temple consultations are not seen as dysfunctional aspects of mantic practices but are fully integrated into the rituals. Although they do not deal directly with the core of the petitioner's request, procedures for assessing the authenticity of the divinatory response are essential as they create a space for doubt. The diviner's proficiency or the god's willingness to answer the query stand as adjustment variables that allow the petitioner to determine what can be trusted as true and what can be rejected as untrue.[6]

In the case of diviners' consultations, such a 'space for doubt' can be linked to the low social status of fortune-tellers. Nobody feels inferior to a fortune-teller and in case of disagreement or inconvenient truth the client is free not to believe the practitioner or to treat him as a charlatan or a swindler. It is indeed to remedy this flaw and to distinguish themselves from 'charlatans' that Taiwanese horoscopists of the 'modern trend' advocate a rational reform of horoscopy which precisely aims at dispelling doubts about practitioners' proficiency.

Judging the Case through Rational Investigation

Having described techniques of doubting that allow the petitioner to judge the reliability of the practitioner's diagnosis or of the divinity's answer, I now discuss the judging process at work in the evaluation of the client's situation and show how practitioners deal with their own doubts during the process of interpreting the horoscope. In this case, techniques of doubting aim at exploring and clarifying the ins and outs of a decision as well as the context in which it takes place. In

6 Which very often depends on personal and/or social interests (see Tarabout, this volume).

particular, I will discuss the method of a so-called 'modern trend' of horoscopists (*xiandai pai*) who since the 1970s have been advocating a kind of 'rationalist' reform of mantic theories and practices in Taiwan.[7]

In today's Taiwan, many fortune-tellers practise only occasionally and have other professions. Working as a fortune-teller does not require any diploma or registration and practitioners do not have to pay any tax. Each fortune-teller has his own way of working and likes to claim it. However, three main types of fortune-teller can be defined. Professional fortune-tellers practise fortune-telling as a profit-seeking full-time activity. They are often disliked by the second category, non-professional fortune-tellers who practise for or teach people who ask for help. They self-identify as the guarantors of a virtuous and technical knowledge and reject accusations of superstition and swindling. Finally, medium-fortune-tellers claim that they do not practise on the ground of learned knowledge but on the ground of innate abilities.

Modernist horoscopists in Taiwan are usually non-professional practitioners of the second type. Most of them do not belong to any hereditary line and are mainly self-taught. They are opposed to professional practitioners who maintain the myth of a secret and selective transmission of divinatory knowledge and whose practices are based on charismatic authority rather than on technical proficiency. To distinguish themselves from these 'charlatans', as they call them, who pretend they can predict anything, modernist horoscopists are careful to make a fair use of their authority and advocate a non-magical, scientific method. To their mind, the only way to dispel doubt about practitioners' integrity is to establish reliable and standardized techniques, which requires two elements. First, the scope of horoscopy must be clearly defined and limited. Second, inside this limited scope, divinatory arts should be as rigorous as science in both their theoretical foundations and their practical application. The degree of authority claimed by modernist horoscopists is directly linked to their mastery of techniques of doubting, and of dispelling doubt: they assert that doubts can be dealt with in a systematic way and that they can be fully dispelled as long as they are precisely circumscribed.

Limited Responsibility

As they highlight the technical dimension of divinatory arts, modernist practitioners take the position of experts whose skills and responsibilities are clearly defined. Thus, if fate is determined by Heaven, methods of fate analysis are created by men and, as such, are not infallible.

The example of name selection is indicative of the limits of practitioners' responsibility and of the corrective procedures that can be provided in case of error. Choosing a name for a newborn baby is a heavy responsibility for the

7 This presentation is based on interviews with and writings of members of the 'modern trend'. In particular, I rely on interviews with a Taiwanese practitioner, Ruli Jushi, and on his books on the eight characters and *ziwei doushu* methods (Jushi 2003, 2010).

parents, who often seek the help of a diviner. Through a technique known as 'name analysis' (*xingmingxue*) based on semantic analysis and on numerology (according to the number of lines composing Chinese characters), the diviner determines a propitious name that must reflect the parents' expectations, discard bad influences and at the same time be compatible with the child's horoscope and that of his parents. In many cases, the diviner does not take the risk of proposing a single name. One practitioner I interviewed explained that he usually suggests no less than twenty or thirty names and asks the parents to test each of them in front of the ancestors' altar at home using divination blocks. After announcing to the ancestors the name they want to test, the parents throw the divination blocks. They repeat the operation until they get three consecutive positive answers, which means that the ancestors have approved the chosen name. In this case, the task of choosing a name requires a combination of deductive and inductive divination. The diviner helps identify a limited number of options but the final choice belongs to the ancestors. Responsibility is thus shared between the diviner and the ancestors, between human and divine judgment.

Although choosing an inauspicious name can have serious consequences, such a mistake is not irrevocable as people can change their names to discard bad influences. The legal procedure is not very complicated and quite common. For instance, a father who relied on 'name analysis' to choose the name of his daughter by himself lamented on the mistake he made, which caused his daughter many misfortunes in her childhood. When he had his daughter's name analysed by a specialist, he discovered that although the sign meaning 'water' in his daughter's name is written with three dots, it is traditionally counted as two lines when computing characters' lines in name analysis. Thus, it appeared that due to this mistake, the total number of lines of his daughter's name was highly incompatible with her birth date. A new name was eventually chosen which freed his daughter from bad luck.

Indeed, such corrective procedures do not only alleviate the responsibility of specialists; they are also used to adapt to an ever-moving environment. For instance, a person can change name several times in her life to fit the different stages of her fate.

Another example shows that fortune-tellers are reluctant to go beyond their competence and the limits of divinatory arts. In Taiwan, many women decide to give birth by caesarean section in order to choose the birth date and consequently the horoscope of their child. It is indeed usual to consult a fortune-teller to settle the most fortunate birth date for a child, and the topic 'caesarean section' is one of the services provided by fortune-tellers. However, many fortune-tellers are reluctant to settle birth dates because they believe humans are not and should not be able to settle their own fate. Because of the rise in caesareans, some fortune-tellers assert that fate is not determined by the date of birth but by the date of conception.

In the mind of modernist horoscopists, acknowledging the limitations of divinatory arts does not reduce their efficacy. On the contrary, they assert that they can only be fully reliable when used correctly, that is to say in appropriate circumstances and according to a rigorous and definite method.

Judging Destiny through a Rigorous Method

Horoscopic methods aim at seeking appropriate courses of action in an uncertain environment, that is to say, at understanding how the acts of a particular individual interact with a particular environment at a particular time. 'Is this action favourable to this person at that particular time?' asks the diviner. The answer – the diviner's diagnosis – does not arise from quick and general impressions. It is built through a rigorous process which takes place during the consultation. This process implies a comprehensive analysis of the petitioner's past, present and future. The horoscope is used to search past conjunctions of personality traits, actions and circumstances which have led to the (often problematic) current situation, so as to make adjustments in the future.

As criminal judges would do in a trial, diviners use every type of proof (oral, material, sociological, psychological) to reconstitute the bundle of factors that determine the situation of a human being at a particular time. When assessing the situation, they also make a clear distinction between elements that depend on the free will of the individual and those that are beyond their control. As experts, diviners go rationally through every component of the case but also rely on their own experience as human beings to build their opinion and convince the petitioner.

From a technical point of view, modernist diviners rely on a rigorous formal pattern which combines theoretical concepts (such as fate), technical devices (such as the horoscope's grid) and open debate (during the consultation) to investigate the situation of a particular person in interaction with a particular environment.

Fate as an Investigative Concept

Fate (*mingyun*), in China, consists of two elements. The *ming* represents the part of fate that is determined at birth and cannot be altered. It is innate (*xiantian*) and corresponds to a person's lifespan. The *yun* is not located in the self but in the moving relations between the self and its environment over successive ten-year periods. It stands for the changeable part of fate, the one that the individual can use to his advantage through his efforts and which is thus acquired (*houtian*). The *yun* represents the good or bad configurations which arise from the confrontation between the *ming* and external circumstances. *Yun* means both movement and fate and can also be translated as 'luck'. Interactions between the two types of fate open the way to many possibilities and divination is a practical tool which aims to discover harmonious and favourable intersections between the *ming* and the *yun*. Thus, *mingyun* is often compared to a plant. The *ming* stands for the seed and the *yun* for the season when the seed is planted. If the seed is of good quality but is not planted at the right time, it will grow poorly. Conversely, a good *yun* can often compensate for a lack in *ming*. For this reason, it is considered that having a good *yun* is better than having a good *ming*.

This concept of fate underlines the diachronic dimension of the individual. A particular situation at a particular time is considered as the result of a moving process involving consequences of past events, evolution of personality and opportunities or obstacles in the environment. As flexible as it may seem, modernist Taiwanese diviners claim that this conception of fate does not elude the problem of determinism. Indeed, although moving, the *yun* is pre-determined, like the *ming*, which leads 'charlatans' to make irrational, excessive and dangerous interpretations. For example, according to modernist horoscopists, the belief that some women pose a threat to the life of their husbands because of a particular horoscope is unworthy of a modern society.[8] To dismiss accusations of superstitions, magic or irrational practices, modernist diviners have developed a concept of fate which clearly states the limits of horoscopy.

Three main factors influence the destiny of a person. The first one is the 'great environment' (*da huanjing*) which refers to the country in which the person is born, its culture, political system and level of economic and social development. The second factor is the 'small environment' (*xiao huanjing*) which represents the context into which the person is born: social status of the family, education, influence of his friends, teachers and so on. The third factor consists of the good and bad aspects of the horoscope as expressed through the vicissitudes of the *ming* and the *yun*. According to this conception of fate, two persons may be born at the same time but they will have a very different destiny if one is born into a peasant family and the other into an upper-class family.

These three factors are also organized into a hierarchy: the first is more important than the second which is itself more important than the third. Not only does the horoscope stand for only one share out of three in the destiny of a person, but it represents the least important one. In contrast to religious determinism, this conception gives full credit to the decisive role of the environment in shaping individuals' personalities and actions.

A Technical Device: The Horoscope's Grid

This general theoretical principle is implemented through the technical device of the horoscope. In the *ziwei doushu* method, the horoscope is a grid composed of twelve houses (see Figure 2.1). One of them represents the individual (House of Destiny) and the others represent either relatives (House of Parents, House of Siblings …) or important issues that are bound to influence the individual's fate (House of Illness, House of Occupation …). Stellar and calendar symbols are placed in the different houses according to the person's birth date. The horoscope repeats the distinction between the two aspects of fate (*ming* and *yun*). Each square corresponds to a ten-year period of the *yun*. The *ming* is represented by

8 In palmistry, such a fate is evidenced by a 'broken palm line' (see Lin 2003).

the horoscope as it is drawn the first time. It depicts both the innate characteristics of the person and the first ten-year period of his fate. The other *yun* periods are analysed by revolving the horoscope so as to place the House of Destiny on the corresponding ten-year period. Stellar and calendar symbols are fixed while houses move, which leads to a different interpretation for each ten-year period.

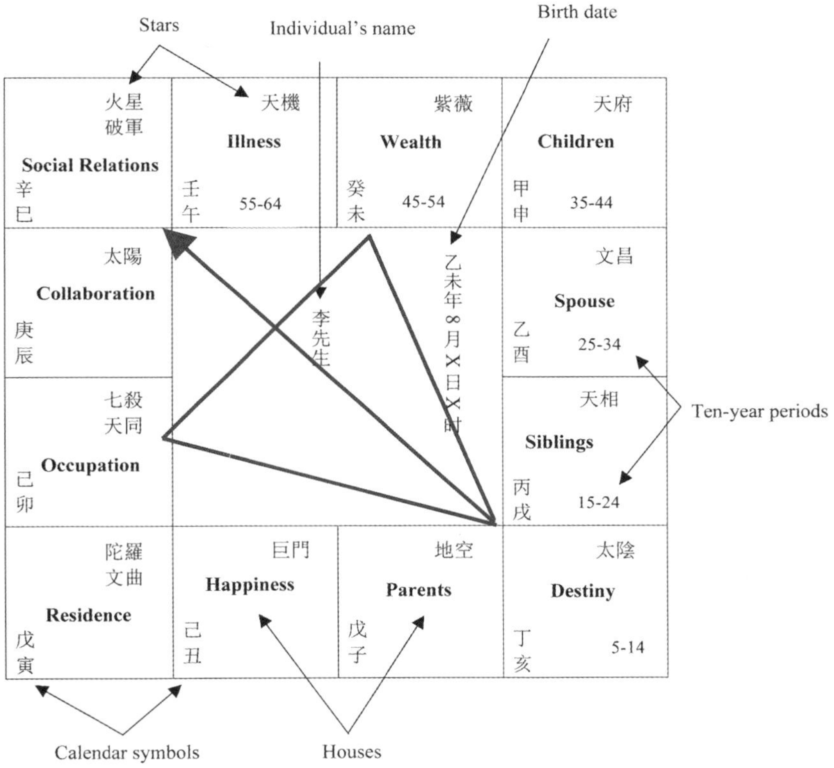

Figure 2.1 The structure of the horoscope grid in the *ziwei doushu* method[9]

The horoscope device and its interpretation display several characteristics that can be used as a model for judging and decision-making.

First, the House of Destiny is the pivot of the horoscope's analysis, which means that the situation is always assessed from the point of view of the individual. However, the House of Destiny – representing the individual – has no meaning in itself: it must be interpreted in interaction with other houses. Indeed, the different stellar or calendar symbols are neutral and become meaningful only when they are

9 This horoscope was calculated by Ruli Jushi during a consultation.

related to each other. Such an interpretation suggests that although it tends to be as unbiased as possible, judging is a subjective and relative act that is embedded in a social context.

Second, this relational interpretation is limited to a reduced number of houses. This particular relationship is symbolized by a kind of triangle which connects the House of Destiny with three other houses: the House of Social Relations, the House of Occupation and the House of Wealth. These houses are the only ones that depend on the individual's will and that he can control and change. This underlines the fact that, although many external factors influence a person's destiny, they can only control a limited number of elements. When assessing the situation, diviners use this triangular relation to make a clear distinction between elements that depend on the free will of an individual and those that are beyond their control.

Thus, occupation belongs to an area that is influenced by the character of a person, along with environmental factors, such as parents' expectations. The adaptation of the individual to their work, which determines failure or success, is the result of a complex set of internal and external conditions. The House of Social Relations indicates the person's ability in human relations. The House of Wealth describes the attitude of the individual towards money (and not directly the amount of wealth, as 'charlatans' would assert, for the wealth of a person depends on many external factors). Other houses are linked with the 'self' in an indirect way and can only lead to very abstract interpretations. For instance, the House of Happiness was once used to determine the predestined lifespan (*yangshou*) of the individual. Modernist horoscopists totally reject this form of determinism and assert that it must be interpreted in connection with the House of Wealth to determine the origin of the person's wealth. Similarly, they claim that consulting a doctor to find the cause of one's illness is far more efficient than analysing the House of Illness. Such principles underline that the factors that depend on the will of the individual are the only fully reliable ones and should be used as the main basis in decision-making. Conversely, factors that are independent of the individual and are thus not controllable should be used with caution.

Third, the different fields listed in the grid allow the diviner to perform a systematic inquiry into the individual's personality and motives. This comprehensive approach leads the petitioner to consider his problems from different angles and to identify factors, risks or opportunities he may have been blind to in the first place. The grid also helps the petitioner express intimate problems: the diviner does not seem to investigate, as a psychologist would do (he only 'reads' the grid) and the petitioner does not have the feeling that the diviner is trying to wring secrets out of him.[10] Thus, the grid device suggests that decision-making should follow a methodical approach including a systematic listing and reviewing of items. These items should not be narrowly restricted to the case at stake but also bring a broader perspective.

---

10 For further elements on the comparison between Western psychologists and Chinese fortune-tellers, see Luo (1993).

Lastly, mantic techniques provide a theoretical model to assess the individual's personality. The different configurations that arise in the horoscopes are classified into broad categories which are in turn detailed in more precise types. Thus, different categories of fate or personality define people who share various characteristics such as personal character, fields of interest, intellectual skills, relational abilities and opportunities for social promotion. Indeed, modernist diviners underline the statistical dimension of mantic techniques: it is only because people who were born under the same configuration have common characteristics that divination is possible. It is interesting to note that, although the horoscope is strictly personal, it can only be understood through the analysis of shared patterns. This suggests that when taking a decision, one should take into account comparable cases and search for similar experiences to assess one's own case. Such a process is similar to judicial decision-making in common-law systems, which justifies the decisions reached with reference to legal precedents.

The horoscope gives a bird's eye view of the bundle of factors that determine the situation of a human being at a particular time. It also records the changing frames of mind with which a person faces life events. Thus, mantic techniques appear to be a powerful tool for life management and decision-making: they teach people how to choose the right path, find the way of life that best suits them and adapt to a moving environment.

Open Debate

The horoscope's grid is not meant to be analysed by the diviner only. It also fosters interaction and debate between the practitioner and his client. Oral debate in public consultations or between the diviner and the petitioner helps dispel doubt and work out the truth collectively.

Modernist practitioners often disapprove of the sceptical attitude of some clients that I described in the first part of this chapter. As these practitioners do not claim any 'magical' ability, they have nothing to 'hide' from petitioners and wish they would fully collaborate to reach a better result. Indeed, familiarity and intimacy are the ideal and most efficient relationships between a fortune-teller and his patron. Practitioners proceed by trial and error and need to dispel doubt through discussion with the petitioner. First, diviners need to assess the factors of the 'big' and 'small' environments which cannot be read in the horoscope but greatly influence the native's fate. Second, they need to evaluate to what extent the general 'fate configuration' expressed in the horoscope applies to the particular situation of the petitioner. Therefore, the more the petitioner reveals about his situation, the more precise and useful the diagnosis.

In opposition to the habit of testing practitioners that I presented above, another petitioner I interviewed has well understood that it is in the client's interest to work with the fortune-teller:

> The more you tell the fortune-teller, the more accurate (*zhun*) the interpretation and the more helpful the advice. If you have doubts about what the fortune-teller says, what's the point of seeing him? If you go to see him, it's because you want him to help you solve a problem. To have a sceptical attitude when consulting a fortune-teller is contradictory (*maodun*).

During the iterative process of the discussion, the diviner and the petitioner work together to reach a fair and acceptable diagnosis of the situation. Indeed, interpretations are seldom unambiguous. For instance, a particular symbol in the horoscope will mean either 'inheritance' or 'promotion'. If the petitioner has no fortunate relatives, the diviner will opt for the second meaning. Faced with two possible interpretations, the practitioner relies on information given by the petitioner to dispel doubts. In some cases, the client does not know the precise hour of his birth, which prevents the diviner from drawing the horoscope. A solution to this problem is to test various scenarios based on different birth hours and compare them with the client's situation to guess which hour is the most probable birth hour.

The quality of the consultation and of the relationship between the diviner and his client depends on the skills and frame of mind of both of them as the diviner's oral performance is stimulated by the interactions with the petitioner.[11] Usually, a 'good' fortune-teller knows how to adapt to the petitioner's reactions and will not stick to an interpretation if it is obviously in contradiction to the petitioner's experience. Conversely, an open-minded client will not reject a seemingly wrong comment but will ponder how it could actually apply to his case and help him consider the situation from a new angle.

Shared Subjectivities as the Keystone of Judging

Diviners and petitioners work together to assess a course of action under uncertain circumstances and on the basis of incomplete information. They have to overcome another core problem of judging and decision-making: how to judge subjective situations as objectively as possible. Petitioners' cases tell the complex stories of human beings embedded in a history, desires and passions, but diviners also have personal histories, ideologies and emotions which influence their judgment.

Divination practices show that far from being an obstacle, human subjectivity can be used effectively. The horoscopic method of judgment that I have presented above takes advantage of the fact that a man's situation is assessed by a fellow man, as it takes into account the subjectivity of both the petitioner and the diviner. Such methods, based on intersubjectivity, require a comprehensive assessment of the situation that includes the personal experience of the subject. Chinese horoscopy gives a complex and multi-dimensional diagnosis of a situation from the point of view of the individual. Through this in-depth investigation, the diviner

11 Luo Zhengxin (1997) analyses the verbal art of fortune-tellers during the consultation.

enters the intimacy of the petitioner and the petitioner better understands their own situation. The resonance between this intimacy and their own inner feelings allows the diviner to dispel doubts, reduce the risks of errors and antagonistic interpretations, and build a reliable diagnosis.

Diviners rely on their own experience as human beings to give advice. During the consultation, the petitioner stands back from their personal situation and views it from a different angle. Thus, in the case of divination, the sharing of subjectivities may be considered as a keystone of the act of judging. This differs from the act of judging in legal contexts, or at least from the positivistic interpretations of decision-making as portrayed in most legal theory. However, Carolina Kobelinsky's study (this volume) of hearings at the French Court of Asylum shows that, in practice, judges do sometimes reach decisions on the basis of their emotional response to an asylum seeker's narrative, which represents a kind of intersubjectivity.

The conception, conveyed by mantic systems, of a human being as a whole, embedded in a complex and unique situation but sharing a common humanity with others, seems to underlie the process of judging in everyday life: what would I do *if I were this person and given the circumstances*? One can thus suggest that the power of judgment – that is, the faculty to cope with uncertainty in everyday life and to make judicious choices – is linked to the ability to consider others as one's equals. This contrasts with legal judgments where the relationship between a judge and an accused or an asylum applicant is clearly unequal, as the judge can impose their decision on the petitioner.

Concluding Remarks – The Sense of Truth

Divinatory practices are particularly useful to ponder how the sense of truth (as opposed to truth as an absolute and inaccessible concept) arises. How does a petitioner get the feeling that a diviner's prediction is accurate (*zhun*)? Why do numerous false predictions not lead to the discarding of divination as a whole? Why do clients still consult a diviner whose predictions did not come true? As already mentioned, when facing erroneous predictions, the petitioner can put the blame on the diviner's incompetence or on errors of interpretation, but actually, some predictions have to be wrong for others to be true and this is precisely why the notion of 'accuracy' is so important.

Indeed, the feeling that a prediction is accurate does not systematically arise a posteriori, after a prediction actually comes true, but most of the time during the consultation, through the relationship between the petitioner and the diviner. The beginning of the consultation, when the practitioner gains the client's trust and establishes their authority by analysing the client's past, is thus particularly important. Among all that is said by the diviner, 'accurate' statements are those which happen to 'make sense' to the petitioner, most of the time during the consultation, or afterwards, when the prediction which has been forgotten actually comes true. In both cases, 'making sense' means giving a special meaning to an event that would not have any particular meaning otherwise. For instance, losing an umbrella takes on a particular meaning if a diviner once told the petitioner that the loss of objects would be a sign of a big change in his life. Conversely, inaccurate predictions are words that do not resonate in the client's mind and therefore are often forgotten. As a petitioner puts it: 'Sometimes, there is no feeling with the fortune-teller'.[12]

This pattern can help us understand the process that shapes petitioners' convictions: among a set of uncertain events, facts and arguments, some elements resonate in their mind, draw their attention, gain the upper hand over other facts and finally give one particular arrangement of reality a feeling of truth. To the client, this feeling of truth is not a mere intellectual satisfaction but provides a guide for action. Thus, a petitioner once explained to me what he calls 'the power of fortune-telling':

> It is like moving in the dark with a miner's lamp or with a lighter. When you hold a powerful miner's lamp, you can see very far, you can know how far you will go and how you will walk. But when you hold a lighter, you can only see one or two steps away, no more. And when you're holding a miner's lamp, you do not walk the same way as if you were holding a lighter and were afraid to make a wrong step and to walk where you should not have walked.

The difference between certainty and uncertainty is a matter of how well-lit one's environment is. Thus, by judging, through a shared process, how petitioners are embedded in their environment, Chinese divination rituals work as a powerful device to dispel doubts and allow them to move in confidence.

References

Berthod, Marc-Antoine (2007) *Doutes, croyances et divination. Une anthropologie de l'inspiration des devins et de la voyance*, Lausanne: Antipodes.

Homola, Stéphanie (2013) 'Pursue good fortune and avoid calamity: the practice and status of divination in contemporary Taiwan', *Journal of Chinese Religions* 41(2): 124–47.

Jordan, David (1982) 'Taiwanese *poe* divination: statistical awareness and religious belief', *Journal for the Scientific Study of Religion* 21(2): 114–18.

12 In his study of fortune-telling in Switzerland, Marc-Antoine Berthod (2007) underlines how fortune-tellers manage to create an 'event' in the petitioner's mind, on which they can build a common history with them during the consultation. Fortune-tellers also express the intuitive feeling that guides their divinatory speech and analysis as an 'extension of their self'.

Jushi, Ruli (2003) *Ziwei Dazhan Tanlang: Xiandai Doushu yu Shengya Guihua* [*Ziwei Star vs Tanlang Star: The Modern Method of the Numbers According to [Ziwei and] the Plough and Career Planning*], Zhonghe: Baishan Shufang.

Jushi, Ruli (2010) *Bazi Guo Wuguan* (*Eight Characters Method*), Taipei: Wuling.

Lin, Szu-Ping (2003) 'The woman with broken palm lines: subject, agency, fortune-telling, and women in Taiwanese television drama', in *Multiple Modernities: Cinemas and Popular Media in Transcultural East Asia*, ed. Jenny Kwok Wah Lau, Philadelphia: Temple University Press, pp. 222–37.

Luo, Zhengxin (1993) 'Suanming yu xinli fudao [Divination and psychological counselling]', *Bentu Xinlixue Yanjiu* 2: 316–37.

Luo, Zhengxin (1997) 'Suanming jiqiaoli de yuyan biaoyan [Language performance in fortune-telling techniques]', *Zhongyang Yanjiuyuan Minzuxue Yanjiusuo Jikan* 84: 37–60.

Pas, Julian (1984) 'Temple oracles in a Chinese city: a study of the use of temple oracles in Taichung, Central Taiwan', *Journal of the Hong Kong Branch of the Royal Asiatic Society* 24: 1–45.

Yi, Ren (1993) *Dangdai Zhongguo de Suanmingre* [*Fortune-telling Fever in Contemporary China*], Beijing: Beijing Shifan Daxue Chubanshe.

Chapter 3

Religious Uncertainty, Astrology and the Courts in South India[1]

Gilles Tarabout

As one of the multiple techniques intended to rationalize decision-making by reducing uncertainty, astrology is regularly sought after in India. A widely shared assumption is that important decisions as well as our day-to-day affairs are part of a general, divine order which, though not immediately perceptible, can be deciphered with the appropriate tools. An astrologer's advice is needed for choosing a spouse, for timing the beginning of an action and for solving a variety of problems. However, interpreting the divine order and deciding the best path of action may prove to be tricky, so that doubts linger everywhere, in the astrologer's own mind as well as in his client's. Astrologers are therefore cautious about the proofs they require and the reasoning they follow (see Vernant *et al.* 1974; also Homola, this volume).

The present chapter describes how such doubts may be expressed, manipulated and tentatively dispelled in the context of an astrological practice dealing with Hindu temples in Kerala, on the south-western coast of India. This practice is called *deva prasnam*,[2] 'divine query'. I present its main characteristics before detailing the process by which astrologers try to clear their own doubts as well as those of their clients – a process which some astrologers like to compare, rather superficially, to a trial in a court. However, astrologers may fail to manage the situation to the satisfaction of their clients: this leads in some cases to accusations against them before an actual law court. The last part of the chapter evokes some cases in which astrology has been involved in trials in Kerala. I suggest that while the procedures in the astrological and judicial contexts may show some superficial similarities, a judgment is enforceable whereas an astrological opinion is not; it can therefore be endlessly questioned. Doubts in astrology are never completely dispelled and their perpetuation depends not so much on the possible failure of the

1 This chapter is a product of the ANR programme 'Just-India: A Joint Programme on Justice and Governance in India and South Asia' (http://just-india.net) funded by the French National Research Agency (ANR-08-GOUV-064).

2 The transcription of technical terms follows the spelling in Malayalam, the main language in Kerala, even for words of Sanskrit origin. Plural forms are indicated by adding an 's'. Place names are spelt according to current Anglicized usage.

astrologers to impress on their audience the rationality of their procedures and of their statements, as on particular interests and expectations.

Temple Astrology in Kerala

Hindu astrology comprises three main branches: birth horoscope (*jatakam*), determination of favourable moments (*muhurttam*) and resolution of questions (*prasnam*). The practice we are concerned with belongs to the third category (for more detailed accounts, see Bhat 1992; Tarabout 2002, 2006, 2007).[3]

Temple astrological consultations are organized in Kerala when devotees want to improve the temple buildings or the ceremonies, or when there is the perception that past unfortunate events point to a divine imbalance. Trustees of the temple committee call an astrologer or visit him in order to formulate their questions.[4] The timing of this first encounter has much relevance for the astrologer, who draws the horoscope of the moment; it gives nearly all the clues for understanding the temple's effective problems according to some practitioners. Indeed, the question put by the temple's committee is seen by the astrologer as a distress signal sent by the temple's main deity, even when the question is about improvements. In all cases, the astrologer will proceed to an exhaustive audit of the temple situation. Who are the deities residing there (sometimes the consultation discloses that their identity has been mistaken or that some were forgotten)? What is the past history of the shrines (the astrologers may go back several hundred years)? What are the causes of present-day misfortune (usually pollution by ghosts)? What is the current state of ritual practice (quite often, the priest's ability is questioned)? How does it fare economically (astrologers may point to mismanagement)? And, eventually, how may the temple prosper in future (astrologers recommend ritual solutions, and eventually answer the question put to them by the committee)?

After this first meeting, the astrologer decides with the committee when and how to hold the main session of the *deva prasnam*, which will be a public event in the temple itself and may last from one to seven or more days; it is often advertised in local newspapers. During this session, the astrologer leads a team of his colleagues and is accompanied by some students in astrology. They all come at the appointed time to the temple, enter its precincts and sit down in front of the inner shrine whose door is left open so that the god or the goddess may directly observe the proceedings. The temple committee and the rest of the audience dispose themselves around them. A complex sequence of ritualized acts follows

3 I rely on ethnographic material gathered during fieldworks in Kerala in 1991, 1994 and 1999. I am particularly indebted to the astrologers consulted for sparing their time in order to satisfy my curiosity, and to my friends N. Rajasekharan Nair, K.P.C. Anujan Bhattattiripad and L.S. Rajagopalan for their constant support.

4 I will refer to an astrologer by using 'he' or 'his' as, to the best of my knowledge, all the astrologers involved in *deva prasnam* are men.

that lasts a few hours, of which every detail takes an ominous importance. This is called the 'ceremony of the eight auspicious objects' (*ashtamamgalam kriya*). It is a set of actions intended to make manifest the condition and the will of the temple's main deity: an oil lamp is lit by the priest who also prepares the eight auspicious objects (typically white rice, turmeric, vermillion, betel leaves with an areca nut, a new piece of cloth, a mirror, a coin or a ring in gold and a book – often a copy of the *Bhagavad Gita*); an astrological chart is drawn on the ground with sacred ashes and a cult is offered there; a small child is then invited to lay down a gold coin in this chart. The astrologers note the time when the child lays down the gold coin, as well as the usual astrological data (rising sign, lunar day, lunar mansion, planetary positions) which enable them to calculate the horoscope of the moment. Besides, the way the chart has been drawn, the name of the child, her native lunar mansion, how she is dressed, how she behaves, in which zodiacal sign she has put the gold coin, the position of the coin (face upward or downward), the direction in which the flame of the oil lamp is bending, the quality of the oil and of the wicks, the number of betel leaves that have been offered, all these elements are charged with significance and play a major role in the interpretation.

When the ceremony of the eight auspicious objects is complete, the interpretation proper begins. It takes the form of a prolonged discussion between astrologers, and between the astrologers and the audience, with little ritualization; it may last several days. A written report (between ten to fifty pages) is drafted at the end of the procedure by the main astrologer. It is countersigned by each member of his team and given to the temple committee.

The whole process is thus a complex social interaction in which stakes can run very high: the sheer cost of ritual remedial measures recommended by the astrologers runs above 100,000 Indian Rupees, and possible modifications of the buildings may cost much more. Besides, astrologers often harshly criticize temple employees, which may lead to their dismissal. A *deva prasnam* is therefore also an exercise in power and astrologers have recourse to a variety of arguments in order to make their point. A major claim in this respect is to operate scientifically.

Astrology as a Science

Astrologers insist that astrological statements can be, and are, empirically verified. Some astrologers whom I met had had a background in science: for instance, one was a former university professor in chemistry, another was working in a space research centre. Others were retired officers from various administrative departments. They were all well-educated people who asserted that, at first, they were sceptics. They became convinced of astrology's reliability when predictions made to them, or to which they were witnesses, were revealed to be stunningly true – there was an element of awe in their narratives. It works, they said, and this is because astrology is a science.

The claim to be a science is often accepted in India and received official recognition by the Indian Government in 2001, at a time when Hindu nationalists were in power: it was made an academic discipline taught in some universities, despite the controversy that erupted (the classification as a science is thus an important political stake). Astrology appears therefore much more rational than other procedures of divination which may still be active, and better adapted to the current evolutions in society. When I pointed out to an astrologer the increasing number of *deva prasnams* organized in Kerala (by comparison with the early 1980s when I did my first fieldwork), he agreed and explained that this was so because 'there is more interest in science' (Shanmugam Master, 12 April 1999). Here, 'science' refers to two domains, astronomy and Sanskrit verses. Astronomy and mathematics provide undisputable data. Normative verses in Sanskrit provide the rules for judging the situation.

It is only recently that astronomy and astrology have become distinguished and astrology relies on this past equivalence to establish nowadays its status as a science. As an astrologer insisted, astrology is 'not about predicting the future as many people believe' but about calculating the position of the planets and studying their effects on our lives:[5] it is the 'calculation when something happens and how' (Narayana Sharma, 24 March 1999). For a *deva prasnam* two different horoscopes are established, one at the time of the first call by the temple committee, the other at the time of the ceremony of the eight auspicious objects. For each horoscope the exact longitudes of the 'planets' are computed, generally by extrapolating from published almanacs and by using pocket calculators or, rarely nowadays, cowries. These published tables constitute a major link between astronomy and astrology and it has been for long the main task of former astronomers to compute them (Pingree 1978: 364). Astrological calculation takes also into account many factors other than the planetary positions: the lunar day (*tithi*), the lunar mansion (*naksatram*), the rising zodiacal sign (according to a sidereal reckoning) and various subdivisions of the zodiac. These are complemented by complex mathematical combinations of relative positions, conjunctions, binds or oppositions, and are carefully mentioned in the final written report given to the committee.

While the use of astronomy and mathematics is part of the very logic of astrology, its display contributes to impressing on the audience the image of a science validated by modern technologies, as most interlocutors were keen to underline; the use of computers and astrological software is publicly advertised by some practitioners for private consultations (though not for *deva prasnams*). This seems to lead to a kind of hypertrophy in mathematical speculations as much so-called astrological data used in temple consultations does not correspond to any effective physical reality and appears to be mere computed derivations from

5 Indian astrology recognizes nine main 'planets': the Sun, the Moon, Mercury, Venus, Mars, Jupiter, Saturn and the ascending and descending nodes of the moon. There are also a few 'subsidiary planets'.

first-level data. Moreover, *deva prasnams* even operate a conversion of omens into astronomical data.

The interpretation of omens is an essential part of the procedure. Omens are called *nimittams*, 'marks', 'causes'; an astrologer aptly translated this as 'witnesses' (Krishnan Nair, 5 April 1999). The list of such possible witnesses is endless and includes signs occurring in or around the temple (a cat crossing the ceremony's space, the crowing of a crow), befalling the astrologer (events in his family, persons he met while coming to the temple) or deliberately produced during the ceremony of the eight auspicious objects (the quality of the oil used for filling the lamp, the stability of the flame, its direction, the quality of the betel leaves prepared and so on). Not all these omens are converted into astronomical data and many are directly interpreted according to widely shared assumptions. Such signs during a *deva prasnam* are considered to be sent by the temple deity in order to make known its condition and its wishes and thus 'prevent [the astrologer] from foolishness' (V. Raghavan Nair, 10 April 1999); they are used in a cumulative way for cross-checking other data and are perceived to be part of the rationality of the procedure.

However, some of these signs become 'astronomized' and transformed into longitudes. For instance, the spatial position of the spokesperson of the temple delegation who meets the astrologer the first time indicates a zodiacal sign and produces an 'ascendant', which becomes astronomical datum computed with the others. Similarly, during the ceremony at the temple, the gold coin put by the child on the zodiacal chart drawn on the ground makes for a 'gold ascendant' determining the first out of the twelve zodiacal Houses framing the whole interpretative process: it will be the main ascendant taken into consideration. There are many other examples: the part of the body touched by the child after laying down the gold coin is put into equivalence with a zodiacal sign; the number of betel leaves prepared is put into equivalence with a planet, with a zodiacal sign and with a House; the astrologer draws cowries to determine a '*prasnam* number' which is put into equivalence with a planet in a given position. As soon as these omens are translated into celestial data, they are submitted to similar computations applying to astronomical data and thus enter the domain of scientific validity of astronomy and mathematics.

All the data require rules for interpreting it. These rules are couched in Sanskrit verses found in treatises (*sastra*, science, treatise), whose authority is not really questioned by most people in India (these verses are also generally not understood) and which are equated with scientific laws. When dealing with questions related to temples, astrologers in Kerala rely on various written sources, most notably on a Sanskrit treatise written around 1650, the 'Path of the Questions' (*Prasnamarggam*; for an English rendition see Raman 1992, 1996). These Sanskrit rules are considered to be *pramanas*, 'norms, authorities, truths, proofs'. As one author puts it, *sastras* 'are pramanik ("proven"), eternally valid and binding on all Hindus' (Parry 1985: 204; see also Pollock 1985). The same word, *pramana*, may also qualify a deed or a document submitted before a court of law as evidence. However, in an astrological context, Sanskrit verses are 'proofs' in a normative sense, rather more like laws or precedents in judicial reasoning than facts or documents submitted. The difficulty is to find the correct applicable rule for a given situation, and to understand it appropriately.

After the ceremonial part of the *deva prasnam* the astrologers hold a lengthy discussion with the temple committee and other devotees during which the interpretation is elaborated step by step. In one temple consultation I observed, which lasted for three days, the chief astrologer quoted and commented on more than two hundred Sanskrit verses. The commentary bears on the proper meaning to be attributed to the verse and involves therefore a discussion about the grammatical rules necessary for understanding the astrological quotations. Sanskrit verses may well have different meanings, up to sixteen according to one astrologer, and the correct choice depends on context and opinion: 'this is a wonder of Sanskrit language … in *deva prasnam* all this is coming under discussion to determine what is applicable to the situation' (V. Raghavan, 10 April 1999).

Astrologers' Uncertainties

Data in an astrological consultation is super-abundant. From the zodiacal position of planets to minute events in the environment, the world is a mass of proliferating signs: but signs of what? While observations are not objects of contestation, their meanings are, and working them out is an operation fraught with hesitations and doubts. Sanskrit rules for interpreting are very numerous. According to one astrologer, there exist more than 400,000 manuscripts of astrology so that it is 'a most complicated science', much more than medicine which has only to manage the human body: 'no wonder if it goes wrong' (Raghavan Nair, 10 April 1999). Interpreting the data requires experience, intuition, caution and divine protection. However confident they may be in their own skills astrologers are aware that they may err in their statements; the procedure is devised so as to limit risks.

The lengthy public debate that follows the ceremonial part of a *deva prasnam* is called *carcca*, 'deliberation, reflection, recollection, debate'. It is this process that enables the astrologers to reach a 'correct way of thinking', to clear their own doubts as well as to convince their audience. As one astrologer explained, a single astrologer, if not endowed with some kind of divine quality, can make mistakes. The collective discussion is intended to 'extract' the results through a debate, thus limiting the risks. This is why the meeting is like a 'court of law, bringing different meanings [of the verses] to the place, discussing, and then coming to conclusions' (Raghavan Nair, 10 April 1999). During this debate, the astrologers detect which planetary relationships are most significant and which are not; which Sanskrit verse should be applied in this case and which not; and what is their correct meaning in the particular context. Data ('witnesses') are patiently sifted one by one, and put into correspondence with appropriate Sanskrit verses, *pramanas* ('proofs'), so that a pattern emerges.

Cross-checking is done in various, complementary ways. One is to tap the knowledge of the audience, which is regularly interrogated. In one instance, astrologers tried to put a name on a ghost whose presence could be deduced from the data; it was the ghost of a man addicted to drinking who had perished by drowning. Somebody in the audience suggested the name of a former president of the temple committee, who had drowned, implying thus that he may have had some liking for the bottle. Someone else immediately protested: this could not be correct as the president had been a good man. He asked the astrologers to be more precise, and the latter now found that the deceased had actually died 'in connection with fire'. The name of another person meeting this updated information was then proposed from the audience, to the satisfaction of all present (M. Kutty, 12 April 1999).

Interactions between the astrologers and the audience thus alternate calculations, articulating rules, making guesses about past or present events, and checking these prognoses in an interrogative form in order to get a confirmation or 'to put names'. This possibility of checking astrological guesses is seen as a great strength: if a testimony from the audience disproves a guess, the astrologers make another try till it fits with the experience of the devotees. Whether guesses are confirmed or challenged by the audience, it helps the astrologers to progressively narrow their diagnosis. One astrologer (Shanmugam Master) compared the process to that of a mechanic listening to a noise in an engine and eliminating one after another its possible causes: making wrong guesses and having them invalidated is part of a dialogical process that helps to get at the final conclusions (see Zeitlyn 1990; Wilce 2001; Guenzi 2013: 158ff.; see also Garfinkel 1967 who analysed such kinds of interaction – in a different context – from an ethnomethodological perspective).

Sanskrit verses, astronomical computation, accumulation of omens and cross-checking may, however, not suffice to reach foolproof conclusions. The procedure recognizes this risk and includes verifications. At regular intervals, for each important statement and for concluding the whole of the discussion, astrologers proceed to a divination test called *ozhivu nokki*, literally 'looking for cessation' – that is, looking for remedies and checking that the problem is over. Having in mind a specific question (Is this conclusion correct? Is the deity satisfied?), the astrologer draws cowries; the resulting number gives an astrological position, itself providing a positive or a negative answer to the question. It is a ritualized way to express and remove possible doubts about the results reached at each step during the debate; at the end of the *deva prasnam* it signals its satisfactory conclusion. These verifications are required by the procedure and are performed whenever needed by the astrologers, quite independently of the explicit reactions of the audience: the astrologers act as if anticipating a doubt about a given statement, while the audience may not have expressed anything of the sort (see Berti, this volume). This is, for instance, the statement made about the last, concluding *ozhivu nokki* in the 1998 report from Thalakkottukkara temple:

> If things are done as mentioned above, will the faults and suffering be removed? And will the divine presence of the Goddess increase? And will there be prosperity and will the people connected with the temple prosper? Is there any sign for it? To know that, praying for the blessings of Jupiter, when it was 4.30 p.m. the 24th in the month of Gemini, 1173 (Malayalam era), the *ozhivu* was seen in Cancer: so it is seen that it is good.

'Praying for the blessings of Jupiter', which the astrologer does just before drawing the cowries in the *ozhivu nokki* process, points to the fact that while astrology claims to be a science, it is explicitly said to be a divine one. Divine intervention is systematic, as its very action produces the signs in need of understanding by the astrologers. Quite naturally, the latter are keen to insist that mistakes can only be averted through God's grace. Knowledge has to be complemented by divine blessings and the astrologer himself has to acquire some divine quality, hence one of his appellations, *devajnyan*, 'one who knows the divine' (Raghavan Nair, 10 April 1999). Other astrologers express the same idea: 'See, mastering the textbook is essential, but we should have meditated on a particular deity always. Only the help of that particular deity will give you intuition. Only through intuition can one say things properly … We have to meditate' (Subrahmania Sharma, 4 April 1999); 'You need god's blessings for choosing between different rules. Good practice and unconditional surrender to the subject and to God enable you to determine appropriate positions' (N. Sharma, 24 March 1999).

Astrologers often appear with their bodies covered with devotional marks, and the whole procedure is imbued with ritual. Some cults are dedicated to deities presiding over the planets and to presiding deities in astrology (gods Siva and Subrahmanyam); others are directed towards the deities of the temple under scrutiny. Ritual purity is required; the astrologer meditates and recites mantras for a long time before the start of the ceremony; the drawing of cowries is always done while murmuring a mantra; the laying down of the gold coin associates the mantras and prayers of the whole audience; finally, reports always include propitiating hymns. The whole logic of the *deva prasnam* is placed under the gods' will and actions and the ultimate verification, the *ozhivu nokki*, is the direct manifestation of the temple deity's approval or disapproval: astrologers have to rely on a divine signal for concluding that there is no more room for doubting.

Manipulating Doubt

Quite often, the conclusions reached by the astrologers may prove surprising or distasteful to some committee members. The *deva prasnam* may reveal that the committee is mismanaging the affairs of the temple; that there is misappropriation or corruption; that the ritual servants are incompetent; that some shrines have to be eliminated; that some ritual practices must be discontinued, others encouraged; that new deities have to be installed; and that the presiding deity of the temple is not, actually, the one devotees believe to be there but some other god or goddess. Conveying this kind of news to the audience requires skilful management of procedure.

Guessing past and present events and situations deemed to be unknown to them is a skill astrologers are expected to display regularly. They should not visit or know the temple beforehand. It is solely through the computation of astronomical data and omens that they should deduce the disposition of all the shrines, the kind of divine image which may be inside the sanctums, the ritual service which is performed and all the characteristics of the temple's routine. They may even be able to discover features hitherto unnoticed by all. For instance, a *deva prasnam* in a Ganesh temple revealed 'the presence of female divinity in the idol', a fact later confirmed by direct examination as 'a faint but distinctly visible carving of a feminine picture was noticed on the back of the idol' (*The Hindu*, online edition, 24 June 2005). Many narratives of this kind circulate and come as strong supports for establishing astrology's validity and an astrologer's particular expertise. We shall see below that such revelations, when overworked, may conversely fuel suspicion about an astrologer's integrity.

The scientific style astrologers profess, and the authority attributed to Sanskrit treatises, make it difficult for the audience to openly question statements during the debate. When astrologers pile up observations one upon another and succeed in bouncing from wrong guesses to admittedly accurate ones, they see themselves as following a 'foolproof' demonstration which should be able to convince their audience on rational grounds. However, *deva prasnam* is also to be seen as a performance involving sophisticated rhetorical skills.

The diagnosis is exposed very gradually (though the astrologer may have reached the conclusions in his mind long before) through various, seemingly disparate arguments narrowing in on the conclusion. Moreover, astrologers systematically depict a catastrophic image of the situation. In all *deva prasnams* temples appear full of pollution and of ghostly presences or unwanted cruel deities; the divine power of the place is about to be lost; rituals are not properly observed; there is mismanagement; gods are suffering. If nothing is done, dilapidation is sure to happen; the gods will go away; misfortune will befall the people of the area. This is not unlike the FUD marketing strategy in which one tries to create Fear, Uncertainty and Doubt in the mind of would-be consumers in order to promote one's own product:[6] indeed, astrologers propose all the required ritual reparations and expiations for restoring the temple to prosperity and the people to happiness.

For instance, in a *deva prasnam* held at the Mettukkada Kamakshi temple in 1999, the astrologers revealed that the goddess Kamakshi, giving her name to the

6 While this strategy in itself (scaremongering) might be as old as commerce, 'FUD' as an acronym was specifically coined during the 1970s in reference to the computer market. It is said to have been practised on a large scale first by IBM, then by Microsoft and others. As commentator Roger Irwin (1998) put it, giving a few illuminating examples, 'the overall message is "Hey, it could be risky going down that road, stick with us"'.

temple, was no longer present and had been replaced by the goddess Rajarajesvari. In order to overcome the visible reluctance of the audience confronted with this change of their main deity's identity, the astrologers displayed a wide range of tactics. They repeatedly referred to inescapable astronomical data, recited Sanskrit verse after verse and insisted upon the presence of ghosts and the coming calamities. Here is a short excerpt:

> (About the goddess) 'The presence of god: the situation is one of adversity. The sign of the Balance is a sacred sign, but it is also a defective sign.'
>
> (About ghosts) 'Mars comes in the sign of Venus … there is an installation of deity here which is inappropriate to the temple, it is the ghost of a Brahman.'[7]
>
> (About calamities) 'The Lord of the Vth House is not the only planet standing in the VIIth. Moon; Saturn and Venus are also standing in the VIIth. If Moon and Venus get bound with Saturn and also get the sight of Mars, the downfall or extinction of women is the result. Quarrels of this kind will arise among worshippers also.' (Mettukkada temple, 1999)

Astrologers thus manipulate doubt, willingly or not, trying to create fear and uncertainty in the minds of their audience in order to disarm possible contestation of their other statements, and to emphasize the risks to which people would be subjected, were they not to follow the proposed remedial measures.

Suspected Astrologers

With all their knowledge and rhetorical skills, astrologers might nevertheless be suspected of being 'counterfeited coins', as one of them put it. Criticism is harsh between astrologers themselves as each is eager to distinguish himself from the others. They and their clients insist on a few values so as to decide between a good and a bad astrologer.

One is ancestry. There are in Kerala families (mostly but not only Brahmin ones) famed for the astrological practice of their members. Claims to a good ancestry in astrology are important and are noticeable in ordinary discussions ('this astrologer belongs to a traditional family of astrologers'), in newspaper reports or in the presentation of books on astrology. According to this discourse, ancestry provides a better education and knowledge in astrology as well as an efficient mantra transmitted from a forefather. As one such astrologer claimed, it

7 In many Kerala temples, a Brahmarakshasa (which I translate here as 'Brahmin ghost'), a terrifying creature, may be installed as guardian deity. However, some astrologers with a reformist agenda (as is the case in the above example) consider these subordinate deities as unwelcome and recommend getting rid of them (Tarabout 2001).

is necessary 'to study a lot of books, it is not possible to master in one birth ... We have to study the text, and we have to get experience, and we have to observe everything in our surroundings. In my case we have that from ancestry; we have got a particular mantra' (Subrahmania Sharma, 4 April 1999). Astrologers who are newcomers, on the contrary, challenge this claim and underline the necessity to democratize astrological practice – in line with the ubiquitous development of astrology courses offered today to interested people in the context of important sociological changes taking place (see Kemper 1980 for Sri Lanka).

Another debate among astrologers bears on the opposition between the 'old way', giving full expansion to the chanting of Sanskrit verses and focusing on astronomical data, and the 'modern way' in which omens are prominent and where the recitation of verses is given less importance. According to 'traditionalists', modernists care more for superficial aspects of *deva prasnam* and rely on cheap tricks to get the audience on their side – such as trying to create fear in their minds.

Astrologers are sometimes suspected of working hand in hand with the ritual specialists who will be in charge of implementing the remedial measures recommended at the conclusion of the *deva prasnam*. Their ethical repute is therefore of great importance (see Budniok, this volume, for a similar preoccupation among judges). Refusing to be paid in a contractual relationship is praised, while being forced to accept gifts is indicative of the highest ethics. Besides, the role of the guru does not limit itself to imparting training and a mantra to his disciples; it is also to develop an ethical discourse.

However, despite all the precautions taken for selecting an astrologer of renowned expertise and high ethics, despite the supposedly foolproof system of data interpretation, the conclusions reached during a *deva prasnam* do not necessarily go unchallenged. Contestation does not aim at the logic of astrology in general; it targets practitioners. This could happen during the procedure itself: in a case I observed, some local astrologers among the devotees strongly objected to what an invited team of astrologers was doing and eventually obtained the cancellation of the *deva prasnam*. This, however, is rare, and contestation usually develops after the consultation. For instance, in implicit disapproval, temple committees do not always implement the astrologer's recommendations and the repetition of *deva prasnams* in some temples, year after year, suggests dissatisfaction with the conclusions of previous consultations. In some rare cases, there can be an outspoken outcry leading to a court petition.

Astrologers in Court

Before examining how astrologers fare in court, it is necessary to recall that, since British times, the judiciary in India has been involved in temple affairs. This was in order to 'protect' temple rituals through a rationalized management of economic and human resources (Presler 1987). As a matter of fact, courts today regulate all the administrative aspects of temple life and rituals, down to the minutest details.

This involvement of courts in (Hindu) ritual matters is more regular and important than a reading of the secular Constitution of India would suggest. This is not necessarily because judges are keen to interfere in religious matters (though some may be), but because there is just no other authority to which litigants may turn in the case of Hinduism.

In this context, *deva prasnams* may be treated as evidence in a trial or be the very object of an accusation. Two cases concerning the Sabarimala temple will serve as illustrations. Sabarimala temple is a major centre of pilgrimage in Kerala, drawing millions of pilgrims and receiving a huge income. It has been for years a locus of confrontation between the state of Kerala (which manages it through the Travancore Devaswom Board), the senior ritual authorities (called *tantri*), the royal family of Pandalam who are the traditional 'protectors' of the temple, feminist movements (women are barred from participating in the pilgrimage, except for young girls and ladies over 50), Hindu rightist movements and environmentalists (the temple is in the midst of a protected forest in the hilly part of the state).

In a series of cases questioning the entry of those women who are said to be barred from the temple, the Kerala High Court quoted *deva prasnams* in support of its decision confirming the ban. For instance, in 1991, respondents were the Travancore Devaswom Board and the Government of Kerala, which had allowed women to celebrate the first rice-feeding ceremonies of their children at the temple, though not during the three main pilgrimage seasons. The Indian Federation of Women Lawyers and a Hindu militant organization were also permitted to participate in the proceedings.[8] In his decision in favour of the petitioner, the judge underlined that the duty of the Travancore Devaswom Board was 'to arrange for the conduct of daily worship and ceremonies and of the festivals in every temple according to its usage … In other words, the Board has a statutory duty to enforce the usage prevalent in the temple'. A *deva prasnam* – he wrote – had revealed that the god (Ayyappa, in an ascetic form) 'does not like young ladies entering the precincts of the temple'. In a rather ambiguous way, much commented upon in the local press at the time, the judge ruled that:

> If the wish of Lord Ayyappa as revealed in the Devaprasnam conducted at the temple is to prohibit woman of a particular age group from worshipping in the temple, the same has to be honoured and followed by the worshippers and the temple authorities. The Board has a duty to implement the astrological findings and prediction on Devaprasnam. The Board has therefore no power to act against that report which will be virtually disregarding the wishes of the deity revealed in the prasnam.

The legal construction of an 'existing usage' is noteworthy. As a matter of fact, women had actually been admitted in the temple for more than ten years outside

8 *S. Mahendran* v. *The Secretary, Travancore Devaswom Board, Thiruvananthapuram And Ors.*, 5 April 1991 [AIR 1993 Ker 42].

the pilgrimage season, on a small scale though not in secrecy. This usage had necessarily received – at least tacitly – the permission of the chief authority on rituals of the Sabarimala temple, its *tantri*, who, we may assume, had to respond to a general evolution in society. The *deva prasnam* took a more rigid, conservative stance, but its conclusions were mere recommendations which, as we have seen, remained open to uncertainties despite all the precautions taken.

By contrast, the judgment transformed the 'existing usage', as it became construed by the judge, into a court ruling. Instead of the more or less fluid situation that astrological consultations usually allow in practice, the judgment substituted an enforceable order. It was no more by 'past usage' that women of a certain age were discouraged to go to the temple; it was by a decision of justice that it became prohibited to do so. A police force had to ensure they would not come. By endorsing the *deva prasnam*'s conclusion, the judgment made it law. A judicial decision can be contested in its validity or justice, as seems to be frequently the case in India where appeals to higher jurisdictions are nearly systematic, but it cannot be doubted in the sense that, until a new court judgement overturns the first, there is no uncertainty as to what should be done.

In the second example, also related to the Sabarimala temple, a *deva prasnam* became the very object of contestation before the High Court of Kochi. The consultation was held in 2006 at Sabarimala, following a fire in a building in 2003 and, in 2004, the rejection of a divine movable image by an elephant which had to bear it during a procession: these were two indications pointing to trouble at the divine level. The *deva prasnam* was performed by a team of twenty-one astrologers under the leadership of the famous Parappanangadi Unnikrishna Panicker, a high-profile astrologer consulted by the President of Sri Lanka, two Chief Ministers of regional states in India and numerous politicians, businessmen and cinema stars. The final report of this consultation criticized the *tantri* of the temple, made proposals that irked the Pandalam royal family and gave a free hand to the Travancore Devaswom Board to install a rope-way for pilgrims in the protected forest area. Opposition was immediate from various quarters. The *tantri* announced he would not implement the recommendations; the royal family petitioned the High Court, claiming the *deva prasnam* was invalid as it attacked its fundamental rights and asking for the organization of a new one. While the *tantri* was soon disqualified on other grounds (he was framed by the police in 'immoral company'), the case developed in another, unforeseeable direction.

One of the revelations of the *deva prasnam* had been that the divine image had been defiled years ago by the direct touch of a woman who, according to the ban, should not have entered the precincts of the temple at all. As soon as this statement was made public, an actress from the neighbouring state of Karnataka, Jayamala, expressed her deep repentance: she had been the involuntary culprit, eighteen years before. However, this rather sensational proof of the chief astrologer's clairvoyance soon became a burden for him as it was discovered that he personally knew the actress. This created the suspicion that the so-called revelation had been pre-arranged and that there had been a conspiracy. The astrologer was publicly accused of having entered into an agreement with the actress and with the Travancore Devaswom Board, and a police inquiry was started. Seeing this, the astrologer petitioned the Kerala High Court in 2009 so as to be granted anticipatory bail (a legal procedure for being bailed out if an official case were to be registered later on).

The text of the petition presented by Panicker is worth looking at, as it expresses the accusation's doubts about the *deva prasnam*, and, as a defence, the reaffirmation by the astrologer of his own high ethics. First the position of the accusation against the astrologer is stated:

> It is alleged that after the Devaprasnam, the petitioner (*i.e.* Panicker) revealed that a lady had touched the idol of Lord Ayyappa. It is well known that women above the age of 10 and below 50 are not permitted to enter into the Sabarimala temple. The prosecution case is that the petitioner was aware that a cine actress by name Jayamala had entered into the sanctum sanctorum at Sabarimala temple and had touched the idol of Lord Ayyappa. It is alleged that the petitioner hatched a conspiracy with the other accused persons and revealed the same after the Devaprasnam with the aim of making fame and money. It is also alleged that with the help of the second accused, the petitioner contacted the cine actress Jayamala over mobile phone and instigated her to reveal the fact and to express regret and repentance … According to the prosecution, all these things were done for creating an impression among the public that the petitioner is a person who could unearth certain events in the Devaprasnam. It was with the aim of gaining fame and money.

Then the astrologer's defence is presented:

> The petitioner states that he is an ardent devotee of Lord Ayyappa. He claims that he is an astrologer of an international repute. He also states that he has conducted … [*deva prasnams*] in various temples in India and abroad. Twenty one astrologers participated in the Devaprasnam and the findings were given after the conclusion of the Devaprasnam and all the astrologers were unanimous on the conclusions. The petitioner states that he has acted bonafide in the matter and the allegations made by the prosecution were denied.[9]

Concluding Remarks

The practice of *deva prasnam* aims at helping people decide about temple affairs in a world perceived as uncertain. This is especially the case when deities are concerned, since their relations with their devotees are construed as ambiguous,

9 *Unnikrishna Panicker* v. *State of Kerala*, 16 June 2009, High Court of Kerala, Bail Appl. No. 3249 of 2009.

polyvalent and largely unpredictable. However, astrology is not necessarily equipped to fully dispel the doubts of all clients. While claiming to be a science, it is also avowedly a divine one. The astrologers' expertise, in their own words, ultimately depends on God's grace – which puts them back at square one. True, astrologers try to minimize the risks by accumulating data, applying 'proven' rules, cross-checking with the audience, trying to reach a collective consensus through a public debate and ritually expressing doubt and its divine resolution. Nevertheless, even if the astrologers, through these techniques of doubting, succeed in dispelling the uncertainty that could exist in their minds, it may not be so easily the case with their audience.

As a matter of fact, the scope of a *deva prasnam* is quite ambitious in its exhaustive scrutiny of a temple's situation, an ambition often incongruent with the kinds of questions posed to the astrologers. Can we change the orientation of the shrine? Build some shops? Buy a new elephant? Explain an accident during a procession? The statements issued during the *deva prasnam* are often quite far from these preoccupations and potentially difficult for the temple committees and the devotees to accept. In addition to their scientific stand, astrologers must also develop rhetorical proficiency, creating and manipulating doubt among their public in order to win their approval.

The good reputation of the astrologer is crucial in this game as his clients will a priori be inclined to have confidence in his statements. It is also at stake each time. Making stunning guesses which are later empirically verified is a key to building fame. However, as the last example shows, it may conversely lead to accusations of malpractice. Indeed, there is a counter-discourse running in India about astrologers, depicting them as unscrupulous shams easily corrupted and engaged in mafia-like agreements with ritual specialists, whom they recommend in the remedial measures suggested in the *deva prasnams*. Astrology per se can also be questioned by some intellectuals, but the more widespread criticism bears on the astrologers themselves. In this respect, in the last case, it is highly significant that critics were less bent on pointing out errors in the procedure than on questioning the morality of the chief astrologer.

Comparison with the judicial process shows some similarities as the purpose of both situations is to extract a hidden 'truth' out of a mass of confused and uncertain data. More specifically, the debate during the *deva prasnam*, explicitly compared to a debate in court (though there is neither prosecution nor defence), displays series of Sanskrit verses whose normative character is not unlike that of laws; they are used in a rather similar manner. However, the astrological 'judgment' is an expert opinion, not a judicial decision, and compares more directly with medical expertise or scientific investigation in its techniques for manipulating and eliminating doubts. It is a consultation, not a trial, and it provides advice and remedies, not enforceable law. This makes for a radical difference between the regimes of truth in these two situations: contrary to a judge's decision which can be appealed against only by following strict and limited procedures framed by the judicial institution, astrological statements may be endlessly questioned. If clients are dissatisfied with recommendations they may not implement them; if they are dissatisfied with an astrologer they may turn to another. In this sense, astrological conclusions always remain open to doubts and to further social negotiation.

Seen as an exercise in power, astrological consultations illustrate well the conflict existing between a largely unquestioned procedure for establishing truths and the tensions of social life. Astrological statements may convince clients only up to a certain point, whatever the data displayed, the rhetoric involved and the procedure approved by the gods. When devotees do not implement recommendations, repeat *deva prasnams* one after the other or sue an astrologer before a court, they seem to be reacting as if their expectations have not been fulfilled. There might be no consensus: feminist associations and Hindu right militants were clearly on opposite sides in the 1991 case already mentioned, in which the judge's decision took a *deva prasnam* as evidence for confirming the entry ban to Sabarimala for some women: the capacity to contest or not an astrological statement appears thus dependent on social tensions and local power relationships. As such, doubt is not solely a cognitive process or a tool within a more or less ritualized process: it also depends on social expectations and on the actual capacity to impose them.

References

Bhat, M.R. (1992) *Essentials of Horary Astrology or Praśnapadavī*, Delhi: Motilal Banarsidass.

Garfinkel, Harold (1967) 'Common sense knowledge of social structures: the documentary method of interpretation in lay and professional fact finding', in *Studies in Ethnomethodology*, Englewood Cliffs, NJ: Prentice-Hall, pp. 76–103.

Guenzi, Caterina (2013) *Le discours du destin. La pratique de l'astrologie à Bénarès*, Paris: CNRS Editions.

Irwin, Roger (1998) 'What is FUD', available at http://www.cavcomp.demon.co.uk/halloween/fuddef.html (accessed 29 December 2013).

Kemper, Steven (1980) 'Time, person, and gender in Sinhalese astrology', *American Ethnologist* 7(4): 744–58.

Parry, Jonathan (1985) 'The Brahmanical tradition and the technology of the intellect', in *Reason and Morality*, ed. J. Overing, London and New York: Tavistock, pp. 200–225.

Pingree, David (1978) 'Indian astronomy', *Proceedings of the American Philosophical Society* 122(6): 361–4.

Pingree, David (1981) *Jyotiḥśāstra: Astral and Mathematical Literature*, Wiesbaden: Harrassowitz.

Pollock, Sheldon (1985) 'The theory of practice and the practice of theory in Indian intellectual history', *Journal of the American Oriental Society* 105(3): 499–519.

Presler, Franklin A. (1987) *Religion under Bureaucracy: Policy and Administration for Hindu Temples in South India*, Cambridge: Cambridge University Press.

Raman, B.V. (ed., trans., commentator) (1992) *Prasna Marga*, Part II (2nd edn), Delhi: Motilal Banarsidass.

Raman, B.V. (ed., trans., commentator) (1996) *Prasna Marga*, Part I (3rd edn), Delhi: Motilal Banarsidass.

Tarabout, Gilles (2001) 'Ancêtres et revenants. La Construction sociale de la malemort en Inde', in *De la malemort en quelques pays d'Asie*, ed. Brigitte Baptandier, Paris: Karthala, pp. 165–99.

Tarabout, Gilles (2002) 'Résonances et métaphores corporelles dans l'astrologie appliquée aux temples (Kérala)', in *Images du corps dans le monde hindou*, ed. Véronique Bouillier and Gilles Tarabout, Paris: CNRS Editions, pp. 135–59.

Tarabout, Gilles (2006) 'La Réparation des fautes. Le Contrôle astrologique de la transformation des rites et des temples au Kérala', in *Rites hindous. Transferts et transformations*, ed. Gérard Colas and Gilles Tarabout, Paris: EHESS, pp. 463–93.

Tarabout, Gilles (2007) 'Authoritative statements in Kerala Temple astrology', *Rivista di Studi Sudasiatici* 2: 85–120.

Vernant, Jean-Pierre, Vandermeersch, Léon, Gernet, Jacques, Bottéro, Jean, Crahay, Roland, Brisson, Luc, Carlier, Jeannie, Grodzynski, Denise and Retel-Laurentin, Anne (1974) *Divination et Rationalité*, Paris: Editions du Seuil.

Wilce, James M. (2001) 'Divining *troubles*, or *divining* troubles? Emergent and conflictual dimensions of Bangladeshi divination', *Anthropological Quarterly* 74(4): 190–200.

Zeitlyn, David (1990) 'Professor Garfinkel visits the soothsayers: ethnomethodology and Mambila divination', *Man* (N.S.) 25(4): 654–66.

Chapter 4

When Judges Feel Misjudged: Encountering Doubt in Ghanaian Courts

Jan Budniok

Techniques of casting and dispelling doubt are common in courtrooms all over the world. But what happens in a judicial setting when the integrity of presiding judges rather than evidence, testimonies and witnesses are in doubt? In Ghana, corruption in the administration of justice is seen as ubiquitous (Ghana Integrity Initiative 2007), and the public often perceives judgments as dependent on a litigant's relation to a judge or other court officers. In particular, allegations of corruption against judges in general and doubts about judges' impartiality emerge frequently. However, judges say that such allegations are often based on hardly any facts; yet once on the table, they cannot be dispelled easily. What is more, such allegations seem perfectly plausible to an alert public who are sensitive to signs of daily corruption by public servants. This chapter focuses on how Ghanaian judges deal with such doubts.

It is based on twelve months of fieldwork in Ghana on judges and the judiciary between 2006 and late 2007. I did research in several courts, from the Supreme Court to district courts, observing their day-to-day workings and conducting interviews with thirty-five judges of different age, status and gender. I also talked to many lawyers and members of the judicial service, studied legal material, observed judges' conferences, visited them in their homes and talked to their friends and families.

The Ghanaian judicial tradition is based on the model of colonial English judges (Amissah 1981). About 250 judges serve in Ghana, including magistrates; they are highly autonomous in their daily work. The system is largely based on self-regulation and self-discipline. About 80 per cent of Ghanaian judges work as single judges, many in isolated courts scattered across the country. Since the 1970s, the administration of justice has been publicly criticized for corruption (Luckham 1977). Many challenges and practices in Ghanaian courts are similar to the so-called functional problems and corruption in the judiciaries of neighbouring countries (Tidjani Alou 2006; Bierschenk 2008). Topics such as the organization of rural trial courts, varying workloads and infrastructure in the northern and southern regions of Ghana, and the motives and perceptions of people bringing cases before a court have been addressed by others before (Lowy 1978; Crook 2005; Crook, Asante and Brobbey 2010).

In this chapter, I focus on the judges' point of view. When interpreting my ethnographic data, I build on Goffman's work (1989, 2003) about interaction order and on Lamont's thoughts on 'boundary work' (1992). Therein, Lamont expands Bourdieu's concept of distinction by identifying different types of symbolic boundaries such as moral, socio-economic and cultural ones. I outline the judges' concept of their work, courts and Ghanaian society. I show how judges strive in their everyday work to construct and uphold an image of judicial integrity and to contain doubt despite constant suspicion. Ghanaian judges see the court users' doubts regarding the legal process as reflecting something larger than structural shortcomings in the court system and moral hazards. Judges at all court levels share a perspective that centres on specific, fundamental challenges to their work in and outside Ghana's courts. Everyday behaviour and social interaction frequently come under the fierce scrutiny of litigants, lawyers and public figures; any doubt, any allegation of improper conduct may discredit a judge and damage the judiciary's reputation.

The judges' perception of their work and the social order in general prompts them to draw rather rigid boundaries to inhibit doubt. In different spaces of action, judges try to anticipate possible disruptions to their purported integrity, any sign that could lead to doubt, including the actions of intruders who try to circumvent their moral boundaries. I analyse how judges use certain signs and attempt to suppress others, and how they employ specific resources to create moral boundaries. To counter doubt, the professional culture of Ghanaian judges is predicated on a complex interplay between self-regulated public appearances and retreats into self-imposed seclusion.[1]

Judges' Views of Ghana's Legal System: The Ideal Type

So, what happens in Ghanaian courts that gives rise to doubt? Judges see the ideal legal process as a well-ordered social interaction in court with a clear set of rules that outlines the procedures minutely. According to judges, in court they are presented with a multiplex reduction of reality – that is, competing and contradicting narratives on events from the past by various actors, evaluations of evidence, proofs, documents and dockets. As judges, they have to make sense of the various narratives, events and documents, and translate them into legal cases and new documents, and make meaning and legal sense to transform them into judgments. This transformation in court proceeds according to legal

1 The judicial profession in Ghana has now endorsed a set of principles in its code of conduct. It asserts judges' belief in their ability to influence positively not only their images, but also the practice and the reality inside the courts – thus preventing doubt, if not creating trust. Proper conduct has been a recurring theme among judges, in addition to general appeals to improve the infrastructure of the courts, salaries, the education and training of judges and judicial personnel, as well as a general overhaul of all aspects of justice delivery.

rules of evidence and is framed by the rules of process. In the sociology of law a funnel model has been used to describe the processing of cases (Blankenburg 1984, 1995). In his reflections about science, Bruno Latour (1996: 238ff.) uses the model of a chain of translations for processing information in science. Similar to Latour's chain, Ghanaian judges believe that the ideal legal process is a continuing chain which can be reversed (see Latour 1996: 239ff.): an appeal allows people to go back one or several steps in the translation process. If a process was faulty, judgment can be overturned.

In Latour's discourse about science, the creation of references is at the heart of transforming acceptable elements, deemed evidence, of an epistemic community into knowledge (Latour and Woolgar 1986; Latour 2002: 234f.).[2] For Latour, the production of fact depends on what an epistemic community deems as acceptable pieces of evidence, and their subsequent translation into truth. In *Laboratory Life*, Latour and Woolgar (1986) conclude that conflicts may arise between different disciplines when they try to communicate about the same phenomenon. According to the authors, different disciplines are predicated on disparate, partly contradictory sub-paradigms for explaining the functioning of phenomena in the world; and deductions from leading paradigms differ substantially at their sub-levels.

In court, legal terminology and procedures are vehicles for judges to cooperate with lawyers and others. Various interconnected boundary objects, such as the various pieces of evidence as well as the social interaction surrounding them, play a decisive role in this process. 'Boundary objects', in Star and Griesemer's terms (1989) connect the different epistemologies and interests of various actors in a single chain. In the case of Ghanaian courts, boundary objects such as different pieces of evidence, dockets and case files are also points of reference to reduce the complexity of reality in court, and to amplify relevant fragments to become significant in terms of the law. Judges cannot accept some narratives as evidence in legal terms; all of them must adhere to legal rules, to be duly translated into legal terms. Only then are they considered for the next step in legal process. How that is done by actors such as defendants, plaintiffs, prosecutors, counsel, judges, court clerks and others is central to the legal process; and judges see themselves as referees and producers of the final result. A judge's legal understanding of reality is the most powerful reading in court: the judgment is presented as a clear deduction according to judicial truth finding. A judgment has several aims and addressees, such as litigants and other lawyers and judges, and it serves as the basis for assessing judicial work. Judges believe the quality of judicial work and the legal thinking behind it can only be appreciated fully by other judges, whether it is during appeal or in law reports. Judges describe a judgment as an intricate document, which necessitates weighing complex arguments; it balances the different sides of the case and justifies the decision (see Jung 2006: 103).

2 The notion of epistemic community can be summarized in this context as referring to a group of people who share criteria for validity and practices to produce knowledge.

Malfunctions in the Court System

Ghanaian judges try to uphold this ideal impression regardless of the everyday disorder and the dysfunction in their courtrooms or the dilapidated state of their court buildings. However, there are a number of structural malfunctions, and Ghanaian judges acknowledge that the court system is far from ideal. They point out that the evidence presented during criminal trials, for example, differs from that in Western countries where sophisticated technology for producing physical evidence is readily available. At present, essential steps such as gathering evidence and documenting a process such as a cross-examination in writing are time-consuming. It takes a long time to fill a judge's case book, and it can take even longer to provide the court administration with a revision as this has to be typed up using an old-fashioned typewriter; computers are often not available.

Judges rely on the cooperation of all other court personnel, such as court clerks, prosecutors, police, lawyers and also litigants, in the everyday courtroom work. They believe that they cannot control the proper functioning of all those involved and thus the impression they make on others in the court. This in turn hampers the smooth functioning of legal processes. A large number of pending cases and a high caseload in many courts are evidence of an overburdening of the current system and its staff. Trials are frequently interrupted for a wide range of reasons: electricity power cuts; a lawyer or a party to the case, a police officer or the prosecutor does not show up; the bailiff fails to serve the case; the docket files are missing and so on. Such disruptions occur frequently. Judges explain such malfunctions with reference to the social and economic situation and the country's poor infrastructure. And yet, every detail that undermines the efficiency of the process or appears odd could be ascribed to a failing in the judge's conduct. Some of the disruptions might give rise to doubts about the judge's integrity as litigants might assume that a case has been adjourned due to a specific social relationship between the judge and a certain party in a case, be it corruption and bribes veiled as 'extra-fees' or some form of social obligation.

According to the judges, case management is a weak point and causes doubt. However, judges do not want to seem too involved in the day-to-day case management as this could undermine their neutrality. Therefore, judges find themselves in a predicament: they argue that they have only limited powers to ensure the speedy delivery of justice, as many shortcomings are due to omnipresent structural defects. This – and the supposed impression of litigants and the public that the court administration is deeply corrupt – leads the judges to amplify a distinct boundary between them and their staff. Hence, they seek to distinguish themselves from the court administration, which in turn hinders their ability to manage court cases. Judges' attempts to ensure integrity thus conflict with attempts to improve the courts' performance.

Judges' Worldview: Ghanaian Society, Litigants and 'Socially Embedded Judges'

Apart from structural malfunctions, social factors also contribute to problems with case management. As judges described the ideal legal process, court work is not only based on cooperation with other legal professionals who present accounts of reality within the legal frame, but also depends on cooperation with plaintiffs and defendants. However, the latter's paradigms and epistemologies, identified by judges as those of Ghanaian society, differ considerably from those of the legal profession. They are even incommensurable in terms of the functioning of courts – that is, the translation of evidence and handling boundary objects – and would ultimately lead to doubt. Structurally speaking, judges face an inextricable dilemma of conflicting expectations, norms and projections from the various groups in court. Already, discontent is inherent to legal process. Judgments can be seen as a zero-sum game: half of all cases are lost, and judges think it is easier for losing parties and their legal counsel to accuse the judge than to admit an error. The way judicial work is evaluated by society at large and parties in court depends on very different sets of criteria. As far as laypersons are concerned, the legal process is also about people's social ties and connections.

Most importantly, judges find themselves confronted with a 'traditional African society' in which a Ghanaian's understanding of a judge's actions is structured by logic inherent to his culture. Judges say that those bringing cases before a court are extremely sensitive to signs of social relationships. Most Ghanaians deem such relations inexorably important. Ghanaians look for them everywhere and try to establish such relationships constantly. A Ghanaian could only conceive his actions within such a framework and would evaluate his agency according to it. As far as that goes against legal norms and bureaucratic rules, it can be termed corruption. Thus, judges use the term 'corruption' as a broad concept. Justice Georgina Tetteh[3] (8 March 2007) explained:

> I think corruption comes firstly from our traditional structures. Our structures are such that: you know, we are so closely knit, if someone had a problem, if I wanted something, invariably something like: I need a school for my child. I want my child to study law. Invariably, if I know anybody teaching or working at the law faculty, I know somebody who knows somebody who knows somebody who works at the law faculty. [We would ask for help.] So, we do that, as a society. Or you go to church with somebody. Then we have a practice, it is part of our culture: you can't go to a chief's house without drink and money. Those open the door for you to speak to the person. So, somebody wants to come and talk to a judge and says: oh, I brought this gift. So, soon the culture of gift would gain. So, I find that when you are in [such] a position then you have to build walls around you. Usually I wouldn't let you sit here by yourself.

3 I use pseudonyms for all interviewees.

> I would insist that somebody is in this room with you; just because I don't want anyone to disturb me. I don't fear that I would be corrupted really, but I am not interested in anybody getting the impression that they can even try. You know, so I have just built that wall. I think the negative perception is because people don't understand how the law works. They imagine things.

Ghanaians suspect that interactions are controlled, reaffirmed or create intrinsic loyalties and that a judge is somehow entangled in wide-ranging social relations. Ghanaians suppose that such loyalties and relations are more important than a judge's ethically motivated professional comportment, even if judges insist that they are bound by such rules. They add that average Ghanaians follow a script when engaging in social interactions with public servants, including judges. They suspect that most people bringing a lawsuit before a court try to enter these webs of social relations by giving presents, mobilizing social relations or by bribing someone with access to a particular set of social relations.

Generally, without experience of the judiciary, most people would automatically draw conclusions from their experiences with other government services and apply these to the judiciary as well. Thus, general suspicion arises from the way in which the rest of the public services function. Judges believe that corruption is rampant in Ghana's public services and that the workings of other public service institutions often result from social interaction and the bending of bureaucratic rules. The judges are adamant that they themselves do not indulge in corrupt practices. Judges assume that law users' dire conclusions are based on an assumed context and 'behind the scenes' action similar to other institutions. Deviations from the assumed ideal are evaluated according to an established episteme of society and bureaucracy in Ghana.

During legal processes, which can take several years in Ghana (as in other countries), the lawyers and judges on the one hand, and the litigants and other actors involved on the other hand, seem to be talking about the same facts, and also believe, to a certain extent, that they are doing so; however, their competing epistemologies mean that their viewpoints clash both during and after the legal process. Judges believe that the laymen's interpretations and misconceptions are exacerbated by arcane laws and procedures, not easily accessible to laymen (see Bierschenk 2008: 119–21). According to judges, first-time litigants have to form their conclusions based on fragile evidence; they rely on what they see in the courtroom, on hearsay and on previous experiences with civil servants. Judges assume that people arrive at this conclusion by interpreting signs in courts like those in other state institutions.

The Use and Interpretation of Signs

Judges and other actors in the legal process translate signs according to fixed or fairly stable rules. Judges aim at arriving at an objective judgment based on clear and convincing evidence. In civil cases they decide on the basis of the 'balance of probabilities', whatever is more likely to be true, while in a criminal case, the judgment must be grounded on reasoning that clearly shows how and why the evidence leads to a guilty verdict that from a judge's perspective is beyond reasonable doubt. While reasonable doubt is a legal category, popular doubt about the courts and the work of judges arises from other factors, criteria and different interpretations. Judges argue that legal processes and the professional actors involved, including the judge, are challenged due to non-professional participants' lack of trust in the legal process. This results from doubting the independence of state bureaucracies in general. How do judges explain that? Doubt arises due to an interpretation of court processes that places events and signs perceived during legal processes in the context of social order and the functioning of public services in general. Most people do not perceive legal rules as the sole and principal guidelines governing judges' conduct – because they are ignorant of them or doubt that they work well. Judges say there is a popular image of an idealized judge. Yet, like most Ghanaian civil servants, judges cannot escape the scrutiny of their spectators and the perception is that legal processes often fall short of the ideal. This seems to validate another image: courts are confronted with the same doubts that bureaucracies in Ghana face in general.

Many small incidents in court could lead to exaggerations by lawyers and their clients. For instance, asking advice from a colleague on the bench or even giving the impression of doing so can be dangerous for a judge, as the case of Justice Farkye shows. In 2007, Dan Kawasi Abodakpi, the MP for Keta, was sentenced to ten years' imprisonment with hard labour for incurring financial losses to the state. He was a member of the National Democratic Congress (NDC), then in opposition. The trial was a major event, but the ensuing hype was not about the sentence itself. His lawyers and political supporters argued that improper, possibly political influence was wielded on the trial judge prior to the judgment. What evidence was there for such an allegation? The presiding judge in the High Court was Justice Farkye, of the Court of Appeal. The opposition argued that on the day judgment was delivered Justice Farkye met another judge for a chat. While the judge argued that he only needed to obtain additional legal documents, the MP's supporters believed that his colleague probably influenced the judgment. Newspapers nationwide reported on the case and the polemical allegations, and a well-known, outspoken lawyer and NDC politician William Mensah told me:

> When I listen to that case, the fact that the judge had to interrupt his judgment to go and see the judge that is in question and that he wanted some legal authorities from the judge: it is the most flimsy excuse that anybody could give. Normally, in matters like that you have court clerks. And the court clerks will be able to get this type of [document] – and you didn't, you were not under any pressure anywhere to start delivering the judgment when you knew you didn't have all your authorities before you. So, to have started and interrupted it is also very unusual. So, the inference and perception that that conversation influenced you

> still stands to my mind. And I think the Chief Justice ought to take a second look at it. I guess that matter might go on further appeal, I suspect so. (interview, 7 December 2007)

In such contexts, a judge must also avoid stammering, nervousness and showing any signs of emotion in court. Reading the judgment confidently is essential for upholding their image. Judges feel forced to gloss over the shortcomings of the Ghanaian judiciary to sustain their integrity and to contain doubt. They have to present themselves as knowledgeable. Appearing calm and competent is the basis for credibility. Judges assume that spectators tend to watch out for little signs and clues, even unintended movements, stammering or gestures. They say such behaviour has no meaning whatsoever, yet they believe that spectators use it as the main basis for interpreting court proceedings.

Thus, they see themselves in a situation where litigants and the public form their perception of judges and the judiciary on the basis of secondary events, behaviour and interactions. If a judge were seen talking to someone, as in the case of Justice Farkye, the existence of a deeper social relationship would be construed immediately. If the judge even smiles or is harsh, if they hesitate when reading a judgment or go into their chambers, such actions are analysed within the frame presented by judges as a specifically Ghanaian understanding and construal of reality. Social interactions suddenly seem more important than they really are.

Appearing self-assured and exuding an aura of unquestionable, professional competence is particularly important when judges are faced with ambiguous cases. They must make their decision appear clear and well founded even though the case could have gone either way. In other words, they have to present the law as clear-cut. Again, trying to create and sustain an appearance of poise, equanimity, self-confidence and professional competence may run counter to the imperative to deliver quickly a sound, legal judgment that would withstand an appeal. In practice, this means a judge must decide whether they should leave the courtroom to consult legal material to back up their judgment (Farkye) or whether they should deliver judgment quickly and self-confidently, as if such a task were second nature to them. Regardless of their choice, either can undermine their integrity.

Some judges suggested that a minority of lawyers might try to distract attention from their own dismal performances by making allegations against the judge. Some lawyers would readily attack judges based on real or imagined faults. At the same time, judges see themselves as an easy target for criticism and allegations, as they never respond publicly to such allegations. Judges speak only through their judgments and not outside the courtroom. They claim that they would never indulge in any mud-slinging, but instead protect their critics' constitutional right to express such criticism (Aikins 2000: 94).

Intermediaries and Intruders

In addition, judges construct and maintain their distance from so-called 'intermediaries' (see Tidjani Alou 2006: 163) who interfere in a bid to earn money. These people undermine the judges' position. Those who try to slip past the judges' boundaries do so to prove that they have access and influence. These are friends or rather people who purport to be friends of a judge. As Mahaman Tidjani Alou (2006) has shown, many people feel lost in bureaucracy, even more so in courts. They place their trust in persons who say that they may be able to help because they know how the system works and claim that they have informal access.

So, apart from the threats posed by the situation in the courtrooms, a twisted *amicus curiae* poses an even bigger threat. The judges are confronted with a situation in which many Ghanaian litigants, or persons claiming to be acting on their behalf, strive to initiate a personal or monetary relation with their respective trial judges. Therefore, judges do not appreciate any attempts to establish relationships with them or conduct that might give the impression that they are socially involved, as circuit court Judge Paul Aikins explained:

> We don't go out to do those types of things that people think that we are doing. Whatever you do, you have to imagine, if your case is very bad, then I would be a fool to collect something from you. Because I can't justify why I am doing a decision in your favour when the case is so bad. But people won't know that, they don't bother. When you come, everything is possible for them. If you come, they will tell, 'No problem, we will see the judge'. Look, when I came first, they used to struggle over who would carry my bag. The idea is for the litigants hanging around to see and assess who is closer to the judge. You see, they do that to say, 'Ah, but, you know, me and the judge, I am normally carrying the bag when he comes. I will take it back to the car, it is no problem. If there is anything I will see him'. (interview, 14 May 2007)

Any attempt by litigants to visit a judge at their residence is considered taboo. Yet, such visits do occur. Some litigants want to have a chance to 'really explain their case', some want to present a gift, others to pay large sums of money. Outside observers may have difficulty distinguishing them from kin who arrive innocently with their problems and presents.

An intruder who ventures to the courts as a middleman presents himself to litigants as a well-connected man, 'knowing his way' in the court administration. Many judges report that such creations of proximity and claims of access to judges often go unnoticed by them at first. They will only realize it when clients of such self-acclaimed intermediaries complain about the judge's non-compliance with alleged agreements. The audience for such an attempt to construe a social relation between an intruder, a judge and clients for their pretended services would be litigants trying to influence the judge through an intermediary. They might get an offer from such a person to arrange it. Such an intermediary could even be a court employee, a clerk or a member of the judge's extended family. Any aspiring intermediary stands to profit from society's impression that the judge's professional work is embedded in social relationships. Based on previous experiences, judges assume that such people will try to create a situation where interaction or even spatial proximity can be interpreted as an existing social relation. Litigants interested in their services may then presume that such a relationship can be mobilized to influence an impending judgment.

Another method used by aspiring intermediaries is to claim that they have influence on the presiding judge, for example lawyers who claim to pay the judge or members of the court staff. Such aspiring intermediaries will pretend that there were behind-the-scenes machinations – and the public and litigants will be inclined to believe that. Judges explain that some court clerks, police officers, lawyers, members of the extended family and self-proclaimed 'friends' have acquired a good sense of how a judge will decide in particular cases. So their claims of being able to influence a judgment can be sustained merely by their correct assessment of the resulting judgment, although no money has ever been paid to the judge, but rather has been kept by the self-proclaimed intermediary.

So, judges' reservations towards people who try to approach them, their reluctance to talk to people in public outside the court setting, is due to their desire to avoid any situation that might be interpreted as a sign of any such relation and that could undermine their image of integrity and neutrality. Judges describe a setting in which cultural presuppositions produce an environment of general suspicion regarding influence or corruption.[4] They have to counter doubt with rigorous boundary work to pre-empt such suspicions.

Encountering Doubt – Upholding Integrity

Judges claim that their behaviour must be superior to that of average Ghanaians, in other words, they have to resist acting according to rules, values and practices governing society in general, and their conduct must be exemplary. Given the importance Ghanaians place on social relations and indicators, judges believe that any minor blunder such as talking to the wrong person could confirm deep-seated scepticism and be seen as proof of corruption. In a situation where Ghanaian judges believe that the smallest 'mistake' can be interpreted as a proof of improper influence on a judge, they have developed well-established habits and patterns of self-presentation encompassing all aspects of their lives. In this section, I look at how judges try to control their image in different spaces and social situations, how they control social encounters, starting with the courtroom. The focus here is on the judges' concept of boundary work, a display of moral otherness through the construction of a boundary, using economic resources and cultural signs. Judges

4 Mahaman Tidjani Alou (2006: 148) describes an 'atmosphere of suspicion' in his analysis of the Nigerien courts.

present this as a form of professional distinction and as the basis for suppressing doubt and maintaining integrity.

The problem for judges is that many signs are produced in court and several different actors interfere in the production of the judicial images. They are not easily controlled or disciplined by the judges, but are nevertheless part of their daily work. The underlying dilemma is that different groups of people grasp courtroom proceedings differently. While litigants, also seen as representatives of 'the society', have distinct criteria regarding judicial work, judges have to bear other criteria in mind at the same time. This includes all those factors taken into consideration by other appeal judges (who are thus other addressees of judicial work) and the judicial service when assessing a judge's work – that is, the quality of their judgment, their legal knowledge and the speed of judgment delivery. Judges have to balance different, often conflicting expectations of their work and they have to prioritize them. When faced with (too) many cases, they might want to speed up and make decisions hastily, even if they have an inadequate grasp of the law.

Therefore, judges have to act on several levels in court proceedings, and with different audiences. However, the various audiences read the same signs differently, according to conflicting epistemologies. To prevent doubt in the proper and undisturbed functioning of legal process, enacting social difference in the sense of professional distinction is essential. This is to prevent another audience, which relies on a different epistemic reading, from misinterpreting insignificant actions and to limit the possibility of social mistranslation of the action and interpretation presented by judges in court. In many cases judges are preoccupied with avoiding or concealing specific actions on their own part and preventing disruptions by other people. One solution to the judges' predicament, since most disruptions seem to be the result of social encounters and apparent or supposed relationships, is to curb the amount of contact with other people in public. However, distance is not the same for all actors: for other judges and members of the legal profession, it is different – and is communicated differently. To create some sort of proximity with members of the legal profession is important, too, both on a professional and a personal level.

In the context of legal processes, judges say other actors often misinterpret their level of social proximity to certain people. Mere friendliness was intended, but some in their audience would interpret that as a sign of social commitment or obligation. Therefore, judges try to keep greater distance. However, as they deal with different groups of people, at times some of their attempts will be misconceived as proximity. Judges believe that in order to control the perception created in response to encounters with other people they have to face such encounters with composure and resolution. Judges suppose that comporting themselves in such a manner helps create an aura of authority that enhances the basis for personal integrity. They feel impelled to produce a coherent and consistent picture of themselves as judges, and to uphold this image in all social encounters, always displaying an aura of competency, reliability, justice and aloofness. To do so, they must establish boundaries between themselves as judges and other people, in many ways.

As I outlined above for the legal process itself, each group that judges address or with which they interact uses different categories to assess the judges. Consequently, judges must use different signs for each group. Often, judges try to address all groups simultaneously. Sometimes they must accord the various groups different priorities. And at other times they have to leave some out because there are simply too many. In many cases, the different groups' understanding is based on contradictory and conflicting criteria. Not all signs and symbols are cumulative or supplementary, or can be substituted by others. Sometimes signs seem contradictory or dysfunctional. Some groups will receive a certain sign that is not intended for them and due to their political inclination they may interpret it adversely. The impression of elitism, for example, so often evoked by judges and their critics, can be regarded as an unintended effect of both professional practices and the setting of moral boundaries, and is thus unavoidable.

Judges always try to avoid the impression that any action or encounter in court could be a hint at the existence of a social relationship. One measure is to create an aura of established routine in court. Thus everything that occurs in full view of the public seems like business as usual and unambiguous. This is crucial. In that respect, judges see equal treatment in public, neutrality, routine and adherence to rules as a means of producing and maintaining integrity through courtroom procedures. Peer-control appears to be less important in the daily production of integrity than self-control. In many courts, the set-up of the building infringes on the judges' attempt to create a border between themselves and others. Using a toilet can prove hazardous. Where should a judge relieve themselves, if there is no private toilet available? Should they use those used also by plaintiffs, defendants and convicts? What happens if they suffer from diarrhoea? Clearly, mundane problems create large-scale moral dilemmas. Moreover, if there is no possibility of having lunch privately, not eating is better than compromising one's integrity. Thus for judges, the daily challenges of natural needs can turn into potential pitfalls in the court setting.

In this context, items or status symbols are not meant to impress the peer group, but rather the public and anyone else trying to cross their boundaries. Every newcomer to a courtroom must believe that the judge presides over the proceedings in a day-to-day manner regardless of the case and those involved. Judges wear wigs and gowns in the court building and also have chambers where they work and reach their judgements. The chambers allow them greater privacy within the court setting. There the judge can receive visitors after they are announced by court staff and have given a reason for their visit. Chambers are also used for official visits or to consult lawyers, whereas the courtroom is reserved for purely public appearances. Such a backstage space (Goffman 2003: 99ff.) is a place to which they can retreat when deliberating a decision. In newer court buildings, chambers have air-conditioning and even washroom facilities. From time to time, judges will order the legal counsel of different parties into their chambers to reach an agreement. Although private litigation is often settled out of court in many other countries, Ghanaian judges prefer to settle such cases in the courtroom, where the public can affirm the openness of the dealings. This diminishes any suspicions of backstage decisions by the court. These signs and symbols underpin their ability to control space and to seclude themselves from the behaviour of and interactions with others. They serve as a means of moral boundary work.

Resources and Social Life

Scholars, the Ghanaian public and even judges themselves perceive judges and lawyers as members of the national elite (Edsman 1979; Luckham 1987). Apart from their political and economic influence, lawyers have shaped other parts of Ghanaian society such as consumption, taste, education and emerging elitist habits. However, Luckham's work and my interviewees' oral accounts paint a picture of an institution and profession that has been in economic decline since the 1970s. Limited economic resources, a diversification of social backgrounds and an increased variety of careers have changed the professional and social biographies of judges since the 1970s. Besides, in the early 1980s, during the 'revolutionary' movement led by Jerry John Rawlings, and especially its experiments in 'revolutionary justice' (Attafuah 1993, Gocking 1996), it became more expedient for judges to keep a lower social profile in order to cope with allegations of elitism and corruption.

For judges a number of items play an important role, and such resources help them to move in different, non-courtroom spaces while still maintaining their judicial aura. Nowadays, most judges have cars – an important resource and also a marker of class distinction. This also serves as a marker of success within the legal profession and to society at large. But judges say it is also a morally important sign. As Justice William Mensah told me:

> If you are a judge, there are things you can't do. For example: you can't join public transports; you know: our system of public transport; *trotro* [Ghanaian minibus; shared taxi] and so on – you can't. It is not possible. And then, ah … even it is not safe to go by taxis. You must have a car of your own. And you see, we don't simply get to work but we represent an image, you know, of justice. And when you haven't got your car and you have to depend on others, and you have to go along with people, you create an image, which is not so positive. It is that you are not that independent person; you are not on your own. You are depending on friends, and you depend on taxi drivers. No, that is not good enough. You see, because: the way the people see us. It is that we are capable of … that we don't depend on anybody else. (interview, 9 November 2007)

Since the late 1990s, superior court judges have been given a much-envied perk, namely a chauffeur-driven car. This helps maintain their integrity. But not all lower court judges can afford cars and they feel their autonomy and integrity is threatened without personal vehicles. One judge recounted a time in the 1980s when he had no car and was forced to use a *trotro* on his way to court and then a motorcycle. He ended up in all kinds of embarrassing situations. Sometimes he bumped into litigants, who would later appear in his courtroom, on the *trotro*. The judge was afraid that other people would think that his fellow traveller had picked him up from his at home or even paid for his ride. Ultimately, he was afraid that observers would assume that there was an improper relation between them. Thus, for judges cars help create important boundaries between the judiciary and other people and are a means for avoiding embarrassing situations. The car takes on a moral meaning, and thus it is an important factor in the judge's management of his integrity.

There are also institutional measures to underpin judges' boundary work and to control social encounters. In order to avoid conflicts, one institutionalized measure is to post judges at some distance from their home region. At the same time, about one-third of all Ghanaian judges are posted to Accra, where most of them have a wide circle of friends and acquaintances. Peer control is stronger in Accra, as most judges work in court complexes housing more than one court. Another measure undertaken by the judicial service to help curb the creation of social networks and accompanying suspicions is to transfer the judge to a new court every four or five years, at least up to the High Court level.

Judges are wary of who they are seen with as it can be difficult to manage their image. As Judge Robin Darko told me:

> There is a Catholic church; it is just by the road here. But I have chosen not to frequent it, because when I am going to church I prefer to go to M. In M, there is a cathedral, you know, it's big. So, people would hardly identify me. But this place is a communal area, if you go they get to know you somehow, and, like: some would have a problem to get to church. So, if a church member, he could be talking about a problem that is likely to come to court, he would expect me to give favours. So, to avoid those kinds of things, I don't attend church here. (interview, 16 May 2007)

Judges fear that anyone they meet outside the court could be in their courtroom at some stage. The only exception is in the very private company of close friends or family members. Only then do they undertake private social activities. But even at funerals, which are important, recurring social events in Ghana (see Lentz 1994: 159ff.) a judge needs to be on his guard and must, for example, take care who shakes his hand. Such a gesture can be interpreted as proof of a deeper social relationship. An apparently innocent act could be construed as something else and used against the judge later in court.

Judges not only establish symbolic boundaries; they also profit from spatial boundaries including private clubs with guards at the entrance, fences and restricted admission often based on rank and status. In their search for friends, one might think that judges would turn to other judges. However, Goffman (2003: 63) argues that high-status groups try to maintain their self-presentation even when they are among their peers – this applies to judges as well. Ghana does not have private clubs exclusively for judges, unlike many other countries. Judges prefer to be active in their church organizations or in groups such as freemasons and associations of their former schools. As soon as they are appointed judges, they cease other social activities and work in organizations or interest groups. Life in urban areas, even in Accra, does not provide the sense of anonymity judges would like from time to time. Goffman's remark seems valid for Ghanaian judges: the higher one climbs in society, the lower the number of people with whom one can be friends (Goffman 2003: 122). Yet, that depends very much on the social status of friends and family, and the composition of their social network depends often on judges' social backgrounds and the economic resources available to them before their professional careers. Judges carefully screen and filter those who can be trusted and will not compromise their integrity. This is very much based on signs of social status; thus judges usually find friends whose status is similar to their own. It is not that all of them are less prone to taking out lawsuits (judges can recuse themselves in such cases), but they are perceived as unlikely to cross boundaries in public. When becoming a judge, the term 'friend' is confined to a nucleus of close friends. Especially in rural areas, judges have less access to such people. Members of freemasons and similar associations say these associations attract judges because they have segregated spaces with strict rules, especially regarding the activities there. Justice Aikins relished such an opportunity:

> You know, it is a place for me to meet friends, from the North, those I attended school with, and many other people. And we, during the meetings, we enjoy ourselves and take off some of the boredom. Yes, I am a member of the freemasons. There I am free. We have our meetings, and after our meetings we have something we call a banquet. It is restricted. So I don't have a problem. They know that this is my work; you don't have to interfere with my work. (interview, 14 May 2007)

Associations with restricted entry and strict rules of conduct protect judges better from outsiders than churches or other groups. At home, judges can keep to themselves, meet old friends and family, and even walk around in jeans, t-shirts and shorts. However, even within the extended family circle, judges must establish boundaries in ways unlike lawyers in private practices.

Conclusion: Countering Doubt in Courts – Upholding Integrity through Boundary Work and Seclusion

In Ghana, there is a complex set of groups, with different expectations and epistemologies, who all make their own interpretations of what they see in court proceedings. Judges argue that there is no monopoly for their ideal of legal interpretation and its linear nature of translation of reality to judgment. Judges see themselves confronted with a plurality of competing epistemologies. As judges understand Ghanaian society, the litigants' view is based on a moral economy of corruption (Olivier de Sardan 1999) and leads litigants to the general assumption that judges, law and legal processes can be influenced like any other public service. Practically any hint of the existence of a social relationship can give rise to allegations of undue influence on a judge. Judges assume that audiences both inside and outside courts will judge every small act. These acts are indicative of the more general disposition of judges, their morals and personalities and the justness of the legal process. This constant, presumed doubt means that judges are permanently on their guard. In order to counter doubt, and stimulate faith in a different order, judges take a firm stance in court and generally in social interactions. This requires a change in their previous social habits and the way they present themselves and interact with people, including their former acquaintances, colleagues and people classified vaguely as 'friends' (see Grätz, Meier and Pelican 2004, Beek 2008). The fewer the resources available, the more important seclusion becomes as judges with poorer family backgrounds have fewer financial resources available to increase their control of social spaces and interactions. Often, they have restricted access to socially and morally adequate people who pose less of a threat to their integrity.

Their role is a totality. Everywhere they go, they have to be on their guard for and seek to prevent situations that might lead to suspicion and doubt. Therein, integrity is not only an abstract moral category; it becomes active boundary work to avoid doubt. Integrity is upheld through different means – dress, body language, means of transport (official or private car), residence, bodyguards and police officers available to judges – depending on their rank within the court system. Outsiders may see these resources as signs of material success or status whereas judges see them as resources for boundary work to create an image of integrity and to prevent doubt. In other words, judges consider them moral signs. If a given action can be construed as inappropriate and give rise to doubts about a judge, this damages the integrity of judges and their profession as a whole. Judges face situations which are beyond their control – they cannot control the behaviour of court staff and colleagues entirely. So, their only strategy is to isolate themselves to an extent that is almost monastic.

Acknowledgments

The research on which this chapter is based was made possible by the financial support of the Volkswagen Foundation for the project 'States at Work: Public Services and Civil Servants in West Africa: Education and Justice in Benin, Ghana, Mali and Niger'. For constructive comments on earlier versions of this text, many thanks go to Carola Lentz, Thomas Bierschenk, Mahaman Tidjani Alou, Mirco Göpfert, Pauline Bougler, Andrea Noll and Sarah Fichtner.

References

Aikins, George E.K. (2000) *The Role of a Barrister as a Practitioner, Bar Executive, Politician, and Judge*, Accra: Advanced Legal Publications.

Amissah, Austin N.E. (1981) *The Contribution of the Courts to Government: A West African View*, Oxford: Clarendon Press.

Attafuah, Kenneth A. (1993) 'Criminal justice policy, public tribunals and the administration of justice in Rawlings' Ghana (1982–1992): a study in the political economy of revolutionary social change and criminal law reform', Unpublished PhD dissertation, Simon Fraser University.

Beek, Jan (2008) '"Every car has an offence on it": Register polizeilichen Handelns bei Verkehrskontrollen in Nordghana', *Sociologus* 61(2): 197–222.

Bierschenk, Thomas (2008) 'The everyday functions of an African public service: informalization, privatization and corruption in Benin's legal system', *Journal of Legal Pluralism and Unofficial Law* 57: 101–39.

Blankenburg, Erhard (1984) 'Mobilisation of the law', *Government and Policy* 2(4): 461–70.

Blankenburg, Erhard (1995) *Mobilisierung des Rechts. Eine Einführung in die Rechtssoziologie*, Springer: Berlin.

Crook, Richard C. (2005) *State Courts and the Regulation of Land Disputes in Ghana: The Litigants' Perspective*, IDS Working Paper 241.

Crook, Richard C., Asante, Kojo and Brobbey, Victor (2010) *Popular Concepts of Justice and Fairness in Ghana: Testing the Legitimacy of New or Hybrid Forms of State Justice*, APP Working Paper 14.

Edsman, Björn M. (1979) *Lawyers in Gold Coast Politics c. 1900–1945: From Mensah Sarbah to J.B. Danquah*, Uppsala: Acta Universitatis Upsaliensis 111.

Ghana Integrity Initiative (2007) *Report on Judicial Corruption Monitoring Exercise in Ghana*, Accra: Ghana Integrity Initiative.

Gocking, Roger S. (1996) 'Ghana's public tribunals: an experiment in revolutionary justice', *African Affairs* 95: 197–223.

Goffman, Erving (1989) 'On face-work: an analysis of ritual elements in social interaction', in *Interaction Ritual: Essays on Face-to-Face Behavior*, ed. Erving Goffman, New York: Pantheon Books, pp. 5–45.

Goffman, Erving (2003) *Wir alle spielen Theater. Die Selbstdarstellung im Alltag*, Munich: Piper.

Grätz, Tilo, Meier, Barbara and Pelican, Michaela (2004) 'Freundschaftsprozesse in Afrika aus sozial-anthropologischer perspektive: eine Einführung', *Afrika Spectrum* 39(1): 9–39.

Jung, Heike (2006) *Richterbilder. Ein interkultureller Vergleich*, Baden-Baden: Nomos.

Lamont, Michèle (1992) *Money, Morals, and Manners: The Culture of the French and American Upper-Middle Class*, Chicago: University of Chicago Press.
Latour, Bruno (1996) *Der Berliner Schlüssel. Erkundungen eines Liebhabers der Wissenschaften*, Berlin: Akademischer-Verlag.
Latour, Bruno (2002) *La fabrique du droit: une ethnographie du Conseil d'État*, Paris: La Découverte.
Latour, Bruno and Woolgar, Steve (1986) *Laboratory Life: The Construction of Scientific Facts*, Princeton: Princeton University Press.
Lentz, Carola (1994) 'Home, death and leadership: discourses of an educated elite from north-western Ghana', *Social Anthropology* 2(2): 149–69.
Lowy, Michael J. (1978) 'A good name is worth more than money: strategies of court use in Urban Ghana', in *The Disputing Process – Law in Ten Societies*, ed. Laura Nader and Harry F. Todd, New York: Columbia University Press, pp. 181–208.
Luckham, Robin (1977) 'The administration of justice', *Review of Ghana Law* 9: 190–228.
Luckham, Robin (1987) 'The economic base of private law practice in Ghana', in *The Political Economy of Law: A Third World Reader*, ed. Yash Ghai, Robin Luckham and Francis Snyder, Bombay: Oxford University Press, pp. 708–17.
Olivier de Sardan, J.-P. (1999) 'A moral economy of corruption in Africa?', *Journal of Modern African Studies* 37: 25–52.
Star, Susan L. and Griesemer, James R. (1989) 'Institutional ecology, "translations" and boundary objects: amateurs and professionals in Berkeley's Museum of Vertebrate Zoology, 1907–39', *Social Studies of Science* 19(3): 387–420.
Tidjani Alou, Mahaman (2006) 'Corruption in the legal system', in *Everyday Corruption and the State: Citizens and Public Officials in Africa*, ed. Giorgio Blundo and J.-P. Olivier de Sardan, Cape Town, London and New York: Zed Books, pp. 137–76.

Chapter 5

Doubt in Action: The Different Times of Doubt in French Assize Courts

Véronique Bouillier[1]

Only a very small percentage of all French criminal offences are judged in Assize Courts (*cours d'assises*).[2] However their complex and lengthy procedures offer an exemplary display on one side of the ideas and ideals governing the French notion of Justice, and on the other side of the way actors and proceedings are supposed to implement these ideals.

A main concern in the Assize trial is the question of truth. 'We are here to discover the truth', said a presiding judge, to which a prosecutor added: 'Perhaps a truth will emerge from the debates, which will be quite close to The Truth'. And witnesses have to swear before making their statements 'to tell the truth and truth only'.[3] What is truth in this context of a courtroom? Whatever the philosophical and sociological considerations on the relativistic nature of truth, the most common shared meaning would be that 'a claim is true if it corresponds to what is so, if it corresponds to the "facts" or "reality", and it is false if it does not correspond to what is so' (Dupret 2011: 155).[4] This truth has to be established, constructed during the trial and then accepted as judicial truth grounded on evidence and reasoning. This process is supposed to progress step by step throughout the hearings and thus implies necessarily the presence of doubt. As Judge Roland Cuer has stated: 'Doubt is inherent to the judicial process' and 'the purpose of justice is to bring to end a doubt and replace it with a judicial truth' (2011).

The aim of this chapter is to show how and by whom, during the lengthy process of an Assize trial, doubt is created and then dispelled, allowing this judicial truth to

1 This research has been made possible thanks to the CNRS/ANR Programme, 'Just-India: A Joint Programme on Justice and Governance in India' (www.just-india.net), directed by Daniela Berti and Gilles Tarabout. With many thanks also to Anthony Good who helped me to improve the text.

2 In 2010 among all judicial decisions made by criminal jurisdictions (1,173,242) only 2,502 were by Assize Courts, the huge majority being by *tribunaux correctionnels* (Ministère de la Justice et des Libertés 2011).

3 Article 331 of the Code de procedure pénale: [The witnesses swear] 'de parler sans haine et sans crainte, de dire toute la vérité, rien que la vérité'.

4 According to 'the correspondence theory of truth', which is held by 'most scientists and many philosophers' (Dupret 2011: 155), but which seems also to characterize what is called 'mundane reasoning' (Dupret 2011: 161–2, quoting Melvin Pollner).

appear and making it possible for the jurors to decide on a verdict. For those who bear the burden of doubt are the jurors: they remain in a situation of uncertainty throughout the hearings and then, at the end of the trial, have the duty to reach a decision on an eventual culpability and to bear the personal moral consequences of a difficult choice.

The presence of a jury is central to the French Assize Court proceedings.[5] The jurors are six, selected at random at the beginning of each new lawsuit, from a panel of thirty people selected for each session, the prosecutor and the defence lawyer having the right to challenge the selection.[6] Unlike proceedings in the USA, the prosecutor and the lawyer have no information about the jurors except their names, ages and professions; thus, they may recuse a juror on grounds based on the aforementioned criteria as well as on their physical appearance. After being selected the jurors take up their places on both sides of the three professional judges, on high chairs facing the room where the public are seated. On their right side, at the same level, stands the public prosecutor (general attorney), who exercises public action on behalf of the State and is the one who accuses. On the other side of the room, the defendant takes their place in the dock with their lawyer before them on a bench. In the courtroom also, close to the prosecutor, are placed eventually the victims, called civil plaintiffs, and their counsel. That the victims are represented by their own lawyers, who are active in the trial, ask questions and plead, is a specificity of the French system.

The jurors have to give the final judgment together with the professional judges.[7] But contrary to the judges, prosecutor and lawyers, they have no previous

---

5 On the history of the jury system since the twelfth century and its initial *raison d'être*, to dilute or avoid the judge's responsibility or sin incurred in the possible condemnation of an innocent, see Whitman (2008). For a more detailed *aperçu* of the French proceedings as viewed by an anthropologist, see Bouillier (forthcoming). For a thorough overview, see Garapon (2001) and Garapon and Papadopoulos (2003).

6 Since the 1 January 2012 reform, there are six jurors, and nine in the appellate court. There were nine and twelve, respectively, before. The prosecutor (*procureur*, *avocat général*) has the right to challenge three jurors and the defence lawyer, four. They do so in the courtroom immediately after a name being announced by the presiding judge who is drawing lots.

7 Contrary to what is done in the USA or the UK, jury and judges deliberate together and have equal voting rights. Moskovitz, in his vivid article retrying the O.J. Simpson case according to the French legal system, portrays the US prosecutor expressing his indignation:

> 'You're not telling me that the judges go into the room with these lay assessors and deliberate with them?'
>
> 'I'm afraid I am. You seem shocked.'
>
> 'Of course I'm shocked. What kind of a jury do you have when judges vote with the jurors?'

information on the case. Whereas the latter arrive every day in the courtroom with huge files that they pile up on their desk and to which they constantly refer, the jurors' only source of information is to listen to everything which is declared, explained and contested by the various actors in the trial and they have to let their opinion emerge from these successive fragmentary oral testimonies. Formally all discourses seem thus to be addressed to the jurors: they are the ones that the prosecution or the defence have to convince. And their opinion evolves as the hearings unfold. As one juror recognizes: 'At the beginning, I was on the side of the victim. Then one goes back, one hesitates, one changes and strangely not in the way one thought'.[8] And quite radically, another juror, Robert Brisart, explains his uneasiness: 'The more the trial went on, the less clear became the facts to be judged' (2002: 423).

This chapter focuses on the ambiguous place taken by doubt in the current practices of the Assize Courts. Doubt has a positive value at the beginning of a trial, it is later alternatively denied and cast according to the speakers (prosecutor and defence) and finally doubt is supposed to be dispelled before any judgment. Examples taken from courtroom interactions will show different moments when, and different techniques whereby, doubt is enacted.

Doubt as Leading Value

At the beginning and at the end of a trial, jurors are reminded of the fundamental principles that have governed any process of judgment since medieval times: '"in dubio pro reo", "in doubt you must decide for the defendant"' (Whitman 2008: 122). It takes the form of a solemn and collective oath taken by the jurors; as soon as they have been selected and the jury thus constituted, they stand up and by turn they raise their right hand and say 'I swear' to the following formula read solemnly by the presiding judge:

> You swear and promise ... to remember that the accused person is presumed to be innocent and that doubt must benefit him; to decide after looking at the

---

> 'Well, the jurors ... can outvote the judges'
>
> 'Look, Professor, I wasn't born yesterday ... When a judge – when *three* judges – tell the jurors what they think, what juror is going to disagree?' (1995: 1125)

The current French system dates from 1941. Before that, it was the same as in England, no professional judges sitting with the jury.

8 Jurors are supposed not to comment on the trial they attended, hence the very general impressions they give when questioned. I quote here from a declaration made to a documentary film maker (S. Lebas and E. Manéglier Dessenne, *Les jurés face au doute*, France 2, 2013).

> charges and the means of the defence, following your conscience and your innermost conviction (*intime conviction*), with impartiality and rightness.

And again at the end of the trial, before the judges and jurors leave the courtroom to deliberate in privacy, the presiding judge reminds them:

> The law does not require judges and jurors to account for the reasons why they are convinced, it does not prescribe rules … ; it stipulates that they have to ask themselves in silence and contemplation and to seek, according to their true conscience, what impression the evidence given against the accused and the means of his defence have made on their reason. The law only asks them this one question, which gives the full measure of their duties: 'Are you firmly convinced?'

The formula used in British or US trials, 'beyond reasonable doubt', is not employed,[9] but reference is made to the inner feelings of the jurors, to their intimate conviction.[10]

A trial is a performance that is the outcome of a long process of judicial inquiry, but whatever the evidence collected or even if there is a confession, great attention is paid to giving full value to doubt – that is, to the possibility of the accused being innocent, at least in the terminology employed. For instance, at every step of the procedure, the choice of words used to designate the person accused must avoid any presupposition. When arrested by the police, the person is called '*mise en examen*' ('placed under judicial investigation', indicted), then '*prévenue*' (charged) when presented to the Investigating Judge and, after being committed to the court, the 'suspect' becomes 'the accused'. Any public declaration prior to judgment that lacks precautionary marks of inverted commas or conjectural words is strongly rebuked. That happens often in politicians' discourses or press declarations. We may recall the scandal following the declaration by Nicolas Sarkozy in relation to the Clearstream court case, qualifying Villepin as culprit before any trial: 'After two years of enquiries, independent judges have considered that the culprits should

9 About this formula, its historical background in pre-modern Christian theology and its ambiguity, see James Q. Whitman who begins his seminal study by observing: 'Attempts to explain the term "reasonable doubt", the Court once dryly observed, do not usually result in making it any clearer to the minds of the jury' (*Miles* v. *United States*, 103 U.S. 304, 26 L. Ed. 481 [1881], quoted in Whitman 2008: 2). See also Good, this volume.

10 See Engel (2008) for a reflection on the subjectivist standard of proof in continental legal orders, and hence the conflicts between (US) common law and (European) continental law regarding an 'apparently technical issue in the law of evidence'. 'At closer sight the conflict roots deeper. US law not only differentiates; it conceptualises proof differently. On the continent, proof is understood as the strictly subjective impression in the judge's mind. By contrast, in US law, proof is an objective concept' (Engel 2008: 2). On *intime conviction*, see also Berti, Kobelinsky, this volume.

be brought before the court'! Or the same Nicolas Sarkozy claiming in 2003: 'The French police have just arrested Yvan Colonna, the murderer of Prefet Erignac'.

The press is also often guilty of the same practices and, by declarations that flout the presumption of innocence, arouses the judges' indignation. To recall a case that I will evoke later in this chapter, the headlines in the newspapers of June 2012 were 'Today starts the trial of the six Somali pirates who hijacked the French sailing ship, Le Ponant'. And even during the investigation, as claimed indignantly by one of the defence lawyers, the arrested men had been described in one report as 'the six pirates' (even though the trial would decide that two were innocent). Thus one recurrent argument of defence lawyers during that case was that the investigation was biased and based on a presumption of culpability instead of innocence.

One may wonder if the careful words and the initial declarations to the jurors are not mere lip service to the presumption of innocence. Considering the course of the trial, the declaration of Judge Cuer (2011) is both provocative and evident: 'We send to the Assize Court people for whom we make a bet on their culpability'. As McKillop summarizes: 'Only those cases in which the investigation reveals strong evidence of guilt are sent to a hearing so that hearings should normally result in conviction' (1997: 565). Thus it has 'sometimes been suggested that there is no presumption of innocence in the French legal system' (McKillop 1997: 578). In fact the notion has to be recast, according to the inquisitorial system whereby the investigation is done before the trial.

Bill of Indictment and Culpability

Immediately after the composition of the jury, their taking of the oath and the setting of the timetable, the court hearing begins. The accused is asked to stand up and give his identity, and then a long reading is done of the 'bill of indictment' or *ordonnance de renvoi*. Since January 2012 the duty of the presiding judge is to write and read a summary of the bill but before the reform the entire reading was done by the bailiff. The text, which was read at great speed and often in a mumbling tone, was supposed to give the accused the reasons why he was in the dock and give the jurors a first survey of the case.

The bill of indictment is a summary established by the Investigating Judge (*Juge d'Instruction*) of the successive inquiries made by the police under his authority and of his hearings of the various witnesses and experts. These proceedings may have taken several months or even years but led to the arrest and indictment (*mise en examen*) of the person now presented to the court. Thus the committal for a hearing before an Assize Court is a decision taken by the Investigating Judge (together with the '*chambre de l'instruction*'), who supposes that the investigation has proved the charges against the accused: the bill of indictment is already a demonstration of guilt.

The Investigating Judge does not attend the trial, but all the documents that his service have collected make up the voluminous dossier in the hands of the prosecutor, the defendant's and civil plaintiff's lawyers, and the presiding judge. The prosecutor's arguments and pleading are grounded on the dossier that he, like the judge, receives a few weeks before the trial, but his opinion, and hence his arguments, can be modified by the hearings.

The bill of indictment demonstrates clearly what was pointed out by Susan Terrio, a US sociologist studying the juvenile courts in Paris; she notes that in French only 'one word "*les faits*" indexes both the charges alleged during investigation as well as the facts established during the trial' (2009: 49). On the contrary:

> In adversarial systems … the facts of the case emerge from a strategic confrontation between the prosecution and defense attorneys … Such systems assume broad equality between the prosecution and the defense. Each side gathers evidence and presents arguments in oral proceedings intended to establish the facts of the case. In the French system, no such equality is presumed between the parties. The facts are established by the JI [Investigating Judge] or the procureur and presented by the state in the person of the trial judge, not by the individual parties to the case. They are premised on a conception of the truth that is established independently of the prosecution and the defense and puts the onus on the accused to prove his or her innocence. (2009: 44)

It is said differently but with the same thinly disguised disapproval by a French sociologist reflecting on her own experience of acting as juror: 'everything is edited, in the cinematic sense, in order to mark out the accused as a culprit … to prove his innocence, he has to "dis-edit" [*dé-monter*, dismantle] the system of arguments [of the prosecution]' (Mozère 2002: 401). The defence, 'has to dismantle one by one the stones of the building that the prosecution has constructed' (Mozère 2002: 407).

Let us take an example of the way the bill of indictment was written (before 2012). Its formula was quite straightforward and aimed at establishing convincingly the reasons why a person was sent to court, even though the word 'guilty' was never employed. This is a case of murder. On the first page of the bill it is written:

> Mrs X was placed under investigation charged with assassination, premeditated murder of a male victim who could be Mr X. The crime was committed on … at … on national territory and at an unspecified time.
>
> Crime listed and punishable according to articles 221-3 AL1, 221-1, 132-72, 221-8, 221-9, 221-9-1, 221-11, of the Criminal Code.

Then all the details of the enquiry are explained and finally comes the formula:

> Whereas the inquiry has helped to establish that Mrs X wilfully killed Mr Y … and that she used all the resources available to achieve her goal.
>
> For these reasons we order the *mise en accusation* of Mrs X before the Assises Court of Seine Saint Denis for having:
>
> In place and day X, with premeditation voluntarily given death to Y.
>
> Crime listed and punishable according to articles … of the Criminal Code.

The complete reading of the bill of indictment has now been suppressed and it is left to the presiding judge (who receives the files before the trial) to write a summary, which he reads himself. The decision was taken to shorten the reading and to avoid stating evidence that would later be given orally by the witnesses, thus preserving the orality of the debates; and perhaps also to water down the impression that the 'crime' is already established and that the judgment in the courtroom is just a confirmation of what has already been stated in the first moment of the trial. This was clear in one presiding judge's declaration when she ended her summary with these words: 'This must in no way prejudge the culpability of the accused person' – a straightforward declaration but not exactly an affirmative support of the presumption of innocence.

Thus when the proper hearing starts, we have, on one side, linguistic turns and advice to the jury, which tend to assert the presumption of innocence, and on the other a bill of indictment, which clearly deals with the presumption of culpability! The task of the prosecution will be to prove this culpability in front of the court, by developing arguments taken from the dossier or born from the hearings, in order to convince the jury. And the accused and their counsel have 'to undermine the evidence to which we had been first invited by the nice construction of the Public Prosecution' (Brisart 2002: 427).

The Defence Lawyers' Role: To Build a Counter-narrative

Thus, during the few days of the trial, the defence lawyers concentrate their efforts on contesting the conclusion of the bill of indictment and the impression it has made on the minds of the jurors. They attempt to show that the enquiries have not been well done, that the conclusions are misleading, that all the witnesses have not been heard; in short to raise doubts in the minds of the jurors, by drawing up another story in favour of their clients. And, if they are good professionals, slowly when the various police officers, witnesses and experts give evidence, they ask questions which, step by step, lead to an alternative narrative, a strategy of which I will give a few examples. But the situation, and hence the lawyers' strategy in raising doubts, has to be different depending on whether the accused recognizes the facts or denies them.

The Defendant Recognizes the Facts

What is the place of doubt when the accused has recognized the facts, admitted his culpability in front of the police or during the investigation and when he repeats his confession in front of the court?

At first sight one may think that doubt is cleared, but the situation could be more complicated and justifies the current legal adage that 'avowal is not proof'. Why would someone confess to a crime that he or she had not committed? A most evident explanation would be to protect someone else, to divert suspicion from the real culprit. But avowal could also be induced by a particular situation, most often during the *garde à vue* (police custody), the first police examination. A study by Lucie Jouvet regarding miscarriages of justice (2010) demonstrates convincingly the process which led the young accused Patrick Dils to claim a horrible murder of which he was recognized to be innocent after fifteen years in jail. She demonstrates very well the psychological pressure, which Patrick Dils describes in this way:

> The police inspector [tells my mother on the phone] that as long as I do not tell the truth, I will not get out of here. But for hours I was telling them the truth, and then I started to understand without really understanding. They didn't want MY truth … I just wanted to go home. I got the impression that, as long as I won't tell them THEIR truth, they won't leave me. (Dils 2002, as quoted by Jouvet 2010: 52–3)

Jouvet, studying the police reports, shows how the suspect is 'talked' (*parlé*) by the policemen: questions are not reported, thus the answers seem spontaneous declarations and are often given with a vocabulary far remote from the one the person uses ordinarily (2010: 70–75).

In these cases, the suspect may retract during subsequent examinations or at the hearing. Thus, whatever the suspect's declarations, the enquiry has to look for objective evidence in order to confirm or challenge his or her avowed culpability.

When the accused recognizes his culpability and gives details that leave no doubt of the facts, the defence lawyer nevertheless tries to challenge the version given in the bill of indictment and supported by the prosecution. He seeks to minimize the facts or the part played by the accused, thus to cast doubt on the circumstances, the context or the motives.

The circumstances may change the *definition* of the crime – that is, the legal category into which the infraction has to be put. For instance, in cases of violence judged in the Assize Court, the defendant could be charged with manslaughter (or 'assault and battery causing death without intention'; *coups et blessures ayant entraîné la mort sans intention de la donner*), 'attempted murder' (*tentative d'assassinat*), 'murder' (*meurtre or homicide volontaire*) or 'premeditated murder' (*assassinat avec premeditation*). The consequences are important since the maximum penalty varies with the definition: from fifteen years for manslaughter to life imprisonment for premeditated murder. The definition is decided by the

Investigating Judge and figures in the bill of indictment, but can be modified. Thus, even before the trial and during the hearings, the lawyers may try to cast doubt, not on the facts, which could appear impossible, but on the intentions of the perpetrator, and thus are striving to have the crime redefined at an inferior level. It falls to the jury to decide in the last resort, given the questions they have to answer during the deliberation (for instance, Question 1: Is the accused guilty of having intentionally committed acts of violence against the victim? Question 2: Have these acts of violence led to the death of the victim?).

Let us take the case of KK, from Sri Lanka, judged at the Seine-Saint-Denis law court. The bill of indictment (established by the Investigating Judge and transmitted in advance to the prosecutor and to the defence lawyer) accused KK of murder, of having intentionally brought about the death of the victim. When he got the bill, the defence lawyer replied to the Investigating Judge by contesting the intentionality of the act, and hence its definition, and claimed that this was a case of manslaughter. But the definition was maintained by the *chambre de l'instruction* and the trial was organized as an accusation of murder. Hence, during the trial, the arguments of the prosecutor attempted to convince the jury that the accused had the intention to kill, that the stabbing was done intentionally to murder the victim. On the other hand, the lawyer tried to refute intentionality: 'Yes, my client has been violent, he has stabbed his friend but he never had any intention to kill him. He hit him deliberately but he had no will to kill. He is not a murderer'. And when the presiding judge gave the accused the right to speak, KK declared:

> This day we had a lot of drinks … When I went back to the apartment, I sat on the bed to take off my shoes, but X pushed the door and got in my room with two knives. He wanted to stab me. I pushed him away two times. He insulted my mother and my sister and all my family. Afterwards I took his knife. I don't know what happened, he was lying down. I stabbed him. I ran outside and phoned a friend to call the emergency services.

The lawyer ended his speech (*plaidoirie*) explaining that the victim's death was an accident with this appeal to the jurors: 'Now you will have to answer the question if KK had the intention to kill the victim, if he had a clear and conscious will to kill. You must decide in your mind if you are sure of his murderous intention'. However, the jurors followed the prosecutor and answered 'Yes' to the question: 'Is KK is guilty of having intentionally killed X?'

It is the prosecution that bears the burden of proof, to convince the jurors of the guilt of the accused, using for that purpose the documents collected by the investigation and the oral declarations made during the hearings. But it is up to the defence to bring in evidence allowing for contestation: in this case, the evidence and arguments of the defence lawyer (that, if KK wanted to kill, why did he strike so many blows, some very superficial, rather than stabbing in the heart) did not suffice to prove his thesis and convince the jurors.

In such cases, when the crime is admitted by the perpetrator and proved by the investigation, the defence lawyers may also try to put forward mitigating circumstances and raise doubt not on the reality of the crime or the fault of the accused, but on the context. In a case of murder which presented many similarities with the previously discussed one, the lawyer tried to convince the bench that the accused was acting in self-defence, that he had been attacked first by the victim who seemed to have been very angry. But the position of the body on the ground and the fact that his murderer stabbed him twenty-two times made it difficult for the lawyer to justify self-defence, thus he was also obliged to have recourse to psychiatry to advance a momentary absence of mind.

The strategy of the defence can be to raise doubt in the mind of the jurors on the legitimacy of punishment, on the fairness of a harsh sentence,[11] in cases of people already mistreated by life (or by the victims).

A women was accused of having killed her husband with a screwdriver: her declaration, without any witness present to support it, was that she took the screwdriver from the hands of her drunken husband, held it in front of her and that, as he jumped towards her, he stabbed himself. The effort of the lawyer was to convince the jurors that she didn't strike any blow, that it was a mere accident, but he insisted also that the woman deserved mercy because of her hard life with this drunkard and the two small kids she had to take care of.

The mitigating circumstances evoked by the defence can be contested by the prosecution. In the case of the murder whose bill of indictment was presented previously, the lawyer made a lot of the violence of the victim towards his mistress, the state of terror in which she lived. And then it was the Advocate General who cast doubts on the lawyer's version, saying that the victim was half crippled and unable to resort to any physical violence. The verbal argument between the defence lawyer and the Advocate General was rather violent, aiming at casting doubt not on the fact, which could not be denied (the accused admitted having killed her lover and cut him into pieces, the pieces were found in a canal, and the saw was found with the accused) but about its context, the life circumstances of the couple.

The Defendant Denies the Charges

The lawyer contests the prosecution evidence

When the defendant denies the charges or goes back on his first confession, the lawyer's task is to demonstrate the emptiness of the files (*l'inanité du dossier*). He tries to refute the charges by looking closely at the investigation.

For instance, during a trial for a hold-up in a postal agency, the lawyer advanced his argument step by step when questioning the first witness,[12] the police inspector:

---

11 In the French procedure the jury, after judging culpability, must also decide the penalty.

12 The witnesses are summoned by the presiding judge; they are supposed to be neutral and take an oath 'to tell the truth and only the truth'. They make a first spontaneous

Lawyer: In your report, you make imprecise and even false statements. Tell us at what time the hold-up ended?

Police Officer: 7h40.

Lawyer: Where do you get that from? Most of the employees talk about 7h45. There was a huge clock in the room. And why don't you talk about the metro ticket? [The lawyer has the files and knows that a RER ticket has been found on the suspect stamped with the time 7h45. If the hold-up was over only at 7h45 and the robber left then, he could not be on the RER counter at the same time.] You say that the hold-up finishes at 7h40 and I say that maybe it is a different man, the one you arrested is not the culprit. Do you know the crowd at the RER station, do you know how much time between the postal agency and the RER station? Did you time the duration of the route?

Police Officer: No, I don't have all these data. They did not look important at first. I was writing a first report.

Lawyer (indignantly): Not important, the ticket!!

Police Officer (very naively): Yes, it is just because the ticket is stamped 7h45 that we inferred that the hold-up was over at 7h40.

The same element has thus been interpreted very differently: the police adapted the elements (like the time of the hold-up) to suit the person they suspected (following the description given by the witnesses) and the lawyer has succeeded in casting doubt on the real identity of the arrested person. Thus the lawyer claimed to the officer: 'Don't you see that you are trying to justify your thesis. This is how one starts on a false basis. Sir, you go too far in misleading justice!'

In the same trial, the co-accused was a 'star' in organized crime. His lawyer used the same technique to crush the accusation by arguing aggressively with the same police officer:

Lawyer: Do you think the enquiry has been well done, that it is satisfactory?

Police Officer: Yes.

---

statement and then are questioned by the judge (who may compare their present oral statements with those already made to the Investigating Judge and listed in the dossier), by the prosecutor and lawyers on the victims' side and finally by the defence lawyer. No witnesses appear specifically for the prosecution or for the defence. The police officers who were the first on the crime scene and who made the subsequent inquiries are the first witnesses to be summoned and give evidence.

> *Lawyer*: Oh yeah … Really? You talk about phone calls made to my client. Do you know where my client was then?
>
> *Police Officer*: I don't know.
>
> *Lawyer*: Why didn't you have the very simple idea of looking for the transceiver terminal for the mobile phone?
>
> *Police Officer*: Maitre, at this time (1999), it was not so simple, it was not among our duties. It was very costly.
>
> *Lawyer*: Don't talk nonsense. You needed only to make a requisition and to obtain the *fadettes* [the detailed bills] from the telephone company. And then you would see that if my client was for instance in Paris at the same time, he will be innocent. Why have you not done that?
>
> *Police Officer*: We did not see the interest in spending a lot of money.

The defence lawyer by a series of sharp questions had succeeded in casting doubt on the accuracy of the process of investigation, in showing the negligence displayed during the inquiries. Thus as soon as the first witness was heard, the construction of culpability carried out by the bill of indictment was shaken.

Resorting to lapses of memory: an ambivalent strategy
Most often when the defendant is subjected to close questioning by the presiding judge who tries to extort from him a clear description of his behaviour and stresses any apparent contradictions between his successive declarations or between his declarations and evidence given by oral witnesses, he resorts to the only way out left: 'I don't know', 'I don't remember', 'I was drunk'. KK, whose trial was mentioned above, gave such answers all through his questioning:

> 'I took the knife [with which the victim was menacing him] and struck him on the face, near his eyes. He started bleeding. After I don't know. I washed the knife. I left the place.'
>
> 'When I pushed him back, a knife was taken out. How I pushed him back, I don't remember.'
>
> 'I was very upset. I lost my head.'

To the judge asking if he remembered how many stabs he made: 'I remember his face then, that is all'.

When the judge asked: 'You are talking about 10 euros the victim asked you for. You didn't talk of this to the policemen?' 'I don't remember.'

'What happened in front of the apartment door?' 'I don't remember.'

'You said that you didn't stab him to death.' 'I don't know.'

'You said that somebody else went to kill him?' 'I don't know.'

'In custody, you said that you were out of your mind to stab like this. Today you say that you didn't.' 'I have not said such thing.'

One can very well understand that, after sometimes several years, people would forget many details or circumstances especially since they were traumatic.[13] As one hostage of Somali pirates said, in the case discussed below: 'I have erased these memories from my mind. I can't be positive'. However the effect of the accused's lapses of memory on the jury may not be very beneficial: the jurors tend to doubt the credibility of the accused, and to punish his or her lack of cooperation. And when the accused, asked if he has some last words to say before the deliberation, replied: 'I just think that I am jailed for nothing', a mere denial which followed many contradictory statements, the jury, even in the absence of material evidence, was not disposed to believe in his innocence.

Some defendants stick to their attitude of denial even when confronted with evidence from video monitoring.

Prosecutor: Do you know Torcy?

Defendant: It is on the RER metro line but I have never been there.

Prosecutor: Your photo has been taken by the video monitoring cameras at 13h50.

Defendant: I was drunk. I don't remember much. It is not me on the photo.

The defence lawyer in this case was trying to raise doubts by questioning the mere presence of his client at the scene of the crime, which is often a good technique when no arrest has been made in *flagrante delicto*. But here the video camera proved at least that the accused was possibly lying.

The sensitive question of identification

Among the techniques used for the identification of the eventual culprit, one which is often used when there are witnesses, is called a '*tapissage*' or 'police ID

13 One may argue that traumatic events should be more vividly remembered, but victims' testimonies inside and outside courtrooms attest the psychological need for, and the frequency of, erasing memory (for many examples in the judicial context of the British asylum courts' quest for 'credibility', see Good 2007, 2011).

(identification) parade'. The suspects are lined up with various people and presented to the witnesses and/or victims. Often this parade is done using photographs.

In the previous case of the 'star criminal', a first parade was done with photos of various suspects but not with his, because the police did not think then that he was involved. A few months later, he was arrested (he was on the run after another hold-up). His photo was published in many newspapers and on television. And later his photo was included in the photo album which was presented again to the witnesses of the postal agency robbery of which he was now accused.

Doubt was cast by his lawyer on the fact that some witnesses then recognized him. They said: 'The photo spoke to me', 'Perhaps it is him, it is difficult but yes, when I have seen the picture …'. Did they recognize him because they had seen his face in the newspaper (he looks familiar) or because he was the author of the hold-up (the robbers wore hoods and masks but took them off at the end)? It was easy for the lawyer to harass the witnesses:

> If you recognized him when his photo was first published in the newspaper, why not call the police? You were not sure? And now you are sure? It is strange, usually memory vanishes with time.

The same questions about identification, photos and lapses of memory were at the centre of the debates regarding the case of six presumed Somali pirates. Most of the indictment rested on the identification by the hostages of the 'pirates' arrested in a truck in the Somali desert by a French commando unit, a few hours after the handing over of the ransom and the liberation of the hostages. The first attempt at identification was done using photographs taken just after the arrest of the 'pirates' and the second, two years later, when the witnesses were brought face to face with their supposed kidnappers.

The results of this identification process varied enormously. Some of the hostages did not recognize anyone. They explained: 'You know, I tried not look at them. They were very nervous. I wanted to save my skin and tried not to provoke anyone'. The reaction of another hostage led to a hot debate between the defence attorneys and the civil plaintiffs' attorney:

> At the first presentation of the photos, he said that he was unsure; at the second presentation, that he recognized two of the pirates. And then suddenly at the court, he declared: 'Now I recognize them all. Now I know, now I can remember. Before, I was too traumatized'.

'Can we remember better after four years?' the attorneys asked the psychologist, who did not answer clearly. Other hostages were affirmative in their identification but mentioned in support of it a minor physical detail that the lawyers were quick to relativize: 'A birth mark on the forehead? But such marks are only marks of the Muslim prayer!'

In short, the evidence given by witnesses regarding identification based on physical appearance often appears doubtful. This was made clear in the case of the hold-up attributed to the star criminal Ferrera: all the witnesses spontaneously talked about the gangster as being North-African or Maghrebian looking. Ferrara is Italian and has a dark complexion. His lawyer thus doubted Ferrara's recognition while the Advocate General tried to minimize the discrepancies among witnesses: 'Maghrebian, that means Mediterranean, Italian that is the same!' The same lawyer continued, questioning a witness and making him and thus the jurors doubt the given evidence: 'Did you see him exactly? Can you be absolutely sure? No, you are not hundred per cent sure, thanks. That is all I wanted to know!'

A Counter-narrative

After having contested the charges, discussed the evidence, destabilized the witnesses, the defence lawyer has then to elaborate a counter-narrative to exonerate his client. This narrative is grounded on the declarations of the accused person who claims his innocence and proposes a different version of the events. The lawyer's duty is to build a credible narrative to oppose the one offered by the prosecution. This narrative has to take into account the incontrovertible elements proven by the accusation, the facts, but to present an altogether different view of the situation, in order to convince the audience of the possible innocence of the accused.

The lawyer's position is sometimes made difficult by defendants who, during the hearings, give alternative versions of what happened. This may be the case with people ignorant of the French justice system, who think that if the judges keep asking them to tell what happened this unfortunate day when they were arrested with a knife in front of a corpse, it is because the judges are not satisfied with the answer; thus such defendants try different versions in front of an exasperated presiding judge who says: 'We are here to know the truth!', and a desperate lawyer who does not know how to defend a client who keeps changing his version up until the last moment.

In the trial of the presumed pirates, the lawyer of one of them, following the account given by his client, challenged the full version of the story given by the prosecution:

> My client has nothing to do with the pirates. If he got on board the sailing boat, it was just to make business, to sell cigarettes. My client is a respected man. He has his business. And later if he was in the pick-up truck [which had been stopped, inspected by the French military and where money from the ransom was found], this was only because he had to see a doctor in the next town. He took the opportunity of this car. This truck was a public taxi. That, in this taxi, there was a pirate carrying money from the ransom, he didn't know. He didn't know the other people. He was just in the taxi, ill. He says that he has been arrested and kidnapped by the white people. Now he is unjustly in jail. He waited for this trial for years to be able to tell the truth to everyone.

The Advocate General's version is rather different:

> This accused man is older and more articulate than the others. He is a leader. I don't believe in his story of being ill. And the doctor who examined him in France didn't confirm anything. Perhaps, yes, he didn't guard the hostages on the boat himself but he was directing the other pirates from the mainland.

Words against words! Truth against truth! No objective evidence here can carry the conviction of the jurors, thus their opinion fluctuates with the credibility of the discourses. Is the jury convinced by the arguments and narrative of the prosecutor or by those of the defence?

The Challenge of the 'Objective Evidence'

The main obstacle to pleading innocence is what is called the 'objective evidence'. This includes first the objects referred to as 'material evidence' which have been found close to the scene of the crime or on a suspect. Often these objects are kept in the courtroom on a table and are presented to the bench when needed. However, in themselves, they are not always sufficient to prove the participation or the intention of the accused.

Is it evidence of criminal intention for a Somali to be found travelling with a firearm? 'The cultural context', said the lawyer, 'explains that if Mr X was found with a Kalashnikov that does not mean he was a pirate! In Somalia everyone has one and even sleeps with it, it does not mean anything'. And this long knife that in another case the suspect had in his bag and with which he stabbed the victim, does it constitute a mark of premeditation? No, he was a cook and always had his long knife with him.

But the exhibition of such material evidence can modify a suspect's attitude and lead him to recognize his culpability. When, in the bag of Mrs X (who cut her lover into pieces with a saw), the police discovered a receipt from a department store which mentioned the purchase of a saw and a date corresponding to the facts, it was considered to be incontrovertible material evidence. And Mrs X then admitted her crime.

Other evidence depends on technical and scientific expertise. As opposed to what was done in the old case of the postal agency robbery presented above, great use is now made of telephony by the investigation department. Mobile phone calls are precisely analysed, location and timetable checked, and the defendant's declarations confirmed or invalidated.

The prosecutor in a case of street fighting between Sri Lankan gangs asked: 'You said that you stayed twenty minutes and left. That is not what your mobile phone says. Where did you go? To the metro? Your phone says that at 19h58 you were in the area'. The defence lawyer replied later in her speech: 'Telephony confirms nothing of what the prosecutor said. On the contrary, the only material elements of this affair corroborate the defendant's declarations'.

A prosecutor declared once: 'Here we have no DNA, no American techniques: we have only telephony!' However 'American techniques' make their entry into courtrooms and various forensic experts are summoned to give evidence. Most often fingerprints and DNA are mentioned as tools of indubitable certainty,[14] but they have to be contextualized, which may give room for challenging them.

During investigations judicial administration spends a lot of time, energy and money on collecting this evidence. Let us take as an example the investigation made on the boat stopped by the pirates. A special team went on the boat to collect a large sample of what could eventually bear prints. At the hearing details were given of the number of bottles, cigarette butts and t-shirts collected and analyzed. Then the forensic expert explained that many pieces had to be rejected because the storage conditions, or heat, or whatever, had blurred the fingerprints and dissolved the DNA. Finally, after one hour of lengthy explanation, the expert said that eleven sets of DNA had been revealed. In the Court, everyone held their breath and thought: 'Finally we shall know the truth, we shall know who was on the boat, and if the six accused now in the dock were among the pirates'. But the expert concluded dryly: 'We compared the DNA collected on the boat with the DNA of the six individuals in the box. The DNA profiles of the six people arrested are different from those under seals'.

The defence lawyers smiled. But the Advocate General questioned the expert and reintroduced doubt:

> We may think that these objects could have been touched by the accused but that the conditions did not allow the DNA to be detected. Or that what they touched could not have been collected. Thus the expert evidence does not accuse any of the six men but the expert evidence does not exclude the fact that they could have been on the boat.

The audience is back to its uncertainty: the lack of material evidence is not a proof of innocence. However, in other cases, the lack of finger or genetic prints, when evidently they should have been found, can be put forward to claim someone

---

14 I am not sure that the Police and Justice officers have knowledge of the many studies on uncertainty and the interpretative nature of fingerprint and DNA evidence. I am very grateful to Anthony Good for the references to the report *The Fingerprint Inquiry*, based on the public judicial inquiry conducted by Sir Anthony Campbell on behalf of the Scottish Government, which concluded: '9. Fingerprint examiners are presently ill-equipped to reason their conclusions as they are accustomed to regarding their conclusions as a matter of certainty and seldom challenged. 10. There is no reason to suggest that fingerprint comparison in general is an inherently unreliable form of evidence but practitioners and fact-finders alike require to give due consideration to the limits of the discipline' (Campbell 2011: 739).

innocent. In the example of the hold-up of the postal agency, the lawyer insisted on the fact that none of Ferrera's fingerprints were found on the cars and motorcycles he was accused of having used (the robbers had no gloves according to witnesses). Too many prints are also no evidence. Ferrera's prints were found on a motorcycle helmet found on the spot, but they were far from being the only ones. Thus they cannot be counted as incontrovertible evidence.

Even in cases of rape where it is very difficult to have incontrovertible evidence or witnesses and where DNA plays a very important part, it has to be contextualized. Presence of the DNA of the accused proves a sexual relationship but not necessarily rape, as in the case related by Marcel d'Ans (2003). Scientific evidence may allow the veracity of a fact to be demonstrated but does not serve to establish culpability. It is only 'an indicative material clue'.[15] 'Scientific evidence from DNA … is only material evidence saying that the trace carrier has been at the place where the trace has been collected at a given moment that science cannot specify. That and only that!' (de Valicourt de Séranvillers 2009: 60). However, the new possibilities offered by DNA analysis have allowed for the reopening of cases and proved the innocence of some people convicted years ago: the DNA found on the victim's body was not theirs.

Scientific evidence such as that demonstrated by forensic or ballistic or other experts is eagerly looked for in most trials. However, it is not always significant. It has to be contextualized and does not suffice to cast off all doubt.

Passionate Speeches: To Carry Conviction with the Jury

Often the situation remains doubtful until the end of the hearing: no clear evidence has been given as there were no witnesses, no traces, as the stabbing was done among a group of people and no sure perpetrator clearly established, as the accused keeps denying the charges. Then the defence lawyers give free rein to their eloquence and may attack rather aggressively the prosecutor or even the presiding judge.

A case of street gang aggression is made rather difficult to judge as the three accused, the victims and the witnesses all belong to the same milieu and use the courtroom as a place for avenging themselves:

> *The lawyer*: 'How can you keep on accusing someone whose file is empty? How to defend someone when one doesn't know exactly why he is accused?

15 'Un indice matériel à valeur indicative' in de Valicourt de Séranvillers (2009: 23), who provides a legal study of DNA and demonstrates that 'La preuve scientifique par l'ADN n'est pas une preuve certitude' (2009: 24) and 'L'ADN n'est pas la reine des preuves' (2009: 5). Reasoning based on fingerprints and DNA suffers also from probability fallacies which can easily sway a jury (I am grateful to Anthony Good for a nice example at http://www.cs4fn.org/biology/prosecutor.php).

> The presiding judge could have dismissed the case. I am ashamed to be here, to comply with this process. Your report uses scary words: axe, blood, gangs. It is frightening, the words are frightening. But I, it is by this justice that I am frightened. Is it like this that people are judged? Do you support this justice? We the lawyers are the last ramparts. One day people will be condemned on hearsay, on possibilities. I am fighting for not judging people on rumours!'

In the case of the Somalis, one of the lawyers declared:

> One doesn't repair a trauma by committing an injustice. M. the Advocate General says: 'H. is lying. I can't check but he is lying'. M. the Advocate General says: 'I don't have any valid proof but I ask you to condemn him as part of a criminal conspiracy. He is part of it as his two brothers are in it'. What is that, M. Advocate General? Are his genes making him a pirate? M. the Advocate General says he has acted with intellectual honesty. I think not: to call for twelve years' penalty, this is not honest.

The defence lawyers as well as the prosecutor appeal to the jury's sense of justice and often insist on the heavy and frightening responsibility of having to decide on someone's fate.

> My client will be condemned on the principle of collective responsibility. But you have to say what was his part in the violence? You have sworn that doubt must benefit the accused! You have to decide on your intimate conviction: that means that you have to decide to answer each question with your life, as if your life was at stake. 'Such a witness could have accused anyone! You, you have to judge and you have no such right.

> To acquit is not easy. It does not mean that the event didn't happen. It is not to choose between two gangs. It is to choose Justice.

> The accused, I entrust him to your care. You have taken an oath that doubt will benefit him.

> On Thursday, you, the jurors, you will gather for deliberation. You will decide, with your intimate conviction, on the destiny of a man who has been uprooted, who had a family and could not see any of them for four years, who is only twenty-one. Don't commit a miscarriage of justice. I ask you to give him back his honour, his liberty. Acquit him!

> The only thing I ask you … would be to tell him only by looking at him: we believe you!

> There are affairs which stand out. You [the jurors] won't leave the courtroom and the deliberation room unscathed!

Concluding Remarks

Throughout the hearings the jurors have been through testing times; they have changed their minds according to successive evidence and convincing arguments, they are constantly switching back and forth between doubt and certainty. And again in his final speech the defence lawyer reminds them of a possible doubt and of their responsibility. However, when they retire to the deliberation room, they are placed under the obligation to choose, with no room left for doubt or uncertainty.

As expressed by one lawyer to the jurors: 'The only choice left to you is to acquit him or to declare him guilty'. No in-between measure: to acquit someone is to declare him innocent, as there is no 'acquittal on benefit of the doubt' in the French criminal code. Someone accused is condemned if, with the majority requested by law,[16] the Assize Court answers yes to the question of his culpability. If not, he is declared innocent.

The questions to which the jurors will have to answer 'yes' or 'no' are put by the presiding judge just before the jury retires to deliberate. These questions repeat in interrogative form the charges presented in the bill of indictment.[17] In most trials I attended the questions were:

1. Is the accused guilty of having killed the victim intentionally?
2. Was it a premeditated murder?

It is also possible for the presiding judge to put a subsidiary question allowing the jury to answer negatively to the first question if they doubt the intention to kill, without clearing the accused:

3. Is the accused guilty of having killed the victim intentionally?
4. If the first question is answered in the negative, is the accused guilty of 'assault and battery causing death without intention' (i.e. manslaughter)?

---

16 The six lay jurors (or nine in appeal) vote together with the three judges (the presiding judge and two assessors), who are not supposed to influence them. Voting is by secret ballot but people express their opinion prior to this, and several turns may be necessary to attain a decisive majority of six votes.

17 The questions can be numerous as they correspond to the different counts of indictment or legal offences. In the case of the Somalian accused, for instance, each of the six was charged with something like thirty different offences, hence thirty questions were to be answered for each defendant by the jurors. Acquittals were pronounced for some of the questions and convictions for others. Needless to say the deliberations lasted several hours.

However, even though doubt is constantly referred to, and even though its possibility gives meaning to the ceremonial of the hearings, as a matter of fact only about 5 or 6 per cent of trials end with an acquittal.[18]

Very seldom is a case presented to the Assize Court with so few certainties that the Advocate General himself can declare in his requisitoire that 'the elements put together constitute a body of clues sufficiently strong [*additionnés, constituaient un faisceau d'indices suffisamment fort*] to accept the culpability of the accused'. It was easy for the defence attorney to reply: 'Condemnation should be grounded on evidence, on certainties, and not "on a body of clues"'. And when the defendant was declared not guilty by the jury, his lawyer congratulated them: 'It is above all a victory for justice as doubt must benefit the accused'.

I shall end with the tricky question of morality. Reference is constantly made to moral values such as conscience, rightness, innermost conviction, fairness, truth. But what makes sense of these references is the possibility of doubting. Doubt is the justification for the trial and the reason why moral values are referred to. James Whitman ends his study with the following words:

> it would be better to openly and routinely instruct jurors that the decision they are about to make is, despite its legal trappings, a moral one … Instructing jurors forcefully that their decision is 'a *moral* one,' about the fate of a fellow human being, is, in the last analysis, the only meaningful modern way to be faithful to the original spirit of reasonable doubt. (Whitman 2008: 212, quoting Eisenberg, Garvey and Wells 1996: 379; emphasis in the original)

I shall add as a counterpoint these few words taken from a heated argument between a presiding judge and a lawyer:

> *Judge* (to the accused): You find it morally good to behave like that?
>
> *Lawyer* (interrupting): Morality has no place here. Here we do law [*on fait du droit*].
>
> *Judge*: The penal code is rooted in moral values. Societies defend moral values.
>
> *Lawyer*: Mr Bailiff, I ask you to note![19]

18 Between 2003 and 2005 the figure was 5.7 per cent according to a study by the Ministère de la Justice. And of the 23 per cent of cases going to appeal, 4.8 per cent of those convicted at first instance are acquitted. See http://www.justice.gouv.fr/art_pix/1_infostat100.pdf (accessed 6 January 2014).

19 Hearings in French courts are purely oral in a sense that they are not recorded or written down. The bailiff only mentions the order of passage of the witnesses and the formal and legal proceedings. Thus the explicit demand made here by the indignant lawyer to write the judge's declaration into the minutes.

If, during Assize trials, verbal references are constantly made to the presumption of innocence, proceedings reveal that it would be more accurate to talk about presumption of culpability. The importance given to the investigation process, to the many pieces of evidence collected by the prosecution during the pre-trial procedures, explains the small number of acquittals. However presumption of culpability is not certainty. As courtroom observation demonstrates, doubt is constantly referred to and gives to the jurors the full measure of their responsibility. Only doubt gives legitimacy to the trial process. Thus the strategy of the defence lawyers is, by various devices, to make the jurors hesitant, unconvinced: the facts are perhaps not those claimed by the prosecution. Lawyers appeal to the jurors' reasoning and sensibility, to their 'intimate conviction'. Yet, though the few days of the trial may lend reality a somewhat blurred appearance, the jurors at the end have to give a straight answer: yes or no.

References

Ans, André-Marcel d' (2003) 'La cour d'assises en examen. Reflexion-témoignage d'un juré sociologue', *Droit et société* 54(2): 403–30.

Bouillier, Véronique (forthcoming) 'From a comparative perspective: criminal cases involving South Asian people in French Assize Courts', in *Anthropology of Criminal Cases in South Asia*, ed. Daniela Berti and Devika Bordia, New Delhi: Oxford University Press.

Brisart, Robert (2002) 'La vérité est ailleurs', *Droit et société* 51–2: 423–32.

Campbell, Sir Anthony (2011) *The Fingerprint Inquiry Report*, available at http://www.thefingerprintinquiryscotland.org.uk/inquiry/21.html (accessed 6 January 2014).

Code de procedure pénale (2010) available at http://www.legifrance.gouv.fr/affichCode.do;jsessionid=E8975D95EA81B0ECBAA3F2A118FD82AF.tpdjo16v_1?cidTexte=LEGITEXT000006071154&dateTexte=20101231 (accessed 6 January 2014).

Cuer, Roland (2011) 'Doute et subjectivité du juge' [Le Bien Commun, with Antoine Garapon, originally broadcast 2 July 2011], available at http://ww.franceculture.fr/player/reecouter?play=4270827 (accessed 20 May 2012).

Dils, Patrick (2002) *Je voudrais juste rentrer chez moi*, ed. Karen Aboab, Paris: Editions Michel Lafon–Paul Ferel.

Dupret, Baudouin (2011) *Practices of Truth: An Ethnomethodological Inquiry into Arab Contexts*, Amsterdam: John Benjamins.

Eisenberg, Theodore, Garvey, Stephen P. and Wells, Martin T. (1996) 'Jury responsibility in capital sentencing: an empirical study', *Buffalo Law Review* 44: 339–80.

Engel, Christoph (2008), 'Preponderance of the evidence versus *intime conviction*: a behavioural perspective on a conflict between American and Continental European law', Preprints of the Max Planck Institute for Research on Collective

Goods, 2008/33, available at http://www.coll.mpg.de/pdf_dat/2008_33online.pdf (accessed 6 January 2014).
Garapon, Antoine (2001) *Bien juger. Essai sur le rituel judiciaire*, Paris: Odile Jacob.
Garapon, Antoine and Papadopoulos, Ioannis (2003) *Juger en Amérique et en France. Culture juridique française et common law*, Paris: Odile Jacob.
Good, Anthony (2007) *Anthropology and Expertise in the Asylum Courts*, Abingdon: Routledge-Cavendish.
Good, Anthony (2011) 'Witness statements and credibility assessments in the British asylum courts', in *Cultural Expertise and Litigation: Patterns, Conflicts, Narratives*, ed. Livia Holden, Abingdon and New York: Routledge, pp. 94–122.
Jouvet, Lucie (2010) *Socio-anthropologie de l'erreur judiciaire*, Paris: L'Harmattan.
McKillop, Bron (1997) 'Anatomy of a French murder case', *American Journal of Comparative Law* 45: 527–83.
Ministère de la Justice et des Libertés (2011) *Les chiffres-clés de la Justice*, available at http://www.justice.gouv.fr/art_pix/1_chiffres_cles_2011_20111125.pdf (accessed 6 January 2014).
Moskovitz, Myron (1995) 'The O.J. inquisition: a United States encounter with Continental criminal justice', *Vanderbilt Journal of Transnational Law* 28: 1121–2.
Mozère, Liane (2002) 'Jurée sous influence ou la résistible jouissance du jugement?', *Droit et société* 51–2: 399–416.
Terrio, Susan J. (2009) *Judging Mohammed: Juvenile Delinquency, Immigration, and Exclusion at the Paris Palace of Justice*, Stanford, CA: Stanford University Press.
Valicourt de Séranvilliers, Héliane de (2009) *La preuve par l'ADN et l'erreur judiciaire*, Paris: L'Harmattan.
Whitman, James Q. (2008) *The Origins of Reasonable Doubt: Theological Roots of the Criminal Trial*, New Haven, CT: Yale University Press.

Chapter 6

'The Benefit of the Doubt' in British Asylum Claims and International Cricket

Anthony Good

Legal proceedings and sporting contests are both highly ritualized forms of activity. Both in their different ways may involve application of 'the benefit of the doubt'. This chapter examines two seemingly very different contexts, refugee status determination procedures in the UK and the Decision Review System in international cricket. It aims to show that although the benefit of the doubt should be applied quite differently in these two settings, in practice it is used in very similar ways, to the detriment of many asylum applicants.[1]

Ritual can be defined as a form of stereotyped behaviour in which the means are of comparable importance to the ends. In the extreme, indeed, the means themselves *are* the ends. Classical anthropology focused on the mythic or symbolic meanings of rituals, but the 1960s onwards saw increasing emphasis on rituals as performances (Turner 1969), and on rituals as performa*tive*, as actually bringing about changes in illocutionary fashion (Tambiah 1973; see also Introduction, this volume). Because their desired ends are generally only achievable if they are performatively and semiologically adequate, many rituals depend for their success on close adherence to rules. These rules normally lie outwith the conventional legal sphere, though this is not always entirely the case – for example, marriage ceremonies are valid only if the officiant satisfies appropriate legal, as well as religious requirements. The links between ritual and law have often been noted by anthropologists (Gluckman 1965). Latour (2002: 251; 2004: 107) has even argued that it is precisely the most obviously ritualized, seemingly trivial aspects of the law – its florid, archaic language, its fancy clothes – that underwrite its claims to 'objectivity', which actually entail no 'object' as such, but rest instead upon the cultivation of dispassion, formalism and indifference.

In both the semiological and performative senses, but especially the second, sport too can clearly be viewed as a highly ritualized activity (Birrell 1981). Sport also epitomizes the ludic element found in many kinds of ritual (Huizinga 1949).

1 Research on the asylum process was supported by ESRC Research Grant R000223352 and AHRC Grant AH/E50874X/1 (with Dr Robert Gibb, Glasgow University) under its Diasporas, Migration and Identities Programme. Thanks go to James Sweeney, panel participants at the 2012 EASA Conference, and the seminar group at MPI Halle, for helpful comments on earlier drafts. Any remaining faults are my own.

One key feature of sport as ritual is that while it is important to win, winning should only be achieved by staying within the rules as *interpreted* by a qualified person (a referee or umpire). Sporting rules are not usually legally enforceable, however. One cannot bring a civil case against a referee for not awarding a goal. Moreover, even for actions that would be considered criminal in other contexts, such as violent tackles, sport's governing bodies are very reluctant to invoke conventional legal proceedings, preferring to employ measures of their own.[2] When injured parties *do* occasionally resort to the formal courts, this is frowned on by their peers as 'breaking ranks' (Roderick 1999).[3] However, even if extra-legal in the strict sense, sporting rules are *legalistic* in form. One can therefore see sporting rules on one hand, and criminal and civil laws on the other, as occupying parallel universes whose similarities are sufficient to justify the comparison attempted in this chapter.

The Benefit of the Doubt in Common-Law Systems

The 'benefit of the doubt' is a core principle in all common-law systems. It is used with its everyday meaning, namely to assume something positive about a person, rather than something negative, when there is no definitive or clinching evidence either way. The notion must, however, be understood in relation to three other distinctly technical legal concepts: standard of proof, burden of proof and – especially in asylum cases – credibility.

The nexus between the first two concepts takes several forms. The *standard of proof* is high in criminal law – it must shown to be virtually certain ('beyond reasonable doubt') that the accused did commit the crime – whereas civil law deals with 'the balance of probabilities' – that is, is it more likely than not that the defendant was liable for the wrong that allegedly took place? In both cases the *burden of proof*, the requirement to prove guilt or responsibility to the required standard, normally falls on the party initiating legal proceedings: the prosecution in criminal trials or claimants in civil suits. In criminal cases this is an onerous burden because the standard of proof is so high; in civil cases, however, the lower standard of proof leads to a more even distribution of the burden of proof between the parties (Murphy 2003: 75). The standard of proof for 'well-founded fear' in refugee law is even lower, given the difficulty applicants have in producing evidence (see diagram in Gorlick 2003: 370). In *Sivakumaran* the British House

2 The international Court of Arbitration for Sport, sponsored by the main sports governing bodies, deals mostly with commercial issues like sponsorship or broadcasting rights, and use of performance-enhancing drugs. See http://www.tas-cas.org/en/infogenerales.asp/4-3-239-1011-4-1-1/5-0-1011-3-0-0/ (accessed 24 December 2012).

3 It is easier to bring criminal prosecutions when actions are clearly outwith the rules of the game (*R* v. *Billinghurst*). When sporting matters *do* come before them, UK courts give short shrift to arguments that sport is immune from ordinary law (Foster 2006: 178–9).

of Lords agreed on the phrase 'a reasonable degree of likelihood', while the US Supreme Court ruled that 'a 10% chance of being ... persecuted' is enough (*INS* v. *Cardoza-Fonseca*).

The common-law notion of 'reasonable doubt' originated in medieval Christian theology. Far from being designed to prevent convictions of innocent people, it served to provide 'moral comfort' for 'judges faced with the anxieties of judging' (Whitman 2008: 11, 15), a hedge against the spiritual consequences of pronouncing a guilty verdict, especially where capital punishment was involved. Although the modern notion is said to be 'inextricably intertwined' with the presumption of innocence, a fundamental principle of criminal law (*R* v. *Lifchus*), English judges are now specifically enjoined *not* to use the phrase in their directions to the jury. Instead, they are advised to say: 'The prosecution proves its case if the jury ... *are sure that* the defendant is guilty' (Judicial Studies Board 2010: 16; emphasis added). The instruction then warns 'Further explanation is unwise', citing *R.* v. *Abdul Majid* where the judge's use of the phrase 'beyond reasonable doubt' caused confusion among the jury. However, it adds, without further comment 'Note: Being sure is the same as entertaining no reasonable doubt'. In other words, the phrase is deemed 'unwise' not because it is inaccurate but because jurors do not understand it. The current English position thus seems somewhat sophistic, bearing in mind the centrality of the term since the 1780s. Moreover, other common-law countries still use the phrase when instructing juries.[4]

In criminal contexts 'the benefit of the doubt' lies in a relationship of binary opposition with this notion of 'reasonable doubt'. For example, the definition of 'reasonable doubt' proposed by the Federal Judicial Center (1987) and described by the US Supreme Court as 'clear, straightforward, and accurate' (*Victor* v. *Nebraska*) reads as follows: 'Proof *beyond a reasonable doubt* is proof that leaves you firmly convinced of the defendant's guilt ... If ... you think there is a real possibility that he is not guilty, you must give him *the benefit of the doubt* and find him not guilty' (emphasis added). Similarly, 'the benefit of the doubt' in civil cases generally lies with the defendant, although because of the lower standard of proof this presents less of an obstacle to the plaintiff than that faced by a criminal prosecutor.

The Benefit of the Doubt in Refugee Law

It is impossible to discuss 'the benefit of the doubt' in refugee law without also examining the notion of 'credibility', which 'works with the benefit of the doubt to compensate for the evidential difficulties faced by asylum seekers, and recognizes

4 See, for example, New Zealand (Young 2003), the USA (*Victor* v. *Nebraska*) and Canada (*R* v. *Lifchus*). For evidence on jurors' understanding of the term, see Diamond (1990: 1722).

the potentially grave consequences of incorrectly rejected applications' (Sweeney 2009: 726).

The 1951 Refugee Convention makes no mention of the benefit of the doubt but the UNHCR *Handbook* (2011), which guides decision-makers on how to interpret the Convention, recognizes that although asylum applicants bear the burden of proof, they are often unable to provide supporting evidence to normal legal standards because of the circumstances under which they fled. Paragraph 196 concludes: 'there may also be statements that are not susceptible of proof. In such cases, *if the applicant's account appears credible, he should*, unless there are good reasons to the contrary, *be given the benefit of the doubt*' (emphasis added). The link between credibility and the benefit of the doubt is reinforced in paragraph 204, which also provides a definition of credibility: 'The applicant's statements must be coherent and plausible, and must not run counter to generally known facts'.

When deciding asylum claims, UK Border Agency (UKBA) case owners follow a manual called the *Asylum Policy Instructions* (APIs). The API relevant here is entitled *Considering Asylum Claims and Assessing Credibility* (UKBA 2012a). This May 2012 version had changed somewhat since (and perhaps because of) Sweeney's authoritative critique (2009). Much of his detailed analysis still applied to this later version, however, and his broader points remain central to the argument offered here.[5]

Sweeney noted that although there was much useful advice in the API, it was 'deeply problematic' regarding the role of credibility findings in asylum decision-making (2009: 701). The problem arose from its 'ambitious but ultimately flawed attempt' to bring together materials of differing legal statuses, including primary legislation, the *Immigration Rules*, the European 'Qualification Directive' (QD),[6] UK case law and the UNHCR *Handbook*, although UNHCR's 'Note on burden and standard of proof' (1998) is a 'notable and unfortunate' omission (Sweeney 2009: 706). Yet these sources do not in fact agree on the relationships between credibility, standard of proof, and benefit of the doubt, so the API's attempted synthesis was inevitably unsuccessful.

In practice credibility assessment is 'often the single most important step' in the refugee status determination process (Kagan 2003: 367), but Sweeney argues that this is only because the term is defined inappropriately. In fact the API's sources

5 This API has since been relabelled *Asylum Process Guidance*. See http://www.ukba.homeoffice.gov.uk/sitecontent/documents/policyandlaw/asylumprocessguidance/consideringanddecidingtheclaim/guidance/considering-protection-.pdf?view=Binary (accessed 10 May 2013). In other words, it no longer constitutes policy as such (James Sweeney, pers. comm.), though the implications of this are unclear.

6 This has since been recast, but at that time it was Council Directive 2004/83/EC of 29 April 2004 on minimum standards for the qualification and status of third country nationals or stateless persons as refugees. See http://eur-lex.europa.eu/LexUriServ/LexUriServ.do?uri=CELEX:32004L0083:EN:HTML (accessed 24 December 2013).

contain two very different interpretations of credibility (Sweeney 2009: 707–8). According to the broad interpretation, credibility is about whether applicants' statements are true and hence whether they merit refugee status: in other words, it is 'loose shorthand for the strength of the case' (Sweeney 2009: 702). However, both Kagan (2003: 369–70) and Sweeney favour a narrower view that sees credibility as 'less about the outcome of the case, or even the conclusive proof of material facts, and more about a pre-requisite evidential step' (Sweeney 2009: 708). A 'credible' statement is unsupported and so not proven, but is plausible and consistent with generally known facts, and so cannot be dismissed when considering whether applicants have a well-founded fear. Taking such statements into consideration, Sweeney argues, is precisely what the UNHCR *Handbook* (2011: §196) means by giving asylum seekers the benefit of the doubt.

The API (§4.1) sets out detailed procedures for 'objective' decision-making. Case owners should 'first … distinguish which facts are material to the claim and which are not' (§4.1.2). They should then assess the *internal credibility* of the applicant's evidence ('whether the applicant's claim is internally coherent and consistent'; §4.3.1); and its *external credibility* (whether the material facts are 'consistent with generally known facts and country of origin information'; §4.3.2).[7] The API then explains that if certain facts are 'unsubstantiated' – that is, 'are internally credible but lack any external evidence to confirm them' – then

> a decision must be made whether to give the applicant the benefit of the doubt on *each* uncertain or unsubstantiated fact – this means that the decision maker must come to a clear finding as to whether the fact can be accepted or rejected. *It is not acceptable to come to a final conclusion that a claimed fact (about which you are uncertain) 'may have happened'* … the benefit of the doubt can only be considered after a finding on the material facts that are to be accepted or rejected has been made. (§4.3.4; emphasis added).

This approach differs markedly from that suggested by UNHCR. Far from it being unacceptable to decide that something 'may have happened', that is precisely what UNHCR (2011) implies decision-makers *should* do (Sweeney, pers. comm.).

Case owners are also required to follow Paragraph 339L of the *Immigration Rules*. This states that an applicant's unsupported statement does not require confirmation when *all* the following conditions are met: the applicant has made a genuine effort to substantiate their claim, with satisfactory explanations for any gaps in documentation; their account has been found coherent, plausible and consistent; they claimed asylum at the earliest possible time; and their 'general credibility … has been established'.[8] The API acknowledges that even if an applicant fails to meet all five criteria, 'an unsubstantiated statement can be

7 This internal/external distinction derives from Weston (1998: 88).

8 The *Immigration Rules* were first issued under sec. 3(2) of the Immigration Act 1971 and have been frequently modified since then. See http://www.ukba.homeoffice.gov.

credible if it is generally internally consistent, compatible with known facts and plausible'. The stumbling block in practice though, almost invariably, is the last point, their 'general credibility'. The API explains that this depends in part on their 'immigration history', such as any unexplained delay in claiming asylum. It adds that for the purpose of paragraph 339L

> a persons [sic] 'general credibility' is considered to be potentially damaged by behaviour that falls within the scope of Section 8 of the Asylum and Immigration (Treatment of Claimants, etc) Act 2004 … if the applicant is unable to provide a reasonable explanation.

Section 8 lists several kinds of behaviour that are to be viewed by decision-makers as damaging to a claimant's credibility. These include: failure without reasonable explanation to produce a passport on request; production of a document which is not a valid passport as if it were; the destruction, alteration or disposal, without reasonable explanation, of a passport or travel document; and failure without reasonable explanation to answer a question. They also include: failure to take the opportunity to make a claim while in a safe country previously; failure to make a asylum claim before being notified of an immigration decision such as a decision to deport; and failure to make a claim before being arrested under an immigration provision, unless the claim relies wholly on matters arising after the arrest.[9]

Notice that these all focus on how asylum applicants travelled to the UK and how they behaved after arrival. *None* of the forms of credibility-damaging behaviour listed in Section 8 is directly connected to any persecution applicants may have suffered in their home countries, although it may of course have been their fear of persecution that caused them to use false travel documents in the first place. Section 8 also adopts a broader meaning of credibility than §4.3.4 of the API (above), because a delayed asylum application or use of a false passport are hardly *unsubstantiated* facts.[10] Section 8 has a valid policy justification (reducing abuse of the asylum system), but seeks to achieve that through the 'unreasonable evidential presumption' (Thomas 2006: 93; 2011: 157; see also Ensor, Shah and Grillo 2006) that the specified behaviour impacts negatively on general credibility. Moreover, although the API mostly refers to 'the credibility of the applicant's *account*', it clearly states that the behaviour described in Section 8 is damaging

uk/policyandlaw/immigrationlaw/immigrationrules/part11/ (accessed 26 May 2012). They 'enjoy a comparable … legal status to delegated legislation' (Sweeney 2009: 707).

9 See http://www.legislation.gov.uk/ukpga/2004/19/contents (accessed 15 January 2014)

10 Like Section 8, Rule 339L is unrelated to risk of persecution. It expresses 'commonsense' assumptions about how those fleeing for their lives ought to behave – not to ensure their own safety, but to maximize the convenience of bureaucrats (see Sweeney 2009: 717).

to '*a persons* "general credibility"' (§4.3.4; emphasis added).[11] Even the one safeguard mentioned, providing 'a reasonable explanation', sets up an additional hurdle to be cleared before the existence of a well-founded fear is even considered (Sweeney 2009: 717).

Section 8 trumped a growing body of case law stating that failure to claim asylum in the 'first safe country' did not in itself undermine credibility (Thomas 2006: 94). Indeed it seems eminently reasonable for people to defer claiming asylum until they reach a country whose language they speak, or where family members already live. Moreover, in *SM (Iran)* the Tribunal found 'no warrant at all' for UKBA's claim that Section 8 should be the starting point of credibility decisions. Overall, the generality of its provisions 'runs against the grain of the independent adjudication of each individual claim' (Thomas 2006: 94), and it potentially violates constitutional principles by 'interfering with the integrity of the judicial process' (Thomas 2006: 95; 2011: 158; see also Sweeney 2009: 716). The Court of Appeal therefore suggested that Section 8 should be interpreted as saying that the listed behaviour was '*potentially* damaging [to] the claimant's credibility' (*JT (Cameroon)*; emphasis added).

While this ameliorates the situation somewhat, the key problem with Section 8 remains 'its potential to put the notion of credibility centre stage' when determining asylum claims, rather than 'confining it to applying the benefit of the doubt' (Sweeney 2009: 718). Section 8(1)'s broad approach 'gives the impression that credibility is a legitimate consideration in relation to believing *any* statement' (Sweeney 2009: 718), not just unsupported statements considered under rule 339L. Moreover, although parts of the passage described as 'surely … wrong' by Sweeney (2009: 718) have been removed, the API (Annex A) still advises case owners that the 2004 Act 'provides a framework for the consideration of credibility issues'.

As interpreted by Sweeney (2009: 711), UNHCR views the benefit of the doubt as:

> an alternative to proof, and not a synonym for it. It is about giving the benefit of the doubt to a credible account in circumstances where proof has not been possible. 'Being credible' is different both to 'being proven' and to 'being true' [and] the threshold of 'credible' is lower even than the low standard of proof applicable in asylum cases.

By contrast, the broad definition of credibility promoted by Section 8 encourages case owners to focus on matters completely unrelated to the ultimate questions of well-founded fear and risk on return. Broad definitions of credibility are superficially attractive for decision-makers because they encourage the use of

11 The API no longer contains the phrase especially criticized by Sweeney (2009: 709), that case owners 'must assess the credibility of the applicant' as well as of their evidence.

apparent common sense, bypass many of the complications of refugee law and, being ostensibly concerned with 'facts', are relatively immune from appeal. For Sweeney, however, citing Twining (2006) and Good (2004: 377), these advantages are illusory because 'establishing past facts' involves 'processes of actively constructing, rather than passively discovering, knowledge' (2009: 725).

An asylum applicant's general credibility should not be relevant here, only their credibility in the narrow sense. The use of broad definitions of credibility in Section 8 and parts of the API, and Section 8's 'worrying … amplification of credibility from an alleviating evidential rule to a decisive factor',[12] permits a whole range of issues, wholly unrelated to the existence of a well-founded fear, to be utilized to undermine applicants' general credibility (Sweeney 2009: 719) and hence deny them the benefit of the doubt.

Applying the Benefit of the Doubt in British Refugee Status Determinations

The discussion so far has stressed defects in principle introduced by measures such as Section 8. This section illustrates how UKBA case owners apply the benefit of the doubt in practice. It is in relation to 'general credibility' that what is often termed UKBA's 'culture of disbelief' becomes most apparent, because case owners deny the credibility of at least part of almost every applicant's story and thereby ensure that the benefit of the doubt is rarely given.

The Reasons for Refusal Letter (RFRL) sent to Mr K[13] illustrates the use of Section 8 to deny the general credibility of an applicant's account:

> As noted previously, an assessment of your general credibility is required in order to assess elements of your claim which you have failed to substantiate with documentary evidence. [Section 8 is then briefly paraphrased.]
>
> Before coming to the United Kingdom, you applied for a student visa, informing the Entry Clearance Officer (ECO) that it was your intention to come to the UK to study … It is therefore considered that if you were coming to the UK to claim asylum, you knowingly misled the ECO when applying for your student visa, and this is considered behaviour that falls under Section 8 …
>
> In addition, it is also noted that once you arrived in the UK you chose to actually follow the course you'd be [sic] signed onto rather than make attempts to claim asylum, despite allegedly only coming to the UK to save your life …

12 'As an alleviating evidential rule, the law on credibility gives applicants the benefit of the doubt by allowing the admission of evidence that would normally be suppressed … To conclude that an unsupported statement is credible should be merely to conclude that it is admissible as evidence' (Sweeney 2009: 713).

13 Passages quoted in this chapter have been redacted to protect applicants' identities.

> Furthermore, it is also considered that you had ample opportunity to claim asylum in Singapore when you entered as a student. The fact that you did not is not consistent with the actions of someone in fear of their lives.
>
> Due to your decision to delay your asylum claim you are not deemed eligible for the benefit of the doubt as per paragraph 339L.

This discussion raises a number of issues. First, despite the initial assertion, there had in fact been no previous mention of credibility assessment in the RFRL. Second, the accusations that Mr K (a) misled the ECO by applying for a student visa, and (b) actually followed the course on arrival in the UK, seem to cancel one another out. Third, Mr K's visit to Singapore took place several years before he came to the UK and preceded his most serious persecution. Fourth, Singapore is not a signatory to the Refugee Convention. Fifth, there is an assertion about how 'someone in fear of their lives' (how many lives is Mr K thought to have?) would reasonably behave. As this exemplifies, the actual use of Section 8 grounds compounds the concerns expressed by Sweeney, Thomas and others, by virtue of its incompetence and illogicality, and often, as with the fifth point though without adverse effect in this particular instance, because of ambiguities arising from grammatical errors.

Perhaps even more extreme is the reasoning in the RFRL sent to Mr N:

> You explain that you fled from Sri Lanka and travelled to the UK to seek international protection. Despite this [sic], you entered the UK on Xth February 2—. You gained entry using your valid student visa, despite having no intention of studying. Within three days you had sought legal advice and been put in touch with some family friends who resided in the UK. You however failed to lodge your asylum claim until Yth March 2—, approximately six weeks later. You have failed to provide any reasonable explanation for this delay in making your asylum claim … Further, it is considered that you have acted in a manner designed or likely to delay the handling and/or resolution of your claim, as well as designed or likely to deceive (the immigration official at the airport upon your arrival). Consequently, your credibility has been damaged under Section 8 of the Asylum and Immigration (Treatment of Claimants, etc) Act 2004.

It is true that Mr N did not claim asylum at the airport, but he did have a valid visa, so it seems a moot point whether this was deception; is 'deception' related to documentation or to future intention? Moreover, the RFRL itself notes that he found a lawyer within three days and the other case documentation shows that within two weeks he contacted UKBA with a completed asylum application, but was sent away and given an appointment to return four weeks later. Consequently, two-thirds of the delay was created by UKBA itself, a 'reasonable explanation' which the RFRL failed to mention.

Negative credibility findings on such flimsy grounds are then systematically used to justify denials of credibility, and repeated refusals to grant the benefit of the doubt, regarding those parts of the story that *do* relate to the claimed persecution. For example, the RFRL to Ms S[14] began its consideration of her claim by referring to Section 8:

> It is noted from your immigration history that you entered the UK on a passport that did not belong to you, and passed through immigration control by deception … It is considered that this behaviour falls under **Section 8(2)(b) and 3(b) of the Asylum and Immigration (Treatment of Claimants, etc.) Act 2004**. It is considered that your credibility has been damaged as a result of this. (bold in the original)

The letter then discusses several incidents mentioned in Ms S's account, and in each case concludes as follows (only one of several examples is given here):

> Therefore, it is accepted that, in light of the objective information, the LTTE did forcibly recruit civilians to fight for them, however, in light of the points above, and the fact that your credibility has been damaged, it follows that it is not accepted that you personally were recruited by the LTTE.

As the RFRL itself acknowledged, Ms S's account accorded with the 'objective evidence' – that is, it did not 'run counter to generally known facts'. Her account was also, in my opinion as the country expert reporting for the appeal, 'coherent and plausible'. In short, while her account was not proven, it did seem to meet the test in §204 of UNHCR's *Handbook*. Moreover, the RFRL's reasoning was based partly on an error; one of 'the points above' involved casting doubt on whether Ms S had fought for the LTTE, which she never claimed to have done. Overall, the RFRL consistently repeated, as a reason for doubting or rejecting her account, the phrase 'Given that your credibility has been damaged...'; yet this 'damage' arose entirely from the manner in which she entered the UK. On that sole basis her account of what had happened to her in Sri Lanka was rejected almost entirely.

The following extract comes from the RFRL to a ten year-old boy whose parents were missing, possibly killed, in Sri Lanka. According to the UNHCR *Handbook*, there should be 'a *liberal application* of the benefit of the doubt' for child applicants (2011:§219; emphasis added). However, the benefit of the doubt was not granted regarding his escape from a refugee camp along with several adults from this home village, because he could not explain fully how this escape took place. At the time, he was aged eight:[15]

---

14 This Refusal Letter is discussed from a different perspective in Good (2011: 113).

15 On the cognitive capacities of children, see Piaget (1955). Eight-year-olds may not be able to give fully motivated accounts of complex events.

> You have provided no details about this escape. Your earlier description of the camp; the camp being restricted, people not being allowed to leave and it being surrounded by soldiers, is considered to be inconsistent with your ability to escape from there given the lack of detail surrounding how you managed to bypass this. Without more, this aspect of your account is found uncertain.[16]

However, judges often use the discretion set out in *JT (Cameroon)*, whereby the weight given to Section 8 factors is a matter for them.[17] For example, Mr A came to the UK on a student visa, but also partly to escape persecution because he was suspected of inadvertent involvement in a bomb attack. Three years later, before his visa expired, he claimed asylum. The RFRL read:

> Your failure to lodge an asylum and human rights claim at the earliest opportunity means that in accordance with Paragraph 339L the [sic] is no obligation for the decision maker to accept your unsubstantiated statements. It is not considered appropriate to afford you the benefit of the doubt.

The judge rejected this assessment however, and allowed Mr A's appeal on both asylum and human rights grounds:

> The [Home Office] has argued that the appellant's claim lacks credibility because of the delays in making the claim … I find that there has been no significant delay which affects the credibility of the appellant … I accept that he genuinely believed that the risk would pass if he remained in the UK to study and do work experience, and that he would be able to return to … his home country.

It is also worth pointing out that A was legally present in the UK up to the point when he claimed asylum. However afraid he was of returning to Sri Lanka, it was arguably perfectly rational of him to use his student and work visas until the last possible moment, not only in the hope (as he himself said) that the situation at home might improve, but also because the moment he became an asylum applicant he would no longer be entitled to work.

UKBA's Independent Chief Inspector (2011) recently identified widespread problems in Refusal Letters' use of country of origin information (COI), involving selective (§7.4) and speculative use of COI (§7.6, §7.7); use of irrelevant COI (§7.11); and poor or non-existent referencing (§9.2). It can be argued, based on

16 RFRLs tend to assume that the behaviour of those committing persecution will be wholly efficient and governed by a self-evident rationality (the notion of the 'reasonable persecutor', Sweeney 2007: 27). Any 'failings' by persecutors, such as allowing internees to escape, are then used to cast doubt on the credibility of the narrative.

17 Judges are, however, often sceptical when asylum claims are not made until a person faces deportation for reasons such as simple overstaying (Jarvis 2000; Thomas 2011: 158).

the – in my experience – entirely typical examples quoted here, that RFRLs are equally defective as regards applying the benefit of the doubt, in their reliance on speculation, faulty logic and factual inaccuracy.

Cricket, Technology and the 'Benefit of the Doubt'

As a schoolboy in the UK, the notion of 'the benefit of the doubt' was most familiar to me in the context of cricket, where umpires gave the batsman the benefit of the doubt if they were uncertain whether he was out. The laws of cricket themselves[18] make no mention of this principle, however, which was a matter of consensual praxis rather than true legality. This praxis has now been called into question by the Decision Review System (DRS) used in international cricket.[19] The discussion here is limited to one form of dismissal, leg before wicket (LBW),[20] and two technological aids, Hot Spot infra-red imaging which shows whether the ball hit the bat; and 'predictive path' technologies like Virtual Eye or Hawk-Eye, which predict whether, had the ball not hit the batsman, it would have gone on to strike the wicket.

A review of an LBW decision may be requested by the batsman, challenging his dismissal, or by the fielding captain, challenging a 'not out' decision (DRS §3.1). The on-field umpire then poses specific questions to a third umpire in a special TV studio (DRS §3.3). This third umpire liaises with the TV director, asking for new camera angles, close-ups, or slow-motion replays. He then

18 The Marylebone Cricket Club (MCC) are custodians of the Laws of Cricket. See http://www.lords.org/laws-and-spirit/laws-of-cricket/ (accessed 8 January 2014).

19 The DRS Regulations, like all playing conditions for international matches, are overseen by the International Cricket Council. See http://static.icc-cricket.com/ugc/documents/DOC_3C93001E02D4B8D59560A80FA18D8F73_1353406591668_138.pdf (accessed 8 January 2014). Paragraphs from the Regulations are cited below in the form 'DRS §X.X'.

20 Law 36.1 states:

> The striker is out LBW in the circumstances set out below. (a) The bowler delivers a ball, not being a No ball and (b) the ball, if it is not intercepted full pitch, pitches in line between wicket and wicket or on the off side of the striker's wicket and (c) the ball not having previously touched his bat, the striker intercepts the ball, either full pitch or after pitching, with any part of his person and (d) the point of impact, even if above the level of the bails, either (i) is between wicket and wicket or (ii) if the striker has made no genuine attempt to play the ball with his bat, is either between wicket and wicket or outside the line of the off stump and (e) but for the interception, the ball would have hit the wicket.

Seen from the bowler's perspective, the 'off side' is the left half of the field for a right-handed batsman, and the right half for a left-handed batsman. The other half of the field (behind the batsman's legs) is the 'leg side'.

communicates what he sees to the on-field umpire. Thus, the latter does not assess the TV evidence himself, although it is displayed on large screens to the spectators. If the third umpire cannot 'answer with a high degree of confidence' he must say that the evidence is 'inconclusive'; he 'should not give answers conveying likelihoods or probabilities' (DRS §3.3[h]). This standard of proof, 'a high degree of confidence', seems comparable to the criminal standard of 'beyond reasonable doubt'. Ultimately the on-field umpire confirms or reverses his initial decision. The umpires' dialogue is audible to TV commentators, but not to ordinary viewers.

Looking at the process in more detail, the batsman can only be out if the delivery was a legitimate one. First of all, therefore, the third umpire is shown a slow motion replay of the bowler's delivery filmed side-on, to verify that at least part of the bowler's front foot landed behind a white line known as the 'popping crease', while he was in the act of bowling the ball. If not, it was a 'no ball' under Law 24 of the laws of cricket, and the batsman cannot be out LBW.

The next question is whether the batsman hit the ball before being struck by it. Even the faintest flick of ball against edge of bat would be enough to rule out an LBW dismissal. Hot Spot technology uses infra-red imaging to detect friction marks on the bat. If a faint white spot suggests that the ball has brushed the edge of the bat, the batsman cannot be out LBW.

If the batsman has *not* hit the ball, several possible situations may arise, just one of which is illustrated in Figure 6.1, in the form shown to the TV audience. The umpire gave the batsman 'out' and the batsman asked for a review of this decision. Virtual Eye *confirmed* that the ball struck the batsman in line with the wickets, and *predicted* (see the final, darker section of the ball's trajectory) that the ball would have gone on to hit the stumps, so the batsman's challenge failed and the umpire's decision of 'out' was upheld. Another possible scenario is that the umpire gives the batsman 'not out' and the fielding captain asks for that decision to be reviewed. If, as here, Virtual Eye predicts that the ball would have hit the wicket, the decision is reversed and the batsman is given 'out'.

It has been argued, especially by batsmen, that use of the DRS system has displaced the benefit of the doubt, so the main beneficiary is now the umpire rather than the batsman (Newman 2012). Certainly, the presumption now is that the on-field umpire's decision stands, barring clear evidence that it should be overturned. For example, it may be possible to show definitively[21] that the umpire was wrong in giving the batsman out; Hot Spot may show that the ball brushed the edge of the bat, or Virtual Eye may predict that the ball would have missed the stumps altogether. The on-field umpire then reverses his decision and gives the batsman 'not out'. In other cases though, even the technology leaves things unclear: it predicts that the ball would only have grazed the stumps rather than hitting them full on. In that case the umpire's initial decision usually stands, as explained in more detail below.

---

21 Assuming, of course, that one accepts the validity of the technology in the first place. In the final analysis all science is interpretative (Bloor 1991 [1976]).

Figure 6.1 Batsman's challenge: umpire's decision confirmed. Source: http://virtualeye.tv/index.php/the-sports/virtual-eye-cricket (accessed 14 January 2014). Used with permission of Virtual Eye

Hierarchy and Interpretation

Umpiring decisions may seem a far cry from refugee status determinations, yet there are features common to both. For example, both are asymmetric: the benefit of the doubt may be given by party A to party B, but not in reverse. Thus, the case owner may give the benefit of the doubt to the asylum applicant if certain preconditions are fulfilled, but no possibility exists for the asylum applicant to give the benefit of the doubt to UKBA. Similarly, in pre-technology times the umpire gave the benefit of the doubt to the batsman, never the reverse. The benefit of the doubt thus operates hierarchically, as an expression of power and authority or, more precisely, a benevolent waiving of a power and authority that could legally and justifiably be exercised otherwise.

A further similarity is that both processes impose arbitrary boundaries upon continuous variables. For example, the DRS process depends upon the accuracy of the technology in predicting the ball's trajectory had it not struck the batsman. Clearly, its margin of error becomes greater the further the ball would have had to travel beyond the point of impact before striking the wicket (see Collins and Evans 2008: 289–92). For this reason the review process was further refined for the 2011 World Cup in India to take account of the distance between impact and wicket. If that distance was more that 250 cm, the third umpire informed the on-field umpire what that distance was, and told him what the technology (in this case, Hawk-Eye) predicted as to where the ball would have hit the stumps. The on-field umpire then applied 'normal cricketing principles concerning the level of certainty in making his decision'. That wording ('principles', not 'laws') encouraged reversion to the pre-technology practice of giving batsmen the benefit of the doubt.[22] In short, the uncertainty inherent in the system under any circumstances was ignored until an arbitrary cut-off point was reached, when the system reverted almost to the pre-technology process, except that the umpire reconsidered his decision in light of the extra information furnished by the technology.

The application of firm, but inevitably arbitrary, limits to continuous variables is very widespread in formal legal systems too. One well-known example arose in the British Human Fertilisation and Embryology Act 1990, which set time limits for experiments on human embryos. Sec. 3(3)(a) prohibited 'keeping or using an embryo after the appearance of the primitive streak'. The 'primitive streak' is the emergent spinal column, the first visible sign of the central nervous system; it appears in a human embryo after about two weeks. That was itself an arbitrary choice, albeit one supported by medical evidence. That legal construction of natural facts was then rendered doubly arbitrary by Sec. 3(4), which fixed the time limit at fourteen days, the average time at which the streak appears, rather than linking it to the empirical appearance of the streak itself (Franklin 1997: 104).

One finds similar examples of the fixing of arbitrary boundaries in asylum law and process too. For example, as mentioned earlier, the benefit of the doubt should be applied more liberally for unaccompanied asylum-seeking children. But who, precisely, is defined as a child in such contexts?

Even if children do not qualify for asylum or humanitarian protection (HP), UKBA's policy is to grant them temporary Discretionary Leave (DL) unless there are 'adequate reception and accommodation arrangements' in their home country. In 2007, however, the way in which this policy was implemented changed significantly:

> For decisions made before **1 April 2007** this was for 3 years … or to their **18th birthday** whichever was the shorter period … For all decisions made on or after **1 April 2007** … DL must only be granted to **17.5 years** (or for 3 years … whichever is the shorter period ...) (bold in the original).[23]

The purpose of this change was to enable any further applications or appeals to be dealt with before the person reached eighteen. If the choice of eighteen as the cut-off point is itself arbitrary, '17.5 years' is doubly so, being imposed purely for administrative convenience.[24]

---

22 DRS §3.3 has since been changed again, to remove the quoted phrase.

23 See http://www.ukba.homeoffice.gov.uk/sitecontent/documents/policyandlaw/asylumpolicyinstructions/apunotices/amendmenttodlpolicyasc.pdf?view=Binary (accessed 14 June 2012).

24 Eighteen conforms to the UN Convention on the Rights of the Child and sec. 55 of the Borders, Citizenship and Immigration Act 2009. That does not render it any less

Arbitrariness is further compounded, sometimes with serious implications for a child's credibility, by the fact that their claimed ages are often unsupported by corroborative evidence. UKBA very commonly questions whether they are in fact 'children' at all. Its age assessment policies are given in the API entitled *Assessing Age* (UKBA 2012b). The mere fact of carrying out age assessments on children may 'taint' their asylum applications with negative credibility, however, and hence undermine the application of the benefit of the doubt, even when they are indeed shown to be children; for example, a child may claim to be fifteen but the assessment concludes she is in fact sixteen (Kvittingen 2010: 35).

It is thus easy to demonstrate arbitrariness in contexts involving quantification, and it seems clear that decisions in non-quantifiable contexts, such as those involving credibility and the benefit of the doubt, must be even more arbitrary. In both refugee status determinations and LBW decisions, binary yes/no decisions are imposed onto highly variable and complexly-nuanced situations (see Collins and Evans 2008: 289).

There is a further complication surrounding LBW dismissals that cannot be resolved by technology. If the batsman genuinely tried (but failed) to hit the ball, he can only be out if the impact of the ball on his body was in line with the wickets, but if he deliberately allowed it to hit him he can be out even if the ball struck him outside the off stump, provided it would have gone on to hit the wicket. This calls for another kind of interpretation on the umpire's part, because some batsmen are skilled at making it appear that they tried to hit the ball when in fact they did not. The umpire is therefore interpreting the batsman's *intention*. This seems very close to the situation of the UKBA case owner deciding whether a person entered the country by deception, and hence whether to give the benefit of the doubt under Section 8.

Holistic and Sequential Decision-Making

The previous section discussed similarities between the application of the benefit of the doubt in international cricket and UK asylum law. In this concluding section, however, we examine one key difference in principle, the contrast between 'holistic' and 'sequential' reasoning.

In an important asylum decision (*Karanakaran*) the Court of Appeal confirmed that the standard of proof, for proving past events *and* assessing future risk, is the *Sivakumaran* standard – 'a reasonable degree of likelihood' – rather than the 'balance of probabilities' civil standard. It also stated that both issues must be considered together in 'a unitary process of evaluation' and that the facts of a case should be considered cumulatively rather than in isolation. As Sweeney

arbitrary, however; the age of sexual consent (Sexual Offences Act 2003) and the minimum age for recruitment into UK armed forces are both set at sixteen.

puts it, 'proving a well founded fear of persecution is *a single composite question* incorporating past and present facts and risk' (2009: 721; emphasis added).

This cumulative process requires decision-makers to add up the weight of all the material evidence. Sedley LJ argued that UKBA case owners do not make truly legal decisions (which involve deciding between two conflicting accounts of events) but administrative ones:

> Such decision-makers, on classic principles of public law, are required to take everything material into account. Their sources of information will frequently go well beyond the testimony of the applicant and include in-country reports, expert testimony ... *No probabilistic cut-off operates here: everything capable of having a bearing has to be given the weight, great or little, due to it* (emphasis added).

DRS decision-making presents a complete contrast to this 'unitary process'. It involves a series of questions that, if answered in one particular way, preclude the need to proceed any further through the assessment process. First, a batsman can only be out LBW if the delivery is a legitimate one. If it proves to have been a 'no ball', the batsman cannot be out LBW whatever happens subsequently. A second potential stopping point is that the batsman cannot be out LBW if he first struck the ball with his bat, however faintly. *Any* contact with the bat is enough to secure a reversal of an 'out' decision; this resembles the criminal standard of proof in that, after reviewing the evidence, the umpire cannot give the batsman 'out' unless he is 'sure' that the ball did not brush the bat. A third such stopping point arises because an LBW dismissal is only possible if the centre of the ball pitches on or inside the line of leg stump. Consequently, the review is aborted if the 'predictive path' technology indicates that at least 50 per cent of the ball was outside the line of the leg stump on pitching. This corresponds to the civil standard of proof, the balance of probabilities. Under any of these circumstances, the process of reviewing the umpire's decision is abruptly terminated and the question of whether the ball would have gone on to hit the stumps is never posed.

The next issue is whether the ball hit the batsman in line with the wickets. Here too the procedure depends on the initial decision. A 'not out' decision will only be reversed if the centre of the ball was between wicket and wicket at the point of impact (that is, more than 50 per cent of the ball was in line with the wicket; again, the civil standard of proof); whereas if the umpire initially gave the batsman 'out', the ball is regarded as having struck in line with the wickets unless the technology shows that no part of the ball was between wicket and wicket at the moment of impact (the criminal standard; DRS 3.3[i]ii). In other words, there is a margin (called 'umpire's call'), equivalent to the difference between the criminal and civil standards, within which the umpire has the benefit of the doubt regarding his initial decision.

The last question is, does the technology predict that, but for this impact, the ball would have hit the wicket? Again the parameters of the review process depend on the umpire's original decision. If he gave the batsman 'not out' his decision is only overturned if technology predicts that the centre of the ball would have hit the stumps at a point inside the *centres* of the two outer stumps; in other words, well over half the ball must be in line with the wickets before the umpire's decision is overturned. Had the umpire's decision been 'out', however, the technology must predict that '*no part of the ball* would have made contact with any part of the stumps or bails' (DRS 3.3[i]iii; emphasis added). Here again, then, there is a (somewhat larger) benefit of the doubt in favour of the umpire.

The DRS decision-making process clearly entails a series of questions and is represented as such in the TV graphics (see Figure 6.1):

(i) delivery: fair delivery/no ball?
(ii) first contact: bat/batsman's body?
(iii) point of pitching: outside/inside leg stump?
(iv) point of impact: in line or not in line with wickets?
(v) predicted trajectory: hitting/not hitting stumps?

The order in which these questions are posed does not exactly parallel the original sequence of events, however, in which stage (iii) preceded stage (ii).

The decision-making process under DRS therefore contrasts sharply with the process set out by the Court of Appeal for asylum decision-making; it is sequential rather than holistic. In practice, however, this difference is largely eroded because the API's 'partial reading' of *Karanakaran* crucially misrepresents its key principles and 'shatters the composite test' (Sweeney 2009: 720). Although the relevant paragraphs have been reworded since Sweeney's critique, the passage from API §4.3.4 quoted above ('a decision must be made …') still merits his criticism by 'both disaggregating the facts and separating their consideration from the question of prospective risk' (2009: 720). Likewise §5, 'Assessment of Future Fear', states that '*Once* the facts have been established consideration must be given to whether there is a real risk of future persecution based on those facts that have been accepted or where the benefit of the doubt has been applied' (emphasis added). Although this wording is slightly less explicit than the earlier formulation quoted by Sweeney (2009: 720), the use of 'once' still implies that these steps are to be undertaken sequentially.

This is clearly at odds with the principles stated in *Karanakaran*, where Brocke LJ stressed that 'it would be quite wrong to exclude matters totally from consideration in the balancing process simply because the decision-maker believes, on what may sometimes be somewhat fragile evidence, that they probably did not occur'. Such matters can and should help towards satisfying the standard of proof even if not thought especially likely to be true. Furthermore, it had been 'quite wrong' for the Tribunal at the earlier hearing 'to consider each matter in isolation as opposed to considering their potential cumulative effect'. Both Brooke and Sedley LJ referred approvingly to Kirby J's dictum in the Australian High Court (*Wu Shan Liang*), that decision-makers 'must not, by a process of factual findings on particular elements of the material which is provided, foreclose reasonable speculation upon the chances of persecution emerging from a consideration of the whole of the material'.

As Sedley LJ himself put it, in wording that seems especially apt in the context of the present chapter, the evaluation of the evidence

> should ... be regarded not as an assault course on which hurdles of varying heights are encountered by the asylum seeker with the decision-maker acting as umpire ... but as a unitary process of evaluation of evidential material of many kinds and qualities against the Convention's criteria of eligibility for asylum.

Refugee status determinations 'should start from the presumption that the claimant is telling the truth' (Kagan 2003: 373).[25] They should also, as UNHCR (1998) suggests, define credibility 'in terms of being *believable* rather than being *believed*' (2003: 381; emphases in the original), thereby requiring the decision-maker to give concrete reasons for doubt rather than relying on impressions and prejudices. In Sweeney's view, however, adopting Sedley LJ's metaphor, 'The Immigration Rules and API turn this simple advice on its head, dissembling it into a series of hurdles each of which could deny the benefit of the doubt' (2009: 716).

It is in this regard, as Sweeney shows, that the instructions given to case owners in the API are legally defective. This becomes even more evident when one looks at actual Refusal Letters. In the DRS process the answers to the initial questions (i) to (iii) may pre-empt altogether the asking of the key questions (iv) and (v). The negative impact is similar, if less absolute, in cases like that of Ms S above, where the initial application of Section 8 led to a subsequent belittling of the well-foundedness of her fear and of the risk she would face on return, through reiteration of the phrase 'in light of your credibility having been damaged'. Credibility assessment in asylum claims should not have this serial character, however. There are not two or more questions to be answered sequentially, whereby at each stage one possible answer obviates the need to weigh some or all of the remaining evidence, but only a single question to be decided on the totality of the evidence.

Cases Cited

INS v. *Cardoza-Fonseca* 480 U.S. 421 (1987)
JT (Cameroon) v. *SSHD* [2008] EWCA Civ 878
Karanakaran v. *SSHD* [2000] Imm AR 271, [2000] 3 All ER 449 [CA]
R v. *Abdul Majid* [2009] EWCA Crim 2563 (12 October 2009)
R v. *Billinghurst* [1978] Crim LR 553

25 The USA's Immigration and Naturalization Service and the Canadian Immigration and Refugee Board both endorse this presumption, unless there is 'substantial reason to reject credibility' (Kagan 2003: 374).

R v. *Lifchus* [1997] 3 SCR 320
Sivakumaran: R v. *SSHD ex parte Sivakumaran and others* [1988] 1 AC 958, [1987] UKHL 1, [1988] 1 All ER 193, [1988] Imm AR 147, [1988] 2 WLR 92.
SM (Section 8: Judge's Process) Iran v. *SSHD* [2005] UKAIT 00116
Victor v. *Nebraska*, 511 U.S. 1, 114 S. Ct. 1239, 127 L. Ed. 2d 583 (1994)
Wu Shan Liang (1996) 185 CLR 259

References

Birrell, Susan (1981) 'Sport as ritual: interpretations from Durkheim to Goffman', *Social Forces* 60 (2, Special Issue): 354–76.

Bloor, David (1991 [1976]) *Knowledge and Social Imagery*, Chicago: Chicago University Press.

Collins, Harry and Evans, Robert (2008) 'You cannot be serious! Public understanding of technology with special reference to "Hawk-Eye"', *Public Understanding of Science* 17(3): 283–308.

Diamond, H.A. (1990) 'Reasonable doubt: to define, or not to define', *Columbia Law Review* 90(6): 1716–36.

Ensor, Jonathan, Shah, Amanda and Grillo, Mirella (2006) 'Simple myths and complex realities – seeking truth in the face of section 8', *Immigration, Asylum and Nationality Law* 20(2): 95–111.

Federal Judicial Center (1987) *Pattern Criminal Jury Instructions*, at http://federalevidence.com/pdf/JuryInst/FJC_Crim_1987.pdf (accessed 24 May 2012).

Foster, Ken (2006) 'The juridification of sport', in *Readings in Law and Popular Culture*, ed. Steve Greenfield and Guy Osborn, Abingdon: Routledge, pp. 155–81.

Franklin, Sarah (1997) *Embodied Progress: A Cultural Account of Assisted Conception*, London: Routledge.

Gluckman, Max (1965) *Politics, Law and Ritual in Tribal Society*, Oxford: Basil Blackwell.

Good, Anthony (2004) 'Expert evidence in asylum and human rights appeals: an expert's view', *International Journal of Refugee Law* 16(3): 358–80.

Good, Anthony (2011) 'Witness statements and credibility assessments in the British asylum courts', in *Cultural Expertise and Litigation: Patterns, Conflicts, Narratives*, ed. Livia Holden, Abingdon and New York: Routledge, pp. 94–122.

Gorlick, Brian (2003) 'Common burdens and standards: legal elements in assessing claims to refugee status', *International Journal of Refugee Law* 15: 357–76.

Huizinga, J. (1949) *Homo Ludens*, London: Routledge & Kegan Paul.

Independent Chief Inspector of the UK Border Agency (2011) *The Use of Country of Origin Information in Deciding Asylum Applications: A Thematic Inspection*, available at http://icinspector.independent.gov.uk/wp-content/

uploads/2011/02/Use-of-country-of-origin-information-in-deciding-asylum-applications.pdf (accessed 24 May 2012).

Jarvis, Catriona (2000) 'For these or any other reasons: an examination of judicial assessment of the credibility of asylum seekers in the United Kingdom', unpublished LLM dissertation, London.

Judicial Studies Board (2010) *Crown Court Bench Book: Directing the Jury*, available at http://www.judiciary.gov.uk/NR/rdonlyres/BE25EBB6-AAD2-ACD-8115-28D3BF613164/0/benchbook_criminal_2010.pdf (accessed 24 May 2012).

Kagan, M. (2003) 'Is truth in the eye of the beholder? Objective credibility assessment in refugee status determination', *Georgetown Immigration Law Journal* 17(3): 367–415.

Kvittingen, Anna Verley (2010) *Negotiating Childhood: Age Assessment in the UK Asylum System* (Working Paper series, no. 67), Oxford: Refugee Studies Centre.

Latour, Bruno (2002) *La fabrique du droit: une ethnographie du Conseil d'État*, Paris: Éditions la Découverte.

Latour, Bruno (2004) 'Scientific objects and legal objectivity', in *Law, Anthropology, and the Constitution of the Social: Making Persons and Things*, ed. Alain Pottage and Martha Mundy, Cambridge: Cambridge University Press, pp. 73–114.

Murphy, Peter (2003) *Murphy on Evidence* (8th edn), Oxford: Oxford University Press.

Newman, Paul (2012) 'I won't let DRS ruin my game, says defiant KP as clock ticks on ODI career', *Daily Mail*, 17 February 2012, available at http://www.dailymail.co.uk/sport/cricket/article-2102795/Kevin-Pietersen-wont-let-DRS-ruin-career.html (accessed 24 May 2012).

Piaget, Jean (1955) *The Child's Construction of Reality*, London: Routledge & Kegan Paul.

Roderick, Martin (1999) '"Hard cases" in court', *Singer & Friedlander Football Review: 1998–99 Season*, available at http://archive.is/EvcpH (accessed 24 December 2013).

Sweeney, James A. (2007) 'The lure of "facts" in asylum appeals: critiquing the practice of judges', in *Applying Theory to Policy and Practice: Issues for Critical Reflection*, ed. Steven R. Smith, Aldershot: Ashgate, pp. 19–35.

Sweeney, James A. (2009) 'Credibility, proof and refugee law', *International Journal of Refugee Law* 21(4): 700–726.

Tambiah, Stanley J. (1973) 'Form and meaning of magical acts: a point of view', in *Modes of Thought: Essays on Thinking in Western and Non-western Societies*, ed. Robin Horton and Ruth Finnegan, London: Faber and Faber, pp. 199–230.

Thomas, Robert (2006) 'Assessing the credibility of asylum claims: EU and UK approaches examined', *European Journal of Migration and Law* 8(1): 79–96.

Thomas, Robert (2011) *Administrative Justice and Asylum Appeals: A Study of Tribunal Adjudication*, Oxford and Portland, OR: Hart.

Turner, Victor W. (1969) *The Ritual Process*, Harmondsworth: Penguin Books.

Twining, William (2006) *Rethinking Evidence: Exploratory Essays* (2nd edition), Cambridge: Cambridge University Press.

UK Border Agency (UKBA) (2012a) *Considering Asylum Claims and Assessing Credibility*, available at http://www.bia.homeoffice.gov.uk/sitecontent/documents/policyandlaw/asylumpolicyinstructions/apis/asylum-assessing.credibility.pdf?view=Binary (accessed 24 May 2012).

UK Border Agency (UKBA) (2012b) *Assessing Age*, available at http://www.ind.homeoffice.gov.uk/sitecontent/documents/policyandlaw/asylumprocessguidance/specialcases/guidance/assessing-age?view=Binary (accessed 14 June 2012).

UNHCR (1998) 'Note on burden and standard of proof in refugee claims', available at www.unhcr.org/refworld/docid/3ae6b3338.html (accessed 24 May 2012).

UNHCR (2011) *Handbook and Guidelines on Procedures and Criteria for Determining Refugee Status*, available at http://www.unhcr.org/refworld/docid/4f33c8d92.html (accessed 24 May 2012).

Weston, Amanda (1998) '"A witness of truth" – credibility findings in asylum appeals', *Immigration and Nationality Law and Practice* 12(3): 87–9.

Whitman, James Q. (2008) *The Origins of Reasonable Doubt: Theological Roots of the Criminal Trial*, London and New Haven, CT: Yale University Press.

Young, William (2003) 'Summing-up to juries in criminal cases – what jury research says about current rules and practice', *Criminal Law Review* 665: 674–89.

Chapter 7

In Doubt: Documents as Fetishes in the Danish Asylum System

Zachary Whyte

The determination of asylum cases in Denmark, as elsewhere, ostensibly rests on the authoritative rationalities of law, country of origin information and medical and linguistic examinations – the steady bureaucratic practices of the sovereign state. And yet, the production and management of doubt play key roles in caseworkers' resolution of asylum claims, as many decisions fundamentally hinge on a judgment of applicants' credibility. In this sense, doubt is at once a property and product of the asylum system, where uncertainty and mistrust also shape encounters between caseworkers and asylum seekers.

To asylum seekers, the asylum process appears a haphazard and uncertain enterprise (Whyte 2009). For them, uncertainty infects every part of their experience of the asylum-seeking period – not least their meetings with the authorities sitting in judgment on them, whose mistrust they are keenly aware of and whom they themselves often in turn mistrust. Anxiety also arises from the sense that their everyday experiences as well as the anecdotes in circulation at the asylum centres jar with the system's self-presentation as rational and impersonal. Here, the asylum seekers' sense of the asylum process as fundamentally uncertain feeds back into the judicial resolution of their cases and can at times become self-defeating.

Doubt, then, flits through the Danish asylum system in various ways. However, it is also concretely materialized at various points, perhaps most significantly in the use of documents in asylum determination. On the one hand, the documents asylum seekers present to authorities can become material expressions of their credibility, precisely because they can be submitted to procedures of authentication in a way that asylum seekers' oral testimony by and large cannot. The vagaries of narrative, context, translation and so on can largely be sidestepped with documents. On the other hand, this focus on documents influences the ways in which asylum seekers understand and approach the asylum determination system. In this sense, documents are a critical point of articulation in the meeting of asylum seekers and asylum authorities. My argument here is that we may usefully think of them as analogous in a number of significant ways to the historical fetishes in use in pre- and early colonial age West Africa, described by Pietz (1985, 1987, 1988).

In this chapter, I examine some of these dynamics of doubt, mistrust and uncertainty, and in particular the role of documents in the asylum system, using a scene from my fieldwork as a starting point. Following this ethnographic scene, I briefly provide some background on the Danish asylum system. I then turn, first, to the centrality of credibility determination in asylum processes and then to the use of documents.

As a first step in this endeavour, let me begin by lining up the three terms – uncertainty, doubt and mistrust – for a very cursory muster. Clearly, they are all related to one another, but for my purposes here, I want to array them to speak to slightly different aspects of a lack of definite knowledge. Uncertainty I understand as the wider term, describing a state of being or context which eludes clear understanding. It is a subject that has amassed a substantial amount of scholarship, particularly among philosophers. The key point for me is less that matters are not definite – when are they ever? – but that their lack of definition is felt and acted upon by actors in specific social fields. Doubt and mistrust denote more specific modalities of uncertainty. While doubt implies a person's inability to make a decision about something, mistrust is more of a moral judgment on other people. Doubting someone or something suggests problems in reaching a specific judgment for lack of convincing arguments, while mistrusting them speaks to a more general social relation. What is immediately clear from these very rough distinctions is that all three terms are fundamentally situated. They must be understood in particular contexts, and they are used and understood differently depending on individual actors' positions.

Meeting the Immigration Service

By the time I got to the asylum centre's cafeteria, the place was packed. The Immigration Service was on an informational visit, and the possibility of meeting the people understood to be actually in charge of the asylum system had created an undercurrent of excitement for the past few days among many of the asylum seekers. At the very least, it was something to do on a cold, late winter afternoon.

Walking up the gravel path to the cafeteria, I had passed the two Immigration Service (IS) people standing by their car, one looking through some papers, the other chatting with one of the interpreters. They were smartly dressed women; one looked to be in her forties, the other maybe a decade younger. Inside, asylum seekers were sitting around waiting. Extra blue plastic chairs had been brought in, and the people still shuffling in, hunched against the cold outside, cast about for friends and empty chairs. Most of the asylum seekers wore the everyday clothes of the camp – jogging pants, a t-shirt, perhaps covered by a zippered sweatshirt – and carried with them the usual mobile phone and packet of cigarettes.

When the event finally started, a Red Cross staff member presented the two IS workers, while people shushed one another to hear. The first was the more senior. She introduced herself as Birgitte Sunesen,[1] giving her title and the

1 All personal names in this chapter are pseudonyms.

office she worked in. She then quickly presented her co-worker, and finally the three interpreters. Speaking in Danish, she asked that the asylum seekers group themselves by language, so as to make it easier for the interpreters, who were trying to make themselves heard over the hubbub. Translations were made into Arabic, Serbo-Croat and Farsi. The last was for the benefit of the Dari-speaking Afghanis, who quickly started muttering their discontent, however, as the interpreter was Iranian, and though they could understand him fairly well, they worried that they were missing important bits of information.

Birgitte then started describing the asylum process with the help of the flowchart model the IS included in its brochures:

> Asylum seekers will first meet with the Danish police, who have four tasks. They must ascertain a) how you arrived in Denmark, b) who you are, c) what nationality you are, and d) whether you have sought asylum in another EU country. This process can take up to six months. I say up to because some countries are slower at responding to Dublin Convention enquiries.

An immediate muttering followed this pronouncement, a few speaking up, the interpreters struggling to keep up with the various comments and questions:

> 'I have a friend who waited eight months for this police interview!'
>
> 'Does Switzerland count as an EU country?'
>
> 'This is not true. The police made an interview with me!'

Birgitte responded by repeating her checklist, adding that the police do include a very short description of applicants' motive for seeking asylum. She ploughed on:

> You then fill out an asylum application form, which together with the police report gives us all the information you have imparted up till that time. You then are called in for an interview at the Immigration Service with your caseworker, who has a law degree.[2] However, there are exceptions with certain nationalities. For example, not all Iraqis and Afghanis are called in. If they are from the government-controlled areas, they may be given asylum automatically as they risk disproportionate punishment should they be returned. Illiterates are always called in for an interview. Otherwise we have nothing on which to base our decisions.

People were constantly mumbling and commenting to each other and the interpreters, while Birgitte continued, occasionally glancing at the papers she held in her hand.

2 While the majority of caseworkers do hold law degrees, this is no longer true of all.

> If the Immigration Service has the slightest doubt, they have the documents verified and/or have a linguistic test performed to evaluate your dialect. We also check the information provided by family members to see if it fits. If we do not believe you after these tests you will be called in for an interview. Here we expect you to know about the situation in the area you say you are from, as well as general conditions in the country.

By now the Arabic interpreter was calling out questions and comments as they were put to him:

> 'I have waited 18 months but have not heard anything yet!'
>
> 'What about Kurdish people? You know, it is hard for us.'
>
> 'I took this language test but now I have not heard anything for four months. Really, I am Iraqi.'
>
> 'What about my family? I want to bring my wife and children, when can I bring them?'

Birgitte tried to respond briefly to some of the questions. 'The reason Kurds may be rejected is that the Kurdish organizations are considered to be in power in the north of Iraq. So unless one has asylum-relevant problems with the KDP or PUK … .' As the translation was heard people clucked and shook their heads, commenting loudly to each other. Birgitte continued, 'I know many of you are not happy with this practice …'. By now one or two people were shouting.

The younger IS worker stepped in and spoke loudly to the interpreter, 'You need to tell people that they can't ask questions yet! Tell them we will answer questions later'. After a few moments, the noise had died down enough that Birgitte could continue. 'Interview dates are set only once we receive the police reports. We have already set the interviews for Iraqis up until June', she added, glancing at the cluster of Arabic speakers:

> If further information about, for example, torture is revealed at a later time, a torture examination must be effected. After the interview a decision is made. This can take longer if the asylum seeker for example presents documents in need of translation, needs to go to a torture examination, or must take a language test. Some cases, however, can be decided immediately. Tests are considered by the caseworker and presented to the head of office.

At this point pandemonium broke loose. Questions kept flying in during Birgitte's presentation, causing the Serbo-Croat interpreter to complain that he could not translate both the questions and the presentation.

> 'Why do 99 per cent of Palestinians get negative? We are tortured and still we do not get positive.'
>
> 'My friend got positive after six months. Why am I still waiting for so long?'
>
> 'What if you don't have a country to return to? How can you deport me?'
>
> 'What if you are sick?'

Birgitte attempted to field the questions as they came. Wearing a somewhat stiffened smile and at times shaking her head slowly, she kept repeating the asylum procedure as laid out by the IS again and again:

> Cases are individually determined. After we get the police report we make a determination based on the material at hand … The Aliens Act's paragraph 9, part 2, number 4 allows for residence to be granted for 'other weighty reasons' or if it is impossible to return the asylum seeker to their country of origin. This has been modified as of July 3, 1998.

When the break finally came, a great number of people rushed to speak with her, while her younger colleague ducked out with one of the interpreters to smoke. Someone put on a tape of Arabic music and cranked up the volume.

The Danish Asylum System

While asylum seekers in Denmark wait for their cases to be determined, they are housed in asylum centres, which – with a few exceptions – are run by the asylum department of the Danish Red Cross. It was at one of these, on the small island of Bornholm in the Baltic Sea, an overnight ferry trip from Copenhagen, that I spent a year doing fieldwork in 2001–2002. The centre housed around 400 asylum seekers in long, pastel-painted, barracks-like buildings, up to six to a room. At the time the average waiting time was about a year, though this figure obscured tremendous variation, with some waiting more than five years for a determination. The majority of asylum seekers in Denmark in 2001 came from Iraq and Afghanistan. They were predominantly men, and most were young, but they were otherwise a quite heterogeneous group, which, when I was there, included an agnostic Afghani shepherd and a devout Iraqi dentist. Their clearest commonality was their relationship to the Danish state.

For asylum seekers, the waiting period was fundamentally patterned by uncertainty. The core uncertainty of the outcome of their cases meant that many of my informants actively refused to speak of their futures, which would be radically different depending on which way the authorities' decision went. As one middle-aged Iraqi man said to me, when I asked him about his plans should he get refugee status: 'How can I make plans? I have to wait for positive, if I have chance. Or maybe I get negative, and then I have to move to a different country. Everything is by chance here. Even my future is by chance'. An important source of this powerful sense of uncertainty was the seemingly opaque asylum determination system, and in particular the systems of doubt caseworkers used to process asylum claims.

As with all other asylum systems, the Danish system is complex and full of exceptions and special rules. I do not go through them in any detail here. Instead, I provide a thumbnail sketch of the main encounters and decisions made in a normal asylum case. One general point, worth making before I do so, is that the Danish asylum system is in significant part more a bureaucratic and administrative than a legal process. That is to say, although it is of course founded in law and all caseworkers have legal training, asylum decision-making is not fully subject to the same standards and requirements that court decisions are. In some ways, asylum determination is closer to decision-making on workers' compensation than criminal cases.

The fieldwork scene I started with has already established a few points about the Danish asylum system. Newly arrived asylum seekers are initially interviewed by the police, primarily to ascertain whether or not they can be returned to another EU country under Dublin system arrangements or to another so-called safe third country. In these cases, Danish authorities are under no obligation to consider the content of asylum claims. In this phase, asylum seekers' fingerprints are taken, their belongings are impounded and searched, language tests may be run to determine their origins from the dialects they speak, their wrists may be x-rayed to determine their age from bone development and medical examinations are routine. If asylum seekers are not considered to be cooperating to the satisfaction of authorities, a range of 'motivation-advancing provisions' (*motivationsfremmende foranstaltninger*) may be applied to them, ranging from the removal of the so-called 'pocket money' they receive to incarceration at a closed camp. Confusingly, as one of the asylum seekers in my initial scene pointed out, police also regularly asked about asylum motives during my fieldwork, and inconsistencies between the statements given to the police and those later given to the Immigration Service have resulted in negative determinations on the grounds that the asylum seekers' stories were not considered consistent and therefore were also considered to be not credible. As will be apparent from even this brief sketch, credibility determination starts early in the Danish asylum system and anticipates asylum seekers' meetings with the IS.

Those asylum seekers admitted to the normal procedure fill out an asylum application in their own language, detailing the substance of their claim to the Danish Immigration Service. Unlike some other European countries, no legal advice or support is provided at this stage of the asylum procedure. There are some limited legal resources asylum seekers can draw on, including free legal aid from the Danish Refugee Council, but the majority do not access or even know of them.

Asylum seekers then wait for interviews to be scheduled. Meanwhile, the IS has the asylum applications translated and begins the process of assessing the credibility and merit of these claims. Credibility is probed for internal consistency and coherence and in relation to the array of 'country of origin' information the IS maintains. At the interviews, asylum seekers' narratives are further probed to clear up inconsistencies and test credibility. Interviews are conducted through an interpreter, whose role is generally considered by the authorities to be mechanical and unproblematic; but for many asylum seekers, the interpreter is an object of concern, with applicants often uneasy about the accuracy of translations or worried that an interpreter has a personal axe to grind. These interviews usually last between three and eight hours with breaks.

If asylum cases are rejected by the IS ('get negative'), they are automatically appealed to the Refugee Appeals Board (RAB), a five-person 'quasi-judicial' body, currently organized with a judge as chairperson and representatives from the Danish Bar and Law Society, the Ministry of Justice, the Ministry of Foreign Affairs and the Danish Refugee Council.[3] Here the asylum seeker is afforded legal representation for the first time, though the quality of this representation varies considerably. While the majority of these lawyers do a professional job, there are no requirements for featuring on the official list of asylum lawyers beyond holding a law degree, and some lawyers representing asylum seekers have little knowledge of asylum law or investment in their clients' cases (Kjær 2003). A representative from the IS (generally not the same person who made the decision) presents the grounds for the negative decision, which is then contested by the asylum seeker's counsel. Unlike the other points of decision in the asylum system, the Board's ruling is presented immediately together with a brief written background for it. While these decisions are considered to function as precedents for the work of the IS, they do not generally include broader deliberations on the intent and reach of asylum law, as one would expect from final courts of legal appeal. There is no further appeal from the RAB, and the Danish Supreme Court has specifically refused to consider asylum cases. A handful of cases have been appealed directly to the European Court of Human Rights. These appeals do not officially have suspensive effects on deportation orders. Final rejection entails a deportation order, but as in other European countries, authorities are not always able to effect these for a variety of reasons (Noll 1999; Andersen, Jacobsen and Olsen 2009).

While waiting, asylum seekers are forbidden to work or pursue an education.[4] They are, with few exceptions, required to remain on site at the centre to which

3 The Refugee Appeals Board has seen a number of changes over the years. Originally composed of seven members, it was reduced to five, then three, and recently increased to five once more.

4 These restrictions, along with the requirement for asylum seekers to stay in centres, can be waived as of January 2013 in certain circumstances. However, the requirements that asylum seekers sign documents promising to leave 'voluntarily' if their cases are rejected, along with the somewhat unclear procedure for approval of jobs and residences (not to mention the difficulty for asylum seekers in finding either), has meant the uptake has been negligible so far.

they are assigned, and are paid a minimal allowance to cover the costs of food, clothing, cigarettes, the all-important phonecards and other expenses. Failure to comply with these rules or to fully collaborate with the asylum authorities as they gather information could result in removal of the allowance, transfer to a 'closed camp' and a range of other sanctions. Some asylum seekers do nevertheless find illegal work, and I observed barter economies in action at the centre I visited, which were especially valuable for people whose allowances had been removed.

The rather lengthy fieldwork scene presented above was by no means a characteristic encounter between asylum seekers and caseworkers, simply because these sorts of meetings are extremely rare. Indeed it is for its atypicality, rather than its representativeness, that I include it here. The meeting was a rare opportunity to address representatives of the asylum system directly. Because it took place in relative anonymity, beyond the reach of identifiable documents, it provides a useful perspective on asylum seekers' understandings of and concerns about the asylum system. Further, the scene speaks to a number of fundamental issues of doubt, mistrust and uncertainty in the Danish asylum field, all of which are fundamental to the uses and understandings of documents there. In particular, it illustrates the differing understandings and experiences of doubt among asylum authorities and asylum seekers, as well as fundamental differences in how to understand the asylum system. While the caseworkers presented it as a coherent bureaucratic system, built on rationalities of law, asylum seekers disputed this presentation with anecdotes and exceptional examples, suggesting a far more uncertain and mistrustful determination process. This also underlines the fact that the asylum system is both an intercultural and an intersocial meeting zone. Not only do asylum seekers and caseworkers not share cultural backgrounds in the vast majority of cases, but their respective structural positions in the asylum bureaucracy also bear quite directly on their encounters in it. Finally, asylum seekers' understandings of the asylum system change significantly over the time they spend waiting for a decision on their cases, in part as a result of their experiences of doubt and mistrust, often leading to frustration and anger.

Doubtful Determinations and Credible Doubts

In one view, the work of asylum determination is fundamentally about the dynamics of doubt. In this sense, doubt functions as a technology for dealing with asylum seekers' stories and thus as a way of processing uncertain cases. This is very much the line Birgitte presented to the asylum seekers at Centre Rønne. Here the more or less dubious stories asylum seekers present to Danish authorities must be considered and weighed. Their documents must be validated, their stories of torture cross-checked with marks on their bodies, their language tested to verify claims of origin and the details of their asylum claims compared with authoritative sources, accepted as facts. This is doubt as a transitive verb, filled in as a crosshatching of the documentary and non-documentary evidence provided by the asylum seekers. Immigration service caseworkers ideally doubt specific documents, details of stories, dialects and so on. If any of these are found to be inaccurate or false, this may be read as symptomatic of asylum seekers' credibility in general, which in turn allows for the resolution of their cases. The logic here is that inaccuracy or lies on one aspect of an asylum case punctures the applicant's credibility in general, thus supporting a negative decision on the case. In this view, 'reasonable doubt' is the necessary starting point for the work of asylum determination (see Good, this volume, for a fuller consideration of the relations of doubt and proof in asylum cases).

There are three points worth making very quickly here. First, this practice in asylum determination is by no means uncontroversial. UNHCR and a great number of other actors (for example Kagan 2003) advocate a much more lenient understanding of what constitutes 'reasonable doubt' in credibility determinations of asylum cases, on the assumption that the risks of unjustified rejection far outweigh the costs of unjustified acceptance. Second, caseworkers are well aware that almost all asylum cases involve inconsistencies. A range of factors may dent the credibility of asylum seekers' stories, and the job of asylum determination is often more about deciding which inconsistencies are significant and so symptomatic of a lack of credibility and which are to do with the general frailty of human storytelling. These factors then at once arise from and entail a degree of discretion on the part of the caseworker. Third, in addition to individual differences in the enactment of doubt, there are institutional ones. Police interviews in the Danish asylum system are more closely related to interrogations, and may be marked by raised voices and direct accusations of lying. By contrast, IS interviews are much more drawn out with more attention paid to the detail of stories and to the relation of what asylum seekers say to what is 'known'. Finally, the Refugee Appeals Board allows for a more court-like procedure, where doubt may be more formally raised and questioned.

For asylum seekers, however, who tend to see the asylum process dominated more by uncertain social relations than by bureaucratic logic, asylum authorities' doubts are often experienced as mistrust. The distinction between doubting details of their case and mistrusting them as narrators, as social beings, is experientially collapsed – and with good reason, as I have just argued, as it is precisely these details that are understood to picture general narrative credibility. While this kind of doubt is then always interwoven with mistrust, the struggles and negotiations of caseworkers to balance the two is generally hidden away from asylum seekers in the name of professionalism. They are instead presented with often fairly idealized presentations of the asylum system as ideal Weberian bureaucracy, as Birgitte did in my starting scene.

In informal conversation, several caseworkers have indicated to me that they also harbour doubts about other asylum authorities, including the police, their peers and the RAB. When presenting cases to the RAB, they occasionally find themselves being made to defend determinations made by their peers that they do not find justified. Similarly, some caseworkers have suggested to me that certain members of the RAB are not sufficiently versed in asylum law and in any case spend very little time deliberating specific cases. These are not doubts that can be easily expressed or even considered in the contexts in which they arise, and the reaction of caseworkers often seems to be to return to the ideal case in much the way Birgitte responded to what might be specific systemic failures by highlighting proper procedure.

A keystone in presentations of the Danish asylum system of the sort I quote Birgitte as making at the beginning of this chapter is that this leveraging of doubt forms a system that applies equally to all asylum applicants and ought only to be of concern to applicants who are lying. Asylum seekers were commonly told to simply tell the Danish authorities 'everything' and not to hold anything back. This of course required a level of trust in the Danish asylum system that was very rare among asylum seekers, all the more so among those who had spent some time in it. In the uncertain context of the Danish asylum system, saying nothing, or as little as possible, often seemed the better strategy.

While asylum seekers were thus doubtful of the motives of the asylum system and uncertain as to its operation, they nevertheless tried to navigate it as best they could. It is from this position that I want to understand the many questions and interruptions in my fieldwork scene. While these interruptions surely indicate the gap between Birgitte's presentation of the ideal system and the everyday experiences of the asylum seekers and their peers, they also expressed the mistrust this gap helped foster. Finding little to connect their personal experiences and the anecdotes of their peers to the official presentation, their mistrust of the asylum system grew. And this mistrust could in turn feed back into the asylum system, when asylum seekers changed the focus of their stories or attempted to downplay aspects of them to match their current understanding of how the system actually worked. This strategy was generally ill-advised, and certainly so if taken too far, as shifting stories often seemed all the more dubious to caseworkers.

Doubt in Heaps

To think a little more about the role of credibility in the asylum determination process, I turn now to classical philosophy. The sorites paradox – or paradox of the heap – speaks to the logical problems that arise when vague categories (the ancient examples include heaps and baldness) are inserted into more binary schemes with (imagined) sharp boundaries (either the sand forms a heap or it does not, you are either bald or you are not). One version of it goes like this: if you start with a heap of sand and remove a single grain, you still have a heap. One grain of sand does not change the heap's status as heap. So if you remove another grain of sand, your heap still remains. Now, logically, you can continue removing single grains of sand without ever crossing a knowable threshold from heap to not-heap. By this reasoning, you might end up with a single grain of sand remaining that you could still call a heap. Conversely, you could start with a single grain of sand, which is obviously not a heap. Adding one grain does not change this status. Again, if you were to continue adding single grains of sand you could – given extensive time and patience – end up with millions of grains of sand piled up without ever having crossed the threshold from not-heap to heap. This paradox has prompted quite an extensive philosophical literature, largely focused on resolving classical logic in the face of vagueness (see Hyde 2011 for an overview), far beyond the scope of this chapter.

I want to use the sorites paradox rather to illustrate a few basic points about credibility in asylum procedures. First, credibility – like sorites paradoxes – is always paired with its negation (heap and not-heap, bald and not-bald, credible and not credible, and so on). Again, as with sorites paradoxes, the central concept is rather vague, but is used in a binary scheme. There is no clear boundary between a credible and a not credible account that is crossed by a single element in it. At least in principle, it is the combined effect of the entire account that determines whether an asylum seeker appears credible or not. By sorites arguments, vague categories like credibility or heaps or baldness do not change through incremental addition or subtraction of elements, which may result in the kind of paradoxical absurdity of calling single grains of sand heaps. In this sense, the process of doubting an asylum seeker's credibility is not attached to the result of this doubting (whether or not the asylum seeker is in fact credible) in any straightforward way.

This speaks to a second basic fact of credibility in asylum determination systems. Different actors assume different starting points on asylum seeker credibility and this fundamentally informs credibility determination. There has been a great deal of literature and policy writing documenting a 'culture of disbelief' in European asylum systems (Eastmond 2007; see Souter 2011 for a review of the term in the UK), suggesting that at least some caseworkers start from the supposition that asylum claims are not credible. The fact that some facts stand up to scrutiny largely does not change this, in the same way that piling up grains of sand does not turn them into a heap. This obviously has profound repercussions for the asylum seekers whose cases are being determined in this way. Conversely, some asylum seekers may insist that their stories are credible, despite the fact that multiplying elements of them are shown to be inaccurate or outright false. An IS caseworker told me of a West African asylum seeker who insisted that he had arrived in Denmark by paddling a canoe from West Africa. The asylum seeker simply did not acknowledge that this story was not credible to the caseworker, nor did he accept that this story should have any bearing on the wider credibility of his asylum claim. In either case, this may lead to seemingly absurd situations where credibility or its lack is claimed, despite any shred of believability.

Unlike in sorites paradoxes, however, in asylum determination the elements of the credible–not credible pair are not mirror images. For the purposes of asylum determination, it is of course the caseworkers' assessments of asylum seekers' credibility that matter most. While the process of establishing credibility may be like piling single grains of sand, if we are to stay with the sorites image, the process of establishing non-credibility is more lumpy than grainy. That is to say, unlike the slow removal of single grains of sand, the systems of doubting instituted in asylum determination may establish non-credibility more quickly than credibility. In effect the process of doubting ends when there is a basis for establishing an asylum seeker as non-credible, whereas no single element of evidence may establish the credibility of an asylum seeker with equal finality. This basic point speaks fundamentally to the process of doubting in asylum cases and structures many asylum seekers' experiences of the asylum process.

However, asylum seekers' understandings of their credibility are not without consequence, if nothing else for the ways in which they may influence their acceptance of verdicts and their strategies for dealing with them.

The Weight of Documents

In thinking about the play of doubt, mistrust and uncertainty, I want to turn now to the place of documents in the asylum process. As Matthew Hull has argued, documents are often overlooked by ethnographers, particularly in bureaucratic settings, in part for their seeming ordinariness. But, as he puts it, 'documents are not simply instruments of bureaucratic organizations, but rather are constitutive of bureaucratic rules, ideologies, knowledge, practices, subjectivities, objects, outcomes, and even the organizations themselves' (Hull 2012: 253).

In asylum determination, documents also play crucial roles, though they figure so diversely that their commonalities may be hard to distinguish. From country of origin information through interview guidelines for caseworkers to the actual written decisions themselves, documents at once inform and form the practice of asylum processing. Rather than address the entire range of documents in use, my focus here is on the documents asylum seekers present to authorities as part of their claims. These are themselves quite heterogeneous, including wedding certificates, photographs, criminal records, educational diplomas and so on. Some are requested by asylum authorities to support aspects of asylum seekers' claims, but others are brought forward by asylum seekers with the idea that they may help their cases, whether or not they were explicitly asked for.

These kinds of documents play key parts in asylum determination, both as authoritative evidence and as touchstones for credibility. The film *Well-Founded Fear* (2000) provides a wonderfully literal image of this, in a scene where a US caseworker taps an enormous pile of papers on his desk, explaining that with files this size, refugee status is almost always granted. While the caseworkers' explanation for this was that these sorts of cases were generally supported by NGOs, and so represented some degree of pre-selection, it was also clear that the simple mass of documents itself had a certain convincing effect. But before I continue, let me just underline that though documents may be very important to asylum outcomes, they are not the only – or even necessarily the primary – factor involved. Questions of internal consistency in the asylum story, proper grounds for asylum, the emotional pitch of the asylum seeker's presentation (see

Kobelinsky, this volume), the applicant's country of origin and general credibility may undermine the most impressive of documents. Nevertheless, documents are important elements in asylum determination and appear particularly so to asylum seekers.

Legal interest in documents tends to focus on them as evidence in a fairly unproblematic way, once they have been established as authentic (Good 2007: 31). In Denmark this work of verification is undertaken by the Documentation section of the Immigration Service, largely through comparison with authentic versions of documents gathered from the relevant countries. If they determine the documents to be authentic, they are accepted as evidence and can be weighty contributions to the positive resolution of asylum cases. Conversely, if they are determined to be false, this may have a – possibly greater – influence on credibility assessments, and thus underpin a negative determination. In either case, documents powerfully shape asylum determination outcomes. This was very much apparent to asylum seekers, who regularly joked that Danish people didn't believe anything unless it was in writing.

However, documents can also be significant by their absence. The failure to produce certain kinds of documents that caseworkers consider easily or commonly accessible may also adversely influence determination (cf. Crawley 1999; Good 2007: 117). Absence here is thus defined largely by systemic expectations. Indeed, there are so-called 'motivation-inducing measures' in place to coerce supposedly recalcitrant asylum seekers to 'co-operate in the resolution of their cases', for instance by producing relevant documents. If nothing else, the absence of relevant documents is often presented as a reason for the drawn-out character of asylum determination (see, for example, Griffiths 2012).

Documents then become a way of focusing doubt in a way that can be resolved – they are, so to speak, 'good to doubt with' in the asylum context. Like medical examinations (Fassin and d'Halluin 2005) and language tests (Eades 2011), their verifiability, or at least their appearance of verifiability, is the source of their potency. Unlike oral testimony with its complexities and inconsistencies, documents can be more easily established as real or fake. This is not to say that documents are in fact verifiable in the way imagined in the Danish asylum system. In countries without the extensive bureaucratic infrastructure of the Danish state, the production and circulation of official documents may be much more haphazard and inconsistent. Nevertheless, the appearance of verifiability allows for doubt to be concretely tested and resolved in the documents asylum seekers bring.

These documents may very well not speak directly to the grounds for the asylum claim. Asylum seekers regularly showed me marriage and birth certificates, identity papers, photographs of themselves and their families, and so on, when they talked about their meetings with Danish asylum authorities. Nevertheless, these documents can function as touchstones for credibility. That is to say, they may help to establish a general sense of the asylum seeker as credible, if the asylum story is consistent with the various documents presented. In this sense, the verifiability of the documents directly or indirectly may help resolve doubts about the asylum seeker's credibility more broadly.

However, while a lack of documents was generally viewed with scepticism, the wrong kinds of documents could seem equally dubious, however authentic they were. Thus I have met a number of asylum seekers who claim that their procurement of legal visas and thus their legal entry into Denmark caused them problems in their asylum cases, on the grounds that if they could access legal documents, were they really so persecuted? In this logic, paradoxically, the very legality of entry into Denmark becomes a seed for doubt.

For asylum seekers, documents focused a variety of different conceptions of their own backgrounds and the asylum system. On the one hand, as what David Parkin called 'transitional objects', documents (including photos, certificates, proofs of identity and even death threats) 'provide the material markers of templates, inscribed with narrative and sentiment, which may later re-articulate the shifting boundaries of a socio-cultural identity' (1999: 313). In this sense, they are held onto as links to a wider, often transnational, social world. They bridge senses of past social identities and possible future lives. They may relate to family, religion, political organization and other factors relevant to asylum determination, but they are often experienced by asylum seekers in a wider social horizon than the narrower one of asylum. Asylum seekers tend to articulate their motives for leaving their home countries not so much in terms of the refugee definition as in terms of the impossibility of their lives in their home countries (Whyte 2011). We may perhaps think of these as 'identity' documents in a purposely broad sense.

On the other hand, the uses of these documents in the asylum process also point to the ways in which asylum seekers must necessarily take account of the narrower views of the asylum system: documents are not just 'transitional objects', but also very much instrumental ones, possible keys to a future life in Denmark or elsewhere. As I have pointed out, asylum seekers were well aware of this usefulness, which they both tried to leverage and occasionally questioned. As Rojhat, an Iraqi Kurd, remarked bitterly to me: 'The ones who really have problems at home have the most difficult time to get positive. How can you go around getting papers and passports if you really have to run for your life? So people like me we have so many problems to get positive'. Another Iraqi man laughed at a fellow asylum seeker, who he said had impressed asylum authorities with a picture of himself in uniform next to a jet fighter: 'This guy, I don't think he can even ride a bicycle! But he will get positive from this'. This sense that the Danish asylum system's valuation of documents was out of step with what could reasonably be expected – and indeed with reality – made documents seem at once valuable and uncertain to asylum seekers.

The focus of Western asylum systems on documents is not lost on people-smugglers either. A recent article in the *Guardian* newspaper describes the expanding business of smuggling-related document forgers. In addition to passports and visas, some entrepreneurial Afghans are now offering forged Taliban death threats (Boone and Bakhshi 2012). This kind of enterprise speaks to an understanding of the fundamental importance of documents in Western asylum determination systems. But it also provides rich justification for the regimes of doubt and verification that these systems implement, despite the impossibility of determining the extent to which Afghan asylum seekers actually make use of these kinds of forgeries.[5] This is very similar to a pattern Macklin (1999: 136) describes from Canada, whereby asylum authorities require particular documents of asylum seekers to resolve their cases. If applicants protest that they are unable to procure them, they are told that others have managed to do so. Then, as asylum applicants learn of their importance and the documents become increasingly widespread, some are found to be forgeries, leading to the documents eventually being dismissed as viable evidence. Paradoxically, it is effectively the requirement to produce certain documents that both leads to their proliferation and eventually undermines their credibility, justifying once more the central role doubting plays in the asylum process.

In a case that provoked some amusement from fellow asylum seekers, one young Afghani man at the centre, who had travelled on a fake Russian passport which he had failed to destroy before meeting the police, was classified as Russian on arrival. This was literally inscribed in his Alien Identification Number, the key mode of identification in the Danish asylum system, where the first three numbers indicate country of origin. While he complained – not least because his chances of getting asylum while classified as Russian were negligible – he was still being addressed by the asylum system as Russian some eight months later. The potency of his fake document seemed to overwhelm the asylum system, underlining to asylum seekers the power of documents, even when they were known and acknowledged to be fake.

For some asylum seekers, this perceived documentary obsession also was assumed to work the other way, making them mistrust the words of Danish authorities. As Moshref, a young Afghani man, told me after he and his brother had just received positive decisions from the RAB, 'I will wait until they send the letter from the *kommune* [municipality]. Then they cannot change their minds. When it is on paper, we will really know we got positive'. Though he said it with a smile, Moshref's comment also emblematizes the erosion of trust in the Danish asylum authorities that many asylum seekers experience as they wait for their cases to be resolved.

While documents then to some extent work to resolve some forms of doubt for asylum authorities, in so doing they also participate in the production and circulation of other dynamics of doubt.

5 Asylum seekers may not be the only ones wielding forged documents. In an unusual twist, allegations have emerged that Dutch asylum officials have, knowingly or not, used forged travel documents to deport failed asylum seekers to Guinea and other countries. See http://www.irr.org.uk/news/cracks-in-the-dutch-deportation-and-detention-regime/ (accessed 21 April 2014).

Documents as Fetishes

Opening the blue, metal cupboard in his room, Abu Minna carefully took out a plastic pocket containing a number of faded, crumpled pieces of paper, as well as newer letters from the Danish Immigration Service. He carefully passed it to me, but kept a thumb and index finger at one corner. I had just asked him about his education in Iraq, and the papers included his diploma. 'I am an engineer. I have proof', he said, tapping the plastic with his other index finger. Then he pulled the papers back and put them away once more in his locker.

I want to suggest that we might usefully think about the place of documents in the Danish asylum system through understanding them as fetishes, in the sense Pietz unfolded across three articles in the late 1980s (Pietz 1985, 1987, 1988); that is to say, as material objects, emerging in cross-cultural contexts, where they are bound up with particular kinds of social relations. Cabot (2012) suggests this approach in her discussion of the place of the 'pink card' in the Greek asylum system. This document, she argues, circulates within and vitalizes both the governance of the Greek asylum system and the everyday lives of the actors involved in it. I want to take a slightly different tack and suggest a perspective on documents in the Danish asylum system that compares them explicitly with the fetishes of early colonial trade encounters.

Caveats immediately threaten to overwhelm this conceit, and I hasten to clarify that I by no means am suggesting identity between these encounters and asylum determination. Rather, it is an attempt to tease out some aspects of the place and use of documents not usually covered in legal approaches. In particular, I am interested in reflecting on the ways in which asylum seekers – like Pietz's early European voyagers – attempt to make sense of and engage with caseworkers as representatives of a social system that they at times find peculiarly difficult to understand, through a particular, valued material form.

Further, as will become clear, the understanding of the fetish Pietz advances is very much bound up in relations of trade and exchange. While this understanding was sometimes applied to the asylum system by my informants (for instance in promises of future good citizenship in return for refugee status), formally and legally there is no exchange here: persons who fulfil the Refugee Convention are by definition refugees. Refugee status is a right, conferred on appropriate persons, not something to be bartered for. This formal understanding of refugee determination is largely fictional, as actual refugee determination procedures vary dramatically across space and time, resulting in much more uneven implementations of who are actually recognized as refugees than the rights-based ideal. However, it is a crucial fiction, because it undergirds important rights of asylum seekers (such as non-refoulement – the right not to be returned to places where one risks persecution) in a situation where they otherwise might be at the mercy of the states processing their claims. All this having been said, there remains a key element of (quite unequal) exchange, if not actual barter, in asylum seekers' meetings with caseworkers.

Let me now turn to Pietz and his detailed treatment of the historical origins and uses of the term 'fetish'. Emerging in the sixteenth and seventeenth centuries in meetings between European merchants (and early colonialists) and West Africans along the coast from present-day Ghana to Nigeria, the idea he argues first appeared in the pidgin word 'Fetisso' (Pietz 1987: 23). This quickly establishes an important point, particularly apposite to asylum determination: the fetish belongs to 'no discrete society or culture, but to a cross-cultural situation formed by the ongoing encounter of the value codes of radically different social orders' (Pietz 1985: 11). In other words, the meaning and use of documents arises not from one setting to be imposed on another, but rather is specific to 'the encounter of radically heterogenous [sic] social systems' (Pietz 1985: 7). This point is particularly important for being so little recognized. That is to say, caseworkers largely proceed from a fairly unproblematic understanding of the place and meaning of documents, once they have been authenticated. But the documents produced, the moments and manner in which they are produced, the systems for validating them and the understandings of their import all emerge from the cross-cultural situation of the asylum determination procedure.

The term 'fetish' brought together a wide array of African material objects and practices, all aimed at a particular form of social interaction across 'bewilderingly different cultures' (Pietz 1987: 23): trade. The idea of the fetish, Pietz argues, was held together by four key features: (1) the fetish has an irreducible materiality, precisely not iconic of 'some immaterial model or entity' (1985: 7), but 'is viewed as the locus of religious activity or psychic investment' (1987: 23); (2) it 'has an ordering power derived from its status as the fixation or inscription of a unique originating event that has brought together previously heterogenous [sic] elements into a novel identity' (1985: 7); (3) it is dependent 'for its meaning and value on a particular order of social relations, which it in turn reenforces' (1987: 23) – indeed it demonstrates the social value of certain material objects and the institutions that mark them, precisely because it is often considered 'trifling' by others; and finally (4) it forms 'an intense relation to and with power over the desires, actions, health, and self-identity of individuals whose personhood is conceived as inseparable from their bodies' (1985: 10).

While it is hardly a perfect fit, I think there is enough resonance with the ways in which documents are understood and used in the asylum determination system to warrant further reflection. Documents are of course material. The pieces of often wrinkled or smudged paper that asylum seekers present to authorities have a value that is very much bound up with their physicality. Their materiality is the basis for examining and authenticating them. Indeed, when they were shown to me at the asylum centre, often as part of some longer narrative, they were often simply held up, like Abu Minna did with his engineering diploma, as if the fact of their material existence alone was corroboration of asylum seekers' stories. That being said, as I discussed above, documents do not necessarily have to be materially present to have an effect. Failure to produce expected documents itself generates and focuses doubt.

Asylum documents also by definition bring together heterogeneous elements. The kinds of documents brought together in an asylum case are not necessarily of the same order, as I discussed above. Birth certificates, marriage licences, membership cards in political organizations, written death threats, pictures of family members or of oneself, and so on, may be gathered and considered together by caseworkers looking to resolve an asylum case. In other words, one's recognition as a refugee is predicated on an ordering of a variety of social relations and identities, a process often mediated by documents.

Asylum documents also demonstrate specific social values of asylum authorities, while at the same time re-enforcing them. This was more than evident in the argument from Macklin, presented above, whereby documents were at first required and then ignored all in the name of a particular bureaucratic system of doubting. This leads to a further point: the kinds of documents that are valuable, in the sense that they are weighty aids in 'getting positive', are not immediately obvious to asylum seekers. This resonates quite clearly with the experiences of early Europeans in West Africa. As David Graeber writes,

> Merchants were always going on about how Africans were willing to accept all manner of junk – 'trifles', 'trash', 'toys' – for gold and other valuable commodities. But at the same time, Africans were clearly not willing to accept just anything, and one could never tell in advance what sort of junk a given group would fancy. Anyone who has pored over 'travelers' accounts' from this period will likely have noticed how much time and energy merchants had to put into figuring out which particular variety of worthless beads, what color or type of worthless trinkets would be accepted at any given port of call. (2005: 412)

Again, not all asylum seekers were equally ignorant of which documents were valued by the Danish asylum authorities, but discussions of the sort I quoted above about the value of a picture of oneself next to a plane were common at the asylum centre and speak at any rate to an ongoing concern with the issue.

Finally, documents relate very directly to asylum seekers' bodies. This is in part because asylum seekers' bodies are increasingly the focus of asylum determination processes (Fassin and d'Halluin 2005). More radically, it may be the case that asylum seekers' bodies are increasingly being treated *as* documents, in the sense that they can be 'read' and 'verified' in bureaucratic systems of doubting. Further, documents shape asylum seekers' understandings of the Danish asylum system, where they are assumed to carry profound power, and thereby also become fundamental to the lives of asylum seekers.

This leads on to a broader point from Pietz's argument: the idea of the fetish also carries with it a certain explanatory power. According to Pietz, early European merchants saw fetishes as key explanatory models for 'African society' in general. They ascribed to Africans an irrational propensity to personify material objects, revealing a false understanding of natural causality, while at the same time attributing causal relations to random associations. This chimes well with asylum seekers' understandings of Danish society in general ("Danish people don't believe anything unless it is in writing") as well as to the specific systems of doubting they were subject to in asylum determination processes. Stories of the inappropriate conclusions drawn from innocuous details (or the inability to provide innocuous details), misunderstandings of the way things work 'back home' and so on were rife at the asylum centre. Much of the frustration of asylum seekers with the perceived obsession of the asylum system with documents may perhaps be read in this light. As Pietz remarks, 'The discourse of the fetish has always been a critical discourse about the false objective values of a culture from which the speaker is personally distanced' (1985: 14). There was a real worry that the asylum authorities in charge of considering their cases were quite simply not up to the task, and this was epitomized by their overwhelming focus on documents over the spoken testimony of the asylum seekers themselves.[6]

But this frustration also has a further horizon, for like the early Europeans piecing together understandings of 'Africa' based on their interactions in cross-cultural zones (for example Pietz 1987: 23), asylum seekers may also tend to assume that documents are central to Danish social order in general. While documents allow caseworkers to focus the process of doubting asylum claims on specific material objects, providing a bureaucratically viable way to deal with the uncertainty of credibility that asylum cases necessarily entail, in so doing they also shape not only the ways in which asylum seekers engage with the asylum process, but also more broadly their understandings and expectations of Danish social order in general. None of this, of course, is set in stone, and individual asylum seekers may have quite divergent experiences with and understandings of the asylum system. The purpose of this comparison is certainly not to claim some inevitable epistemology of asylum, but rather to find a way to take seriously the kinds of concerns asylum seekers expressed to one another – and very occasionally to visiting caseworkers – about the asylum system, and in particular the systems of doubt that characterize it.

Concluding Remarks

Doubt is at once a property and a product of the Danish asylum system. Pursued by authorities as a way of determining the validity – and in particular the credibility – of asylum claims, doubt also informs asylum seekers' understandings of both individual caseworkers and the asylum system in general. These doubts in turn feed back into the asylum system, in what we may think of as a dynamic system of mutual, if highly asymmetrical, doubting. Documents provide a very concrete way of resolving some doubts, though they simultaneously can generate others, among both asylum authorities and asylum seekers.

6 Elsewhere, I have discussed this as the result of a near-sighted system of surveillance I call the myopticon (Whyte 2011).

Thinking about asylum documents as fetishes, in Pietz' sense, speaks to a particular understanding and function of documents. It by no means exhausts the uses and understandings of documents in the asylum system or among asylum seekers. Rather, multiple understandings clash and overlap, as asylum seekers and caseworkers negotiate the processing of asylum claims. But it may usefully frame one way of using documents to navigate mistrust and uncertainty in the asylum system.

For asylum seekers, the value of their documents is overwhelmingly to do with the value the Danish asylum system places in them. That is to say, documents are valuable because the asylum system fetishizes them, and having the right ones and presenting them correctly can help asylum seekers 'get positive'. The powerful belief of caseworkers in documents (again, I am leaving aside here the question of the objective reasonableness of this position) all but forces asylum seekers to attend to them. This overlays rather than replaces the values asylum seekers may ascribe to their documents in other contexts. While certificates of education or birth certificates would likely be kept in any case, written death threats were of a different order (and, of course, rarer).

My argument, then, is that the use of documents is not merely an aid in credibility determination, but powerfully frames the asylum process as an intercultural encounter with particular consequences for the practices of both caseworkers and asylum seekers. Indeed, perhaps the key point to be drawn from this comparison across centuries and continents is that particular ways of relating to cultural others through material objects can have repercussions far beyond the immediate encounter.

References

Andersen, Lisbeth Garly, Jacobsen, Anette Faye and Olsen, Birgitte Kofod (2009) *Afviste Asylansøgere og Andre Udlændinge i Udsendelsesposition i Danmark*, Copenhagen: Danish Institute for Human Rights.

Boone, Jon and Bakhshi, Nooruddin (2012) 'Boom time for Afghanistan's people smugglers', *Guardian*, 18 January, available at http://www.theguardian.com/world/2012/jan/18/afghanistan-people-smugglers-taliban-europe.

Cabot, Heath (2012) 'The governance of things: documenting limbo in the Greek asylum procedure', *PoLAR: Political and Legal Anthropology Review* 35(1): 11–29.

Crawley, Heaven (1999) *Breaking Down the Barriers: A Report on the Conduct of Asylum Interviews at Ports*, London: ILPA.

Eades, Diana (2011) 'Testing the claims of asylum seekers: the role of language analysis', *Language Assessment Quarterly* 6(1): 30–40.

Eastmond, Marita (2007) 'Stories as lived experience: narratives in forced migration research', *Journal of Refugee Studies* 20(2): 248–64.

Fassin, Didier and d'Halluin, Estelle (2005) 'The truth from the body: medical certificates as ultimate evidence for asylum seekers', *American Anthropologist* 107(4): 597–608.

Good, Anthony (2007) *Anthropology and Expertise in the Asylum Courts*, Abingdon and New York: Routledge-Cavendish.

Graeber, David (2005) 'Fetishism as social creativity: or, fetishes are gods in the process of construction', *Anthropological Theory* 5(4): 407–38.

Griffiths, Melanie (2012) 'Anonymous aliens? Questions of identification in the detention and deportation of failed asylum seekers', *Population, Space and Place* 18(6): 715–27.

Hull, Matthew S. (2012) 'Documents and bureaucracy', *Annual Review of Anthropology* 41: 251–67.

Hyde, Dominic (2011) 'Sorites paradox', in *The Stanford Encyclopedia of Philosophy*, ed. Edward N. Zalta (Winter 2011 edn), available at http://plato.stanford.edu/archives/win2011/entries/sorites-paradox/.

Kagan, M. (2003) 'Is truth in the eye of the beholder? Objective credibility assessment in refugee status determination', *Georgetown Immigration Law Journal* 17(3): 367–415.

Kjær, Kim U. (2003) *Flygtning i Danmark. En kommenteret introduktion til det danske asylsystem*, Copenhagen: Akademisk Forlag.

Macklin, Audrey (1999) 'Truth and consequences: credibility determination in the refugee context', in *The Realities of Refugee Determination on the Eve of a New Millennium: The Role of the Judiciary*, ed. International Association of Refugee Law Judges, Haarlem: IARLJ, pp. 134–40.

Noll, Gregor (1999) 'Rejected asylum seekers: the problem of return', *International Migration* 37(1): 267–88.

Parkin, David J. (1999) 'Mementoes as transitional objects in human displacement', *Journal of Material Culture* 4(3): 303–20.

Pietz, William (1985) 'The problem of the fetish, I', *RES: Anthropology and Aesthetics* 9: 5–17.

Pietz, William (1987) 'The problem of the fetish, II: The origin of the fetish', *RES: Anthropology and Aesthetics* 13: 23–45.

Pietz, William (1988) 'The problem of the fetish, IIIa: Bosman's Guinea and the enlightenment theory of fetishism', *RES: Anthropology and Aesthetics* 16: 105–124.

Souter, James (2011) 'A culture of disbelief or denial? Critiquing refugee status determination in the United Kingdom', *Oxford Monitor of Forced Migration* 1(1): 48–59.

Well-Founded Fear (2000) dir. Shari Robertson and Michael Camerini, USA: POV, DVD.

Whyte, Zachary (2009) 'In process: an ethnography of asylum-seeking in Denmark', D.Phil. thesis, University of Oxford.

Whyte, Zachary (2011) 'Enter the myopticon: uncertain surveillance in the Danish asylum system', *Anthropology Today* 27(3): 18–21.

Chapter 8

Emotions as Evidence: Hearings in the French Asylum Court

Carolina Kobelinsky

The ritualized character of legal proceedings has been the subject of numerous studies. In courtroom sessions, everyone plays a particular role; this almost always involves a mode of dress and a predetermined place to occupy in the court. There is also a considerable literature by classical anthropologists on the importance of emotions in ritual behaviour. As rituals, legal hearings both produce a dramatization of the moral relations of the group concerned (Gluckman 1965) and elicit emotions from their participants. In fact, there is an articulation between norms and emotions within ritual. In his study of the ritual system of the Ndembu people of north-western Zambia, Victor Turner showed that in the action situation of ritual, '[n]orms and values, on the one hand, become saturated with emotion, while the gross and basic emotions become ennobled through contact with social values' (1967: 30).

In recent years, in reaction against legal positivism, social scientists have also begun dedicating their attention to the study of emotions in legal proceedings, especially from a feminist perspective (Abrams 2002, 2005) and from psychological or neuroscience-based approaches (Blumental 2005; Maroney 2006). Some philosophers and legal scholars have focused on emotions such as revulsion or disgust in criminal cases involving rape, torture or war crimes (Nussbaum 1990). These studies have illustrated the impact of such negative emotions caused by the victim's testimony (Bandes 1996). Other studies have examined the desire for vengeance as expressed and satisfied by law (Solomon 1990) or the ways in which legal responses to mass violence have channelled emotions away from vengeance (Minow 1998).

In this chapter I move away from criminal courts and examine the emotions at stake in the French National Asylum Court (Cour nationale du droit d'asile or CNDA). This administrative jurisdiction was set up to review appeals against decisions of the French Office for the Protection of Refugees and Stateless Persons (OFPRA), whose responsibilities included granting, refusing and withdrawing refugee status and subsidiary protection. I do not focus here on coping strategies to manage the emotional challenges arising in asylum decision-making, as Baillot, Cowan and Munro (2013) have recently done in the UK context. Instead, I explore the role of emotions in French proceedings and argue that 'benign' emotions felt by adjudicators help explain the success of some applicants in obtaining refugee status. In other words, I show how judges' reliance on their own emotions serves as a technique for dispelling doubt. This chapter is based on ethnographic research conducted at the CNDA in 2009 and 2010.[1] Most of the material was collected from observation of public hearings, *in camera* deliberations (when judges allowed me to attend meetings taking place behind closed doors) and the in-depth work of examining the cases. I also conducted formal interviews and had informal conversations with judges, rapporteurs, lawyers and interpreters.[2]

The chapter is divided into two main parts, each composed of three short sections. The first part deals with the political discourse and bureaucratic organization of asylum in France. In the first section I examine the public discourses surrounding asylum and the central role that suspicion plays in contemporary representations regarding refugees. In the second, I offer a description of the appeal procedure that takes place in the CNDA, displaying the different actors involved in decision-making. The third section provides a description of an ordinary hearing with the aim of illustrating the routinization of adjudication in asylum proceedings. The second part analyses the role of emotions in the courtroom. The first section unfolds an ethnographic vignette where compassion is at stake. The second examines a case of admiration and the third, one of esteem. In all three cases, I show how emotional expressions are channelled into the recognition of state protection. In the conclusion, I point out the ambivalent role of these benign emotions and claim that although the positive emotions studied in the chapter are not displayed very frequently in the everyday practices of the Court, they are crucial if we are to understand how the *intime conviction*[3] of judges is built and how it operates.

Political Discourse and Bureaucratic Practices

The modern legal concept of the 'refugee' was born in the interwar period, when the League of Nations appointed a High Commissioner for Refugees in charge

1 The research on which this paper is based was supported by the European Research Council (n° 230347; ERC-2008-AdG) under its 'Towards a Critical Moral Anthropology' Programme, led by Didier Fassin at the Institut de recherche interdisciplinaire sur les enjeux sociaux (IRIS-EHESS), Paris.

2 I would like to thank the Court authorities for allowing me to carry out fieldwork freely and its agents for sharing their experiences with me. I also want to thank Tony Good for his generous comments on the first version of the chapter and his careful English proof-reading.

3 I shall not problematize this term, employed by the judges, here. I merely note that the notion – which could be translated literally as deep-seated or inner belief – appears in the French Code of Criminal Procedure, based on the idea of 'moral proof' that arose during the eighteenth century (Leclerc 1995). It is then employed in Assize Courts (see Bouillier, this volume). Although it does not appear in any asylum legislation, judges and rapporteurs use it on a frequent basis. Although it is not exactly the same, the equivalent role is played in common-law contexts by the concept of 'standards of proof' (see Good, this volume).

of organizing the assistance provided by some countries and humanitarian organizations to Europeans displaced during the Great War and the Russian Revolution. The conception and practice of asylum changed with the Second World War, however. Since the signing of the 1951 Geneva Convention Relating to the Status of Refugees, the system of recognition and protection of refugees has been developed in each signatory country.

Although France has always shown some economic concerns about the impact that excessive generosity towards refugees would have on the national labour force, refugees generally benefited from a positive outlook during the first decades after the signing of the Convention. As briefly elaborated in the coming sections, this legitimacy has been seriously undermined and has been instead displaced by suspicion. Disbelief has indeed become a key feature of representations and institutional practices concerning asylum seekers. The study of decision-making in the CNDA reveals the central role of suspicion understood as an attitude of mistrust (see Whyte, this volume) or incredulity towards requests for asylum, based on intuition or feelings fuelled by preconceived notions.

Political Discourse and Institutional Figures

Since the Second World War, asylum has been institutionalized in European countries – and elsewhere – under the Geneva Convention of 1951, which provides a formal definition of a refugee in Article 1A(2). The term 'refugee' applies to any person who

> owing to a well-founded fear of being persecuted for reasons of race, religion, nationality, membership of a particular social group or political opinion, is outside the country of his nationality and is unable or, owing to such fear, is unwilling to avail himself of the protection of that country; or who, not having a nationality and being outside the country of his former habitual residence as a result of such events, is unable or, owing to such fear, is unwilling to return to it.

In France two institutions were created to deal with the postwar refugee population: the French Office for the Protection of Refugees and Stateless Persons (OFPRA) and the Appeal Commission for Refugees, which in 2007 became the French National Court of Asylum. These institutions spent the first few years both organizing the asylum system and managing the large influx of European refugees. In 1971, France ratified the 1967 New York Protocol that expanded the scope of the refugee definition, in both a geographic and a temporal sense, opening the possibility of hosting refugees from all over the world.[4] The impact of this development, in terms of volume of requests, however, was not immediate.

---

4 At the time of the ratification of the Geneva Convention, each state could choose between a definition limited to events taking place in Europe before 1 January 1951 or an

When in July 1974, the French government decided to suspend labour migration, applicants for refugee status continued to be admitted in the territory. At the time, the number of asylum applications did not exceed 2,000 and the rate of recognition of status exceeded 85 per cent. Twenty years later, it had dropped to less than 28 per cent for 27,600 claims. According to the OFPRA, the number of applications for the year 2003 was 54,429 while the rate of positive outcomes in the first examination was only 9.8 per cent and reached 14.8 per cent when including the positive decisions made by the Appeal Commission.[5] The increase in the number of applications over the last few decades is often interpreted as evidence that applicants are using indirect means to obtain residence permits. This increase is thus associated with a strategy to circumvent the closure of borders to immigration labour. These assumptions, however, neglect two important realities: (1) the lifting of restrictions of time and space in the Geneva Convention and (2) that until the suspension of labour immigration in 1974 it was easier and faster to get a work permit than refugee status, so many potential candidates for protection under the Convention did not claim asylum as they already had legal residence in France (Spire 2004).

Today a large majority of applicants are refused protection under the Geneva Convention or the Subsidiary Protection regime.[6] Issues of asylum, and more generally issues concerning migration, have become highly politically contested in France and elsewhere in Europe. Suspicion has become a fundamental characteristic of contemporary representations and practices regarding asylum in wealthy countries (see, among others, Daniel and Knudsen 1995; Good 2007; Bohmer and Shuman 2008; Valluy 2009; d'Halluin 2012). Asylum has been constructed as a 'threat' (see, for the UK discourse, Squire 2009) and the public discourse associates asylum seekers with 'bogus refugees' who come not for 'political' reasons but for purely 'economic' motives. Although many scholars have argued that the distinction between political and economic causes of exile is difficult to sustain (Zolberg 1983; Castles and Miller 1993; Schuster 2003), this interpretation appears in most political discourses and in parliamentary debates at both European and national levels.

The discussions in Strasburg, just before the vote that enacted EURODAC, are a good illustration of this. The EURODAC system for the comparison of asylum seekers' fingerprints across the European Union was created, it is said, to facilitate the application of the Dublin Regulation, which established the principle that

expanded definition including events 'in Europe or elsewhere' over that period. The 1967 Protocol then removed the time limit to include more recent events too.

5 These figures are in the 2003 OFPRA report, available at http://www.ofpra.gouv.fr/documents/OFPRA_Rapport_2003.pdf (accessed 8 January 2014).

6 The Immigration Law of 10 December 2003 introduced subsidiary protection as a protection regime which can be granted – by the OFPRA and the Court – to those who are subject to serious threats in their country. More precarious than conventional asylum, subsidiary protection requires an annually renewable residency permit.

only one EU Member State is responsible for examining an asylum application. The objective is to avoid asylum seekers being sent from one country to another. During the debate at the European parliament, the representative of the committee that was asked to study the creation of the system asserted that it was also being created in order 'to prevent multiple applications and thereby also to stop social abuse'.[7] Interestingly, the same discourse associating asylum seekers with abusers of the system also appears in the French context. Speaking about the reform project meant to lead to the so-called Sarkozy Law on Immigration (of 2003), Dominique de Villepin asserted in front of the members of Parliament in 2003, that the persons 'who are truly persecuted are far from representing the majority of the asylum seekers'. De Villepin, Minister of Foreign Affairs at the time, relied heavily on OFPRA statistics, which showed that asylum had been granted to only 13 per cent of applicants. More explicitly, he explained that 'many foreigners petition our system of asylum, not to obtain the protection of our country, but to remain there as long as possible, their motivation being economic in nature'.[8] In the vein of EU harmonization, the 2003 Immigration Law substantially modified the asylum procedure with new restrictive notions – 'application manifestly unfounded' and 'safe country of origin' – effectively allowing the *préfectures* to reject a large number of cases even before their examination by the OFPRA. These rejections relied heavily on the assumption that asylum was a path of economic immigration. Eight years later, Claude Guéant, then Minister of Interior, announced a new reform policy, arguing that the 'asylum system [was] in danger because the *dispositif* [was being] used to enter and remain in our country'.[9]

Appeal Bureaucracy

The atmosphere of distrust towards asylum seekers at national and European levels is also prevalent in the everyday practices of adjudication in the French National Asylum Court. Formerly known as the Commission des recours des réfugiés (CRR – Refugee Appeals Commission), the Cour nationale du droit d'asile (CNDA) examines claims filed by asylum seekers and evaluates whether or not the rejection pronounced by the OFPRA should be upheld or overturned. Although the CNDA is currently under the supervision of the Conseil d'Etat,[10] since 1952

7 European Parliament debates, 18 November 1999, available at http://www.europarl.europa.eu/sides/getDoc.do?pubRef=-//EP//TEXT+CRE+19991118+ITEMS+DOC+XML+V0//EN&language=EN#creitem5 (accessed 19 January 2014).

8 *Comptes rendus des séances de l'Assemblée nationale*, 5 June 2003, p. 4590, available at http://www.assemblee-nationale.fr/12/cri/2002-2003/20030227.asp (accessed 8 January 2014).

9 Quoted in *Le Monde*, available at http://www.lemonde.fr/politique/article/2011/11/25/claude-gueant-annonce-une-reforme-du-droit-d-asile_1609352_823448.html (accessed 8 January 2014).

10 The highest administrative court in France.

the CRR had been under the administration of the OFPRA and therefore reported directly to the institution whose decisions it judged.

When an appeal is recorded by the registry and the case file is requested from the OFPRA, the Court first of all evaluates whether or not it is admissible. The Court can give a direct ruling to reject certain cases due to foreclosure (that is, when the deadline for appeal has expired) and, since 2004, it can also reject cases after an initial evaluation of the well-founded nature of the claim (for example when applications for re-examination do not present any new facts). This process allows a certain number of files to be dismissed very quickly (without a collegial – collective – decision). After this initial selection, a case will be assigned to a rapporteur who will be in charge of investigating the file.

Rapporteurs work for the Court either under contract or as civil servants after obtaining a *concours de la function publique*. Most of them are women under the age of 40. The majority of rapporteurs have degrees in law or political science. They are the only members of the Court to study the cases in depth. They examine the documents provided by the claimant (and his or her legal representative) as well as the documents provided by the OFPRA when the application was initially examined. They must then write a report suggesting in conclusion whether or not the appeal should be rejected or approved and, if approved, which kind of protection should be granted. The rapporteurs sometimes reserve their judgment, either because they are not able to come to a conclusive judgment on the case or because of their reluctance to state a position before certain judges.

The claimant is then summoned to a public hearing where he or she can be provided with an interpreter on oath, in the language of his or her choice, and the advice of a legal representative. It is hardly necessary to emphasize that in general claimants are not aware of the complexity of French administration and law, nor of asylum case law. From 1 December 2008 onwards, all claimants have access to a lawyer paid for by the state, whereas prior to that date only claimants who had entered France legally had access to legal aid. During the hearing, after the court secretary calls the case, the rapporteur summarizes the facts cited by the claimant and the decision made by the OFPRA, presents the supporting documents and suggests a solution. The board of judges then listens to the lawyer and questions the claimant.

The usual board of judges is composed of three members: 1) a Chair, appointed by the vice-president of the Conseil d'Etat from the sitting or honorary members of the Conseil d'Etat or the bodies of the Administrative Tribunals and Administrative Courts of Appeal, or appointed by the first president of the Revenue Court (Cour des comptes) from the sitting or honorary magistrates of the Revenue Court and Regional Revenue Chambers (Chambres régionales des comptes), or appointed by the Minister of Justice (garde des Sceaux), among the sitting magistrates and the honorary magistrates of the judiciary; 2) a 'qualified individual'[11] of French

11 The expression appears as such (*personne qualifiée*) in the official documents and is never clearly defined, but court officials consider that this means someone who, as a rapporteur explained to me, has 'a serious career path, a substantial CV'.

nationality, appointed by the UN High Commissioner for Refugees (UNHCR) upon agreement from the vice-president of the Conseil d'Etat; 3) a qualified individual appointed by the vice-president of the Conseil d'Etat upon the suggestion of one of the ministers represented on the governing board of the OFPRA. The judges making up the board are very often on temporary contracts. This is the case for all the assessors but also for the majority of chairs, despite the fact that, since 2009, twelve permanent magistrates from administrative and legal jurisdictions have been posted to these functions on a full-time basis.

In some exceptional cases, three boards of judges can meet in *sections réunies* (combined sections) in order to evaluate cases referred there by the president of the Court or a board of judges which require the introduction of new case law. The issues at stake here are substantial as the decisions made are intended to then be followed by other judges and to crystallize the position of the Court not only on judicial elements but also, more generally, on political issues, whether in relation to the situation in certain countries or regarding how to deal with a set of claims with the same characteristics.

Decisions – for both ordinary and extraordinary sessions – are made during *in camera* deliberations after the hearing and the rulings are posted three weeks later in the entrance hall of the Court. The CNDA either overturns the OFPRA's decision and grants refugee status or upholds the negative evaluation and the dismissed person is asked to leave French territory within thirty days. In the case of rejection, the dismissed person has one final opportunity to request that the case be re-opened. This procedure entails applying to the *préfecture*, which evaluates the existence of new evidence. In this case, the OFPRA provides a certificate for re-examination and the *préfecture* has to extend the residency permit. The case then passes via the OFPRA and finally back to the Court, where the claimant is given a new public hearing. If this is not successful, the rejection of the application is final. The foreigner then has thirty days in which to leave the country before the *préfecture* issues an 'Obligation to leave France', which, after the thirty days, is a binding measure of removal and can be enforced immediately without any further decision from the administration. The decisions of the Court can be appealed before the Conseil d'Etat for matters of procedure or law. To be admissible, such appeals must be presented by a legal representative before the Conseil d'Etat and the Court of Appeal (Cour de cassation) within two months of notification of the decision. This is a non-suspensive appeal, therefore no residency permit is delivered to the claimant during the assessment period and removal decisions can be enforced. If the Court of Appeal overturns the decision, the appeal is referred back to the French Court of Asylum for re-examination.

Suspicion as Routine

Most of the hearings I observed during my fieldwork started with a rapporteur recommending rejection of the appeal on the basis of the 'vagueness' of the applicant's statements, the lack of evidence provided supporting the narrative or discrepancies between different stories told by the applicant at different times in the procedure. The smallest detail that seems inconsistent, or as Susan Coutin (2001: 84) put it, the smallest 'plot hole in the narrative', is raised by the rapporteur to justify a recommendation to dismiss the appeal.

Miss Abayomi,[12] a 28-year-old Nigerian sits in front of the board composed of a male chair in his sixties, a woman in her fifties and a young male UNHCR assessor. The rapporteur (a man with a law degree who has been working at the Court for five years) starts reading: 'The applicant affirms her father was an IT engineer working for the XXX petrol company and an activist of the MEND [Movement for the Emancipation of the Niger Delta]. He disappeared in 2007 and since then she has been in danger. The different narratives are incomplete and inconsistent. She explains in her written story that she had suffered aggression on 23 June 2007 … but in her oral interview with the OFPRA she stated the episode took place in August 2007. She does not provide any documents to support her narrative concerning either the threats or the disappearance of her father'. He thus recommends rejecting the appeal as the facts stated are not established. The Chair gives the floor to the legal counsel, who says that 'when we provide documents it is suspicious and when we don't it is a problem because we do not have them …'. He explains that his client is not an 'economic refugee' because her family has money in the country and there was no other reason to flee than the threats for her life after her father's disappearance. 'By the way, he may be dead now.' The Chair thanks the lawyer and gives the floor to his colleagues.

UNHCR assessor: 'What did your father do in the MEND?'

The interpreter explains, the claimant answers and the interpreter says: 'He provided information'.

UNHCR assessor: 'Is that all you can say? What kind of information?'

After translation, the woman says, in English: 'I don't know'. Without waiting for the translation, the UNHCR assessor raises another question: 'What was your father's job?'

After translation, the claimant replies in a feeble voice, and the interpreter says: 'I don't know'.

The Chair: 'Do you know your father's degree?'

The interpreter translates, she answers and he says: 'He is an engineer'.

12 All the asylum seekers' names are pseudonyms.

> The Chair: 'So do you have an idea of what he did in the petrol company?'
>
> The interpreter speaks, she replies and then he says: 'No, she says she doesn't know'.
>
> The legal advisor intervenes: 'Please, let me remind you that my client is in a state of shock'.
>
> The Chair: 'I understand, but all this does not seem very credible to me'. And addressing himself to the assessors: 'Do you have other questions?'
>
> They don't and the hearing ends. (field notes, public hearing, July 2009)

I did not have the chance to observe the *in camera* deliberation that day but the administration assessor commented during a session break that there was 'nothing to say' about Miss Abayomi's case. The rapporteur told me afterwards that 'it was obvious that the whole thing was fake'. Most of the hearings are marked by suspicion, especially with regard to the truthfulness of the narrative, the sincerity of the applicant and the authenticity of the documents when they are available.[13]

Like Miss Abayomi's hearing, Mr Muntasir's illustrates a very ordinary day in the courtroom.

> The clerk calls the next case. The young man, from Bangladesh, sits in front of a board of judges composed of a male chair in his fifties, a female UNHCR assessor who seems to be around forty years old and a male assessor from the administration who's been retired for ten years. The female rapporteur (a law graduate, who has been working in the Court for three years) summarizes the case saying that Mr Muntasir states that he belongs to the Bangladesh Nationalist Party (BNP) and that he describes two major violent episodes against him and his family. Nonetheless, he does not provide any evidence to support his statement. She concludes by recommending the rejection of the appeal as 'the facts stated are not established'. The chair of the board of judges thanks the rapporteur and gives the floor to the applicant's counsel who focuses on the 'deplorable and unacceptable' conditions of the interview made by an OFPRA officer who was 'really suspicious of the claimant'. He then briefly emphasizes the difficulties faced by his client in Bangladesh. The Chair thanked the lawyer and starts questioning the claimant.
>
> The Chair of the Board of Judges: 'Why did you join the BNP [Bangladesh Nationalist Party]?' The claimant speaks, the interpreter relates: 'He says he agreed with the ideas of the party'.

13 On credibility assessment in the British context, see Good, in this volume.

> The Chair: 'OFPRA indicates that you have no knowledge of the BNP's organization. How can it be?' The claimant speaks, the interpreter says: 'He says he has knowledge. It is not true what OFPRA says'.
>
> The Chair: 'You have been violently assaulted. Can you give more details? Because, well, the rest of the case is a bit classical among your countrymen: there is a case, you are charged with something, arms sales … It's always like that. Today we had four cases and they all say the same thing'.
>
> The interpreter communicates with the applicant who begins speaking in French, but nobody understands him. He then addresses the interpreter who listens and explains: 'He said I came because I have problems in Bangladesh. I was attacked, I was injured, and my family was threatened'.
>
> The Chair, talking to the other two judges: 'Do you have questions?' Each assessor asks one question. The hearing closes after exactly thirty minutes. (field notes, public hearing, March 2010)

During the deliberation, the Chair of the Board – who is known for being among the most severe – asked the assessors what they thought about the Bangladeshi man. The UNHCR woman replied 'For me it is clearly a no'; the other assessor agreed. The chair concluded: 'This is a rejection for me too. It is always the same thing'.

As with the ethnographic vignettes above, oftentimes the applicants do not present – or present few – documents in support of their narratives. Legal counsel do not often raise significant legal arguments and only sum up the adduced facts insisting on the necessity of granting a particular form of protection. Apart from asylum seekers' difficulty in obtaining evidence to present to the Court in order to support their story, observations of the hearings also convey the inequality of asylum seekers' competences, which seem to be based on social class, level of education and the comprehension of what is really at stake during the hearing. The way the claimant speaks, looks and sits, the way he or she talks, are important elements that help judges to construct their *intime conviction*. In most of the observed hearings, the judges seem to show no emotion or feeling. Comments such as 'we know this story' or 'it is the tenth time we've heard the same thing' are openly expressed by judges during hearings or in the deliberations, showing a sort of frustration with requests which 'are always the same'. The repetitive nature of the cases, together with the routinization of the process of decision-making, lead to an erosion of emotions (Fassin 2001). The indifference of the civil servants (Herzfeld 1992) articulates very often with the economy of suspicion towards asylum seekers, in that narratives that are similar are almost immediately considered fake.

Emotions at Work

In spite of the general absence of emotion during the hearings described above, judges expect a lot from the encounter with the asylum seeker and, in this sense, the Court can still be seen as an 'emotional bureaucracy' (Graham 2002). Sometimes it is a look, a gesture or a word that provokes a reaction and convinces the board of judges of the well-founded nature of an application. Such was the case for a Tamil asylum seeker who, as the judge and rapporteur noted during the deliberation, 'lowered his eyes' as he took from an envelope a photograph of his family, who had been assassinated, and was reluctant to follow his lawyer's request to show it to the judges. This attitude was perceived as a sign of reserve and self-consciousness, emotions attesting to the asylum seeker's sincerity.

Applicants who have been advised by NGO advocates or legal representatives know that the hearing is a staged event (a *mise en scène*; see Garapon 1997) and that they have to somehow perform their *refugeeness* or, to put it more simply, borrowing the terms of an applicant, '[they] have to convince'. Sometimes claimants and lawyers may turn to '*dispositifs de sensibilisation*' (Traïni 2010) – that is, material support, objects, performances, to evoke an emotional response.[14] In so doing, they sometimes deliberately encourage judges' reliance on emotions as a technique for dismissing suspicion.

Before analysing the emotions at stake in the courtroom, it seems important to clarify how I consider this notion. In accordance with anthropological works on emotions since the 1980s, I do not understand emotions as mere physical reactions opposed to reason, as was conceived by a 'Euro-American middle-class' (Lutz 1988). I do not oppose them either to any kind of subsequent mental work – usually called sentiment.[15] Rather, I consider emotions, following Michelle Rosaldo, as 'embodied thoughts, thoughts seeped with the apprehension that "I am involved". Thought/affect [that] bespeaks the difference between a mere hearing of a child's cry and a hearing *felt*' (1984: 143). These 'embodied thoughts' appear as interpretations of the objects or situations that arouse emotion.

Ethnography – both as a method and as a practice of knowledge – does not provide the tools to penetrate the mental processes of the judges. I cannot know exactly what someone else is feeling in the same way as I cannot exactly know what someone else thinks when he or she says something. In both cases, as John Leavitt (1996: 529) put it, I interpret, I postulate meaning for the words, gestures or tears. I will then try to articulate here my interpretations of what the judges felt and thought with what they remembered and spoke about. In this sense, I attach great importance both to what I observe that seems to express emotions and to the judges' narrative on their own feelings (see Crapanzano 1994).

---

14 Similarly, the judges will be more or less sensitive and 'emotional' regarding their own careers, trajectories and social characteristics.

15 In this sense, following Hochschild (2003) I use the terms 'emotion' and 'sentiment' interchangeably.

According to the judges' comments, it seems that the emotional expressions that arise during the face-to-face encounter with the applicant are based on three factors: 1) physical aspects of the performance offered by the claimant during the hearing: his or her way of speaking, his or her 'bodily hexis' (Bourdieu 1977), his or her tears, and so on; 2) the evocative power of the narrative that appears in the report and in the counsel's speech referring to the story told by the applicant; and 3) prior images that judges may have concerning the geopolitical context of the claim, linking the particular claim to a more general (and news-media-based) imagery.

In the following section, in order to understand the role of judges' emotions in decision-making at the Court, I analyse these factors in three cases where the applicant was granted asylum despite the rapporteur's recommendation that the case be rejected, or his or her reserve of judgment (*réserve d'avis*).[16]

Compassion

The following vignette summarizes the hearing of Mr Samir, a 34-year-old Sudanese man from Darfur, which took place in April 2010.

> The applicant sits facing the judges. The rapporteur starts reading: 'This Sudanese man, Berti and Muslim, has always lived in Darfur. After completing two months of military training in Khartoum, he returned home and did not report for military service. Unable to obtain a high school degree, as a result of this failure, he devoted himself to working in agriculture. Then, thanks to money sent by one of his two brothers, who lives in Libya, he started a business selling cattle. Shortly after, he got married. When, in 2005, his village was attacked by Sudanese government forces, assisted by Janjaweed militiamen, he managed to flee with his wife, but his sister, his half-brother, his father and grandmother were killed in these events. A few months later, two government agents posing as members of the rebellion came to his shop and tried in vain to make him confess sympathy for the rebellion. He was then arrested by soldiers and was taken to a military camp. There he was abused, and accused of belonging to the rebel group JEM [Justice and Equality Movement]. Having been quickly interviewed, he was subjected to forced labour in the camp, where he was the only prisoner. After months of detention, he managed to escape during an attack by the rebels. He walked to a nearby village where a cousin told him that his village had been completely destroyed and that his wife and daughter were in West Darfur. He then went to Al Fasher to get money from an uncle (2,000,000 Sudanese pounds, or about 650,000 euros), and from there went to Mallit where one of his two brothers resides. He then decided to leave the country. With

16 Although in the three cases presented the asylum seekers are male I by no means imply that these positive emotions only arose with male candidates.

> the help of smugglers, he made it to Tripoli. He then travelled to Algeria and to France'.
>
> 'In sum', says the rapporteur, 'the applicant claims to be persecuted because he escaped from a military camp where he was detained after being falsely accused of belonging to the Sudanese rebellion, and because of his refusal to do military service'. In his conclusion, the rapporteur indicates that the claim raises difficulties in ascertaining the nationality and origin of the applicant. Although his oral statement at the OFPRA broadly confirms his written narrative on the description of the geography of his home region, this is not supported by any documentary evidence. The claimant reports that all his documents were destroyed during the attack on his village. The rapporteur stresses that the applicant has no evidence to support his narrative. Finally he notes that the claimant provided no specific evidence to establish that he would be persecuted. Therefore he recommends dismissing the appeal on the grounds that the alleged facts are not sufficiently established.
>
> At the end of the reading, the applicant's counsel takes the floor emphasizing the chaotic situation in Darfur and his client's distress, especially since he lost his entire family. The board of judges then proceeds to ask questions regarding the death of his family and the situation in Darfur. One judge inquires about the conditions of detention and the applicant describes the forced labour and the torture he was subjected to. He starts crying and is no longer able to speak. He lowers his head and says, 'I was treated like a slave'. There is a moment of silence. When he seems recovered, the UNHCR assessor affirms, 'That's what has happened; it is tragic, we have all that on file. But I would just like to ask a question concerning his fear of return. What are his fears if he returns?' The interpreter translates and the man answers in a very feeble voice. The interpreter explains that he fears the Janjaweed militia. There are no further questions. During the deliberation, the discussion about this case does not last more than two minutes. All board members agree to grant him asylum.

Several factors come into play here to help overturn the initial recommendation of refusal made by the rapporteur. The report and the counsel's speech give a picture of the applicant's history as 'particularly difficult', in that his family has died or disappeared, and he himself was subjected to degrading treatment. His tears during the hearing arouse emotion from the board, composed of a young male assessor with a background in law and two women aged about forty, known to be severe in their judgments. The rapporteur, a 34-year-old man with a law degree and much experience at the Court, was also very affected, as he told me later in the afternoon. People in the room seem touched by the situation as well, not a sound was heard for several seconds. I was also stirred. The man slumped in a chair, weeping, a hand over his face, his voice broken, embodies the victim who suffers. The pathos here is the spring that propels the proposal from negative to positive status.

The emotion caused by the applicant's image, but also by the dramatic narrative, and the prior images that the judges may have had about the widely publicized conflict in Darfur, lead to a form of compassion. As Luc Boltanski (1993) points out, the possibilities of being affected feed on collective images from the media, fiction narratives, art pieces, political pamphlets and so forth. When I spoke with one of the judges some days after this hearing, she emphasized the 'chaos' and 'all we've seen and all we've heard', implicitly referring herself to the media images of the Darfur conflict.

Despite the lack of documentary support, the applicant's expression appears here as an indicator of his sincerity, as the young assessor pointed out during the deliberation. It embodies his suffering and the emotion he evokes is the sign of the truthfulness of the story.

Admiration

The vignette that follows describes the hearing of Mr Begum – a 32-year-old Bangladeshi – in June 2010.

> The applicant sits, following the interpreter's directions. The rapporteur starts reading: 'Very young, Mr Begum joined the youth wing of the Awami League, in high school and then in university. He served as the secretary for the literary and cultural affairs division. He was particularly involved in theatre activities. He became secretary of propaganda for the League in an area of his hometown; he was then elected to the District Executive Committee. In addition to his political activities, he also worked with his father as a furniture manufacturer. He says he was assaulted along with his comrades after a theatrical performance. A few months later, he participated in a demonstration that was attacked by members of the Bangladesh National Party and Jammaat-E-Islami. He was wounded and hospitalized for six days. He filed a complaint with the police after the death of a comrade during this incident. Nevertheless, nobody was arrested. In retaliation, he was then threatened and forced to withdraw the complaint. Following the discovery of a concealed weapon (planted in his home by his opponents), he was put on trial for illegal possession of weapons. After being arrested by the police, he was brought before the court and was sent to the city prison. He was released on bail after six months. Following his release he continued his political struggle but also invested in social initiatives. He participated in a protest against the attacks of August 2005. The protest was then attacked by members of opposing parties but he managed to escape. Soon after, he learned by telephone that he was accused of causing the death of one demonstrator, a member of Jammaat-E-Islami, and a new case was launched against him as well as eleven of his comrades. Knowing that he was wanted by the agents of the Rapid Action Battalion, he left his city and hid with distant relatives. With violence erupting throughout the country he was no longer able to continue living under these conditions, so he left Bangladesh for France with a fake passport'.

> In support of his narrative, the applicant has provided his party membership card, complaints and rulings against him as well as medical certificates indicating the existence of physical injuries. In his conclusion, the rapporteur adds that the written and oral statements of the claimant reflect a good knowledge of the Awami League and the structures of the party. If the actual level of responsibilities held by the applicant is difficult to define with certainty, the fact remains that Mr Begum was entrusted with certain responsibilities that seem very plausible, especially given his long-term activism. His remarks on his persecution are relatively accurate and his description of his detention in prison is convincing. Nonetheless, the rapporteur decides to reserve his opinion because of political changes that had just brought the applicant's party to power. [The Awami League came to power in December 2008.]
>
> The claimant's counsel takes the floor emphasizing the applicant's ten-year prison sentence. He also notes that the Court has given asylum to League members even after their rise to power. The Chair then begins to ask the claimant many very specific questions – nine to be exact – on the party's organization, its coming to power, details of the events in which he participated and his responsibilities within the Awami League. The man answers easily and at length; the interpreter translates. The administration assessor asks him why he would have problems if he returns to his country. He explains that despite the change at the head of power, things remain precarious in Bangladesh. The UNHCR assessor has no question and the Chair ends the hearing.
>
> When the case is discussed during the deliberations, the chair comments, 'This is a true activist', '*lui, chapeau!*' The UNHCR assessor indicates that the petitioner 'could have trouble if he returned'. The other judges agree. The administration assessor says that 'he answered passionately!' 'There is no problem of authenticity [concerning the documents].' The three judges agree to reverse the OFPRA's rejection and grant him asylum.

The rapporteur also seems to agree with the decision. She will later explain to me that she was 'leaning towards giving him a cancellation [a favourable decision for the claimant]' when she examined the case but she was not '100 per cent sure', which is why she chose to reserve her judgment. Political commitment by the applicant appears to be sincere because it is attested by both the documents provided (from the Awami League, the claims and rulings against him, the medical certificates of physical injury) and the ease with which he was able to provide details of the party's organization during the hearing. The fluidity of his speech and the absence of hesitation are seen as a form of spontaneity, interpreted by members of the board as a sign of truthfulness. The documents and the narrative provided seem afterwards convincing even for the rapporteur. The spontaneity and fluidity of the applicant's speech made him a man worthy of admiration. I use the term admiration here as it implies approval of something or someone that is respected, whose qualities are emphasized. Indeed, the applicant embodied the figure of the refugee par excellence, namely the activist persecuted for his political beliefs, or as one judge exclaimed, the 'activist' ('*le militant*').

Esteem

The final vignette summarizes Mr Jackson's hearing, which took place in May 2010 The claimant was a 25-year-old man from Cameroon.

> The young man greets the judges and proceeds to take a seat. The rapporteur starts the reading: 'Mr Jackson asserts he is the son of a former senior judge and a former Minister for Territorial Administration, who presented himself as a presidential candidate and died under mysterious circumstances shortly after the announcement of his candidacy. His mother has tried to send him abroad to continue his graduate studies, but the authorities refused to issue him a passport. He began to study international business in Yaoundé where he met the son of the head of the opposition party Social Democratic Front (SDF), responsible for the mobilization of youth in the 6th district of Yaoundé. The claimant says he took part in a demonstration where he was arrested, detained and subject to abuse. He explains that, through bribery, he managed to escape and leave Cameroon'. The rapporteur explains that the OFPRA rejected his request and that while his statement regarding his family was credible, it was vague and imprecise with regard to his political commitments and activities in the opposition.
>
> In his conclusions, the rapporteur recommends the dismissal of the appeal arguing that although the applicant's narrative is credible concerning his links with the SDF, it lacks details regarding the role and daily activities of the party's members. After the counsel's very brief remarks, the judges ask several questions regarding the status and activities of the petitioner's father. The applicant is fluent in French and does not need the help of the interpreter. The Chair asks about the threats he was subjected to and about the death of his father. The claimant replies explaining how he was constantly being watched. There was one question about his involvement with the opposition party. Following that, there are only four additional questions before the Chair of the board of judges closes the hearing.
>
> During the deliberation, when this case is discussed, the Chair immediately states that 'the young Cameroonian is all good', and nodding his head, the UNHCR assessor affirms. The rapporteur indicates that nobody questioned him about his political activities and the Chair replies: 'It is nothing; he is the son of his father'. The administration assessor adds: 'This young man is very good'. They all agree to reverse the OFPRA's decision and to grant him refugee status.

Unlike the rapporteur, the judges are more flexible with regard to this young man's political commitments. For the judges, what seems to matter is that he belongs to a prominent family in the country and is openly engaged in politics. Based on the Chair's assessment, particularly his statement 'he is the son of his father', one might assume that Mr Jackson's father was somehow linked to the claimant's fear of persecution. However, during the hearing, there was no indication of such a connection, at least not a clear one. It is important to know that the Chair is known as a generous judge, an opinion he explicitly has of himself. The focus of the judges seems therefore to have been less on facts, as the assessor of the administration explained to me later, than on their positive view of this young 'educated' and French-speaking individual who evidently came from a 'cultured family'. Behind this lies the idea – often openly admitted by some judges concerning particular asylum seekers, but implicit in this case – that the cultural capital of the applicant can facilitate his 'integration' into French society. The criterion of integration is an important element for the assessor of the administration who participated in this hearing. This assessor, a retired teacher, repeatedly asks questions with regard to the claimant's level of French and often makes comments in this regard during the deliberations.

Esteem operates here as a positive feeling that one attaches to a person of value (or considered as such) and his or her qualities. It is a feeling that establishes a relationship of empathy between the judges and the applicant as individuals sharing the same language and a set of codes and manners specific to their social class. Esteem is then a way to establish class affinities, a form of complicity that can be recognized by the other. Here, perhaps more than in other cases, the sympathy felt by the judges works, following Adam Smith's theory of sentiments (2009 [1759]), as a mechanism to share one's joys and sufferings with others. The image of the young man works like a mirror, the applicant becoming a kind of alter ego.

The Ambivalence of Emotions

The hearings in the French Court of Asylum can be seen as rituals that articulate certain norms and values and that may elicit emotions among judges. My previous work among asylum seekers showed that the court hearings also provoke particular feelings – namely anxiety and fear – among claimants (Kobelinsky 2010). Concerning adjudicators, despite the routinization of their work leading to the erosion of emotions when listening to stories of persecution, or perhaps because of this routine's nature and this indifference, face-to-face encounters with applicants occasionally arouse emotions that come to be treated as evidence and can in fact dispel suspicion. This is worth noting, considering how suspicion is, as shown in the first part of this chapter, a strikingly important feature of representations and practices on asylum in France nowadays – as in other rich countries that select the 'real refugees' from among thousands of claimants.

I argued in the second part of the chapter that hearings are occasionally interpreted by judges through positive emotions, dispelling suspicion and opening the possibility for a decision favourable to the claimant. This is indeed a quite simplified outline of what in fact happens in the courtroom. However, it helps us understand the actual process of adjudication. The applicant's way of speaking or sitting, the narrative synthesized by the rapporteur and the counsel, the judges' prior understanding of the geopolitical and social context of the case – all these elements contribute to decision-making. It seems that the judges can sometimes feel a certain connection with the claimant – because of a sort of class affinity and the esteem it creates, the respect and approval that come together with admiration, or the wish to protect that resides in compassion. Avoiding the classical dichotomy between the spontaneous reaction (considered an emotion) and the following mental work (considered a sentiment), I could have used both terms here interchangeably. However I just referred to emotions thus emphasizing that it is all about 'embodied thoughts', and not mere physical reactions, which lead to the desire to protect the applicant, thus allowing the judges to bypass 'weaknesses' in the cases (for example the absence of supporting evidence, the inconsistency of the narrative). Judges' reliance on their own feelings during the encounter with the claimant (and his or her story) works then as a technique for dispelling suspicion. However, it is not a tool deliberately encouraged as such by judges or rapporteurs. Most judges I talked to reject the importance of emotions in decision-making while at the same time they may talk to their colleagues – and even to me – about how affected they were when listening to a particular narrative or the admiration they felt in front of a particular claimant.

These rare emotions, however, are ambivalent. The truth which they seem to attest can in fact lead to the granting of refugee status; nonetheless, their absence in most other cases strengthens the legitimacy of frequent refusals, as the majority of the claims (and claimants) do not elicit positive feelings. In this sense, judges' belief in emotions serves at the same time as a technique for dispelling and creating suspicion. I suggest that this ambivalence characterizes the everyday practices of adjudication in the French Court of Asylum.

References

Abrams, Kathryn (2002) '"Fighting fire with fire": rethinking the role of disgust in hate crimes', *California Law Review* 90(5): 1423–64.

Abrams, Kathryn (2005) 'Legal feminism and the emotions: three moments in an evolving relationship', *Harvard Journal of Law & Gender* 28: 325–44.

Baillot, Helen, Cowan, Sharon and Munro, Vanessa E. (2013) 'Second-hand emotion? Exploring the contagion and impact of trauma and distress in the asylum law context', *Journal of Law and Society* 40(4): 509–40.

Bandes, Susan (1996) 'Empathy, narrative, and victim impact statements', *University of Chicago Law Review* 63(2): 361–412.

Blumental, John (2005) 'Law and the emotions: the problems of affective forecasting', *Indiana Law Journal* 80: 155–238.

Bohmer Carol and Shuman, Amy (2008) *Rejecting Refugees: Political Asylum in the 21st Century*, Abingdon: Routledge.

Boltanski, Luc (1993) *La souffrance à distance. Morale humanitaire, médias et politique*, Paris: Métailié.

Bourdieu, Pierre (1977) *Outline of a Theory of Practice*, Cambridge: Cambridge University Press.

Castles, Stephen and Miller, Mark (1993) *The Age of Migration: International Population Movements in the Modern World*, London: Macmillan.

Coutin, Susan B. (2001) 'The oppressed, the suspect, and the citizen: subjectivity in competing accounts of political violence', *Law & Social Inquiry* 26(1): 63–94.

Crapanzano, Vincent (1994) 'Réflexions sur une anthropologie des émotions', *Terrain* 22: 109–17.

Daniel, E. Valentine and Knudsen, John Chr. (1995) *Mistrusting Refugees*, Berkeley: University of California Press.

d'Halluin, Estelle (2012) *Les épreuves de l'asile. Associations et réfugiés face aux politiques du soupçon*, Paris: Editions de l'EHESS.

Fassin, Didier (2001) 'Charité bien ordonnée. Principes de justice et pratiques de jugement dans l'attribution des aides d'urgence', *Revue française de sociologie* 42(3): 437–75.

Garapon, Antoine (1997) *Bien Juger. Essai sur le rituel judiciaire*, Paris: Odile Jacob.

Gluckman, Max (1965) *Politics, Law and Ritual in Tribal Society*, Oxford: Basil Blackwell.

Good, Anthony (2007) *Anthropology and Expertise in the Asylum Courts*, Abingdon: Routledge-Cavendish.

Graham, Mark (2002) 'Emotional bureaucracies: emotions, civil servants, and immigrants in the Swedish welfare state', *Ethos* 30(3): 199–226.

Herzfeld, Michael (1992) *The Social Production of Indifference: Exploring the Symbolic Roots of Western Bureaucracy*, Oxford: Berg.

Hochschild, Arlie (2003) 'Travail émotionnel, règles de sentiments et structure sociale', *Travailler* 9(1): 19–49.

Kobelinsky, Carolina (2010) *L'accueil des demandeurs d'asile. Une ethnographie de l'attente*, Paris: Editions du Cygne.

Leavitt, John (1996) 'Meaning and feeling in the anthropology of emotions', *American Ethnologist* 23(3): 514–39.

Leclerc, Henri (1995) 'L'intime conviction du juge: norme démocratique de la preuve', in *Le for intérieur*, *Actes du colloque AFSP/CURAPP*, Paris: Presses universitaires de France, pp. 206–13.

Lutz, Catherine (1988) *Unnatural Emotions: Everyday Sentiments on a Micronesian Atoll and Their Challenge to Western Theory*, Chicago: University of Chicago Press.

Maroney, Terry (2006) 'Law and emotion: a proposed taxonomy of an emerging field', *Law and Human Behavior* 30(2): 119–42.
Minow, Martha (1998) *Between Vengeance and Forgiveness: Facing History after Genocide and Mass Violence*, Boston: Beacon Press.
Nussbaum, Martha (1990) '"Secret sewers of vice": disgust, bodies, and the law', in *The Passions of Law*, ed. Susan Bandes, New York and London: New York University Press, pp. 19–62.
Rosaldo, Michelle (1984) 'Toward an anthropology of self and feeling', in *Culture Theory: Essays on Mind, Self and Emotion*, ed. Richard A. Shweder and Robert A. Le Vine, Cambridge: Cambridge University Press, pp. 137–57.
Schuster, Liza (2003) *The Use and Abuse of Political Asylum in Britain and Germany*, London and Portland, OR: Frank Cass.
Smith, Adam (2009 [1759]) *The Theory of Moral Sentiments*, London: Penguin Books.
Solomon, Robert C. (1990) 'Justice vs. vengeance: on law and the satisfaction of emotion', in *The Passions of Law*, ed. Susan Bandes, New York and London: New York University Press, pp. 123–48.
Spire, Alexis (2004) 'Les réfugiés, une main-d'œuvre à part? Conditions de séjour et d'emploi, France 1945–1975', *Revue européenne des migrations internationales* 20(2): 13–38.
Squire, Vicki (2009) *The Exclusionary Politics of Asylum*, Basingstoke and New York: Palgrave.
Traïni, Christophe (2010) 'Des sentiments aux émotions (et vice-versa). Comment devient-on militant de la cause animale?', *Revue française de science politique* 60(2): 335–58.
Turner, Victor (1967) *The Forest of Symbols: Aspects of Ndembu Ritual*, Ithaca and London: Cornell University Press.
Valluy, Jérôme (2009) *Rejet des exilés. Le grand retournement du droit d'asile*, Bellecombe-en-Bauges: Editions du Croquant.
Zolberg, Aristide R. (1983) 'The formation of new states as a refugee generating process', *Annals of the American Academy of Political and Social Science* 467(1): 24–38.

Afterword

Tobias Kelly

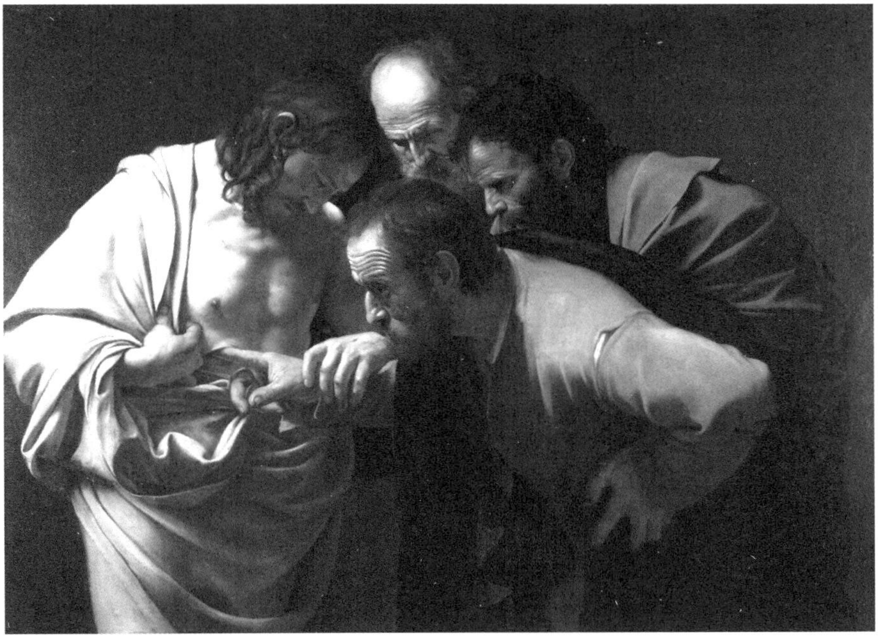

Figure A.1 ***The Incredulity of Saint Thomas*, Caravaggio (1601–1602). Reproduced by permission of the Stiftung Preußische Schlösser und Gärten Berlin-Brandenburg. Photographer: Hans Bach**

Doubting Thomas

Caravaggio's seventeenth-century painting *The Incredulity of Saint Thomas* is one of the most iconic depictions of doubt in European art. The picture portrays Thomas leaning towards a partially robed Jesus (Figure A.1). Thomas's face shows what might be taken as a slightly quizzical, even surprised, look, his right hand is outstretched and his index finger is poking into an open wound on Jesus' right flank. Caravaggio's famous picture refers to the even more famous biblical story. In this story, Thomas is supposed to have questioned the resurrection of Jesus, saying 'unless I see the nail marks in his hands and put my finger where the nails were, and put my hand into his side, I will not believe it'. When Jesus later appeared before Thomas, he is reported to have told the apostle to touch the wounds and end his doubts.

The picture, painted in Caravaggio's characteristic dramatic style, can be seen as a portrayal of deep scepticism, of the original Doubting Thomas, who would not believe until he had actually thrust his finger into the bleeding body of Christ. However, there is another reading of the picture. It can also be interpreted as an image of certainty, rather than disbelief. The art historian Glen Most (2005) suggests that Caravaggio's painting should be seen as a depiction of conviction. The thrusting of the finger into the open wound provides Thomas with the evidence he needs to firmly believe in the resurrection, and therefore forms the basis of Christian faith. The painting is not therefore an image of disbelief, but of certitude and verification.

I start this Afterword with *The Incredulity of Saint Thomas* because it points to two of the central points raised by this insightful and thought-provoking collection. First, it shows how doubt and conviction are not inherently opposed. The doubt of the apostle Thomas is not pure scepticism, but is based on, and ultimately leads to, a strong faith. Thomas' doubt is central to his belief. Speaking more broadly, the Latin root of the word doubt, *duo*, implies a doubling. To doubt therefore means to be in two minds (MacGregor 1989; see also Pelkmans 2013). Doubt is therefore distinct from disbelief and scepticism, as it still implies a measure of commitment, however torn. Indeed, commitment can actually be sustained in large measure by doubt. Belief is not undermined by hesitation and uncertainty, but can be strengthened by it. By being in two minds, rather than none, there is always an alternative decision to make, a different path to take and second commitment to make. While this can lead to anxiety and indecision, it is a very different emotional experience and social phenomenon from apathy or cynicism. Doubt is a social process forever on the move. It does not retreat into languidness. As the chapters in this collection show, commitment and doubt can therefore be tied up with one another. What is important is how this sense of 'being in two minds' is controlled and channelled in particular directions.

Second, Caravaggio's painting highlights the ways in which claims of doubt, and indeed any form of knowledge, are caught up with what might be called particular sensory economies. The evidence of the senses produces their own culturally and historically specific forms of conviction and uncertainty. For Thomas, the verbal claims of the other apostles were not, on their own, enough to help him believe. He could only believe once he had not only *seen* the resurrected Jesus, but also *touched* and *felt* the wounds of the crucifixion. However, the prioritization of sight and touch as pathways to knowledge is far from universal. Even within Christianity, Thomas' prioritization of physical affirmation has been read either as part of a tradition that emphasizes the physical experience of faith or as an example of the failure to understand that 'true faith' does not require physical evidence. Taken together, the chapters in this volume explore the ways in which the sensory and emotional assessment of different forms of evidence can both produce and overcome doubt.

Doubt and the Social

Doubt is a crucial, although often unexamined, part of the anthropological endeavour. The sense that things can always be otherwise, the search for surprise or what Jane Guyer (2013) has called, paraphrasing the writer Ben Okri, 'the quickening of the unknown', is what motivates much anthropological enquiry. Guyer draws our attention to an 'epistemology of surprise', which explicitly seeks out those moments of cognitive dissonance, where we are not entirely sure what is going on. Indeed, the sense that we do not know is a central motivation for many anthropological projects. If we knew what we were going to find out, if we were certain about our assumption about other people and their way of life, there would be no point in being an anthropologist.

Anthropology, with its scepticism towards universal categories, can be seen as part of a wider intellectual tradition that sees 'honest doubting' as the only solid basis for rigorous convictions (Dewey 1934: 87). As is pointed out in the introduction to this volume, Handelman (1987) has praised the central role that doubt can play in anthropology, by showing where theories, models and assumptions break down. Doubt then is central to the production of anthropological knowledge. This is a doubting that does not necessarily descend into nihilistic scepticism, although at times it certainly can. Rather, it is an epistemological stance that assumes things are never entirely as they seem. Crucially, at the same time, most anthropologists recognize that complete scepticism would make anthropological enquiry impossible. Most anthropologists are ready to accept some things as given, to hold them in place, even if their status is not entirely settled and we never take them entirely for granted. This is doubt in the tradition of Wittgenstein, who saw doubt as taking place within a realm of belief. As he wrote: 'If you tried to doubt everything you would not get as far as doubting anything' (Wittgenstein 1972: 18). To doubt everything would get you nowhere, and would undermine the very grounds upon which you base your doubts.

Doubt is central to anthropology in other ways too. It may well be that the central object of anthropological enquiry, namely the possibility of social and cultural life, is inherently shot through with doubt. Hannah Arendt, for example, saw social life as fundamentally built on uncertainty. She argues

> that he who acts never quite knows what he is doing, that he always becomes 'guilty' of consequences he never intended or even foresaw, that no matter how disastrous and unexpected the consequences of his deed he can never undo it, that the process he starts is never consummated unequivocally in one single deed or event. (Arendt 1958: 233)

For Arendt, social life is a gamble, whose outcomes are always unknown, but we have no choice but to play the odds. Predicting the future is notoriously difficult, as soothsayers, economists, weather forecasters and other prophets know only too well, but we are under pressure to do so nevertheless.

However, it is not just the future that is unknown, or even unknowable. The past and present can be equally inscrutable. For anthropologists such as Veena Das, for example, building on the work of Wittgenstein and Stanley Cavell, social interaction is built on uncertainty in the unknowability of others' minds, and as a result we take a leap of faith whenever we put our trust in others, as we inevitably must do. For Das, there is a fundamental hesitancy 'in the ways in which we habitually dwell amongst our concepts of culture, of everyday life' (1998: 172). Stanley Cavell (1988) has similarly stressed how even our most intimate relationships are caught up in a struggle to read each other (see also Segal, forthcoming). We do not have to have Cavell's and Das's apparently tragic disposition to recognize that doubt can play a foundational role in our social and cultural interactions. Conversations where we were certain what people would say would be rather pointless. Intimate relations that were entirely predictable would soon lose their attraction, or at least they would for many people. Political and economic exchanges where the results were predetermined, and known to be so, would soon wither and die. On a day-to-day level, the trust we place in others is also premised on doubt. We trust precisely because we are not sure. Things could go either way, but we hope we know which way that will be.

The chapters in this volume focus on two particular forms of doubt. The first is doubts about other people. These types of doubts are doubts about the people we have in front of us and whether they really are all they seem to be. In this volume these doubts often take the shape of questions over expertise. Does the judge or diviner, for example, really know what they are talking about, have they mastered the arts they practise, are they acting out of good faith or are they hiding something? This can be seen as part of the scepticism that for scholars such as Das and Cavell can run through all social interactions. As Budniok shows in this volume, Ghanaians constantly question the integrity of the judiciary, seeing behind their every action possible corruption. People simply do not believe what they take to be the pretence of neutral, objective and independent legality claimed by the judges. Similarly, in a very different context, Homola shows, also in this volume, how the clients of Taiwanese diviners often fail to trust those claiming superior knowledge. Diviners are often suspected of being charlatans or fraudsters.

The second form of doubt, which is linked to the first, concerns whether the scraps of evidence upon which we build our judgments about the world have been interpreted correctly. This is a form of doubt described most famously by Max Weber (2013 [1904–1905]). Weber's ascetic Protestants might (or might not) have been certain of their own faith, but what they were less certain about was whether they were among God's chosen. They were therefore forced to read the material world for signs of God's grace, but were forever anxious that they had read these signs incorrectly. At stake in such doubts is our ability to interpret the clues, to construct theories and assumptions out of partial shards of evidence, to reason inductively and to be aware that we might always have interpreted things wrongly. We think we have it right, but we are not entirely sure.

Doubts caused by the limits of inductive reason can concern the past or the future. Divination, for example, seeks to decipher traces of information about the past in order to uncover otherwise hidden forces and processes. As Tarabout shows in this volume, astrologers try to make sense of a mass of potentially cryptic signs in order to interpret events in the present and put in place remedies for any potential future misfortune. In a very different context, as Good also shows in this volume, cricket umpires have to predict where the ball might have gone had it not hit a batsman. Until recently all umpires had to go on is what happened in the past, but no two balls are exactly the same, and the art of a good bowler is precisely to deceive the batsman by varying the flight of the ball. More recently, the introduction of technology has meant that predictions can be based on computer simulations. However, even with these simulations there is a margin of error, creating new spaces for doubt, especially when computer technology contradicts the expectations of the naked eye. Sometimes, legal judges too are forced to project into the future, to make predictions about the risk to asylum seekers, for example, based solely on events in the past or present. Most commonly, though, the law is concerned with the past. Judges and juries, for example, must piece together the evidence to try to come to a decision about 'what happened' at a particular time and place that has since passed. Either way, doubts inevitably remain over whether the necessarily incomplete pieces of evidence have been interpreted correctly.

Managing Doubt

The important point to make is that doubt does not, necessarily, imply that scepticism is overwhelming and all encompassing. The crucial contribution that these chapters make is to show the varied ways in which we are able to put these uncertainties to one side and to move on. This is where the sense of doubt as being 'in two minds' is important. In all of the chapters in this volume, at some point, a decision is made to choose between one of these 'two minds', and then people act 'as if' certainty has been reached. To point to uncertainty, anxiety, hesitation and confusion is one thing, and even risks being banal. What is much more interesting is to recognize that people still continue to make decisions, to have firm convictions, to believe in other people, despite, or even because of, these uncertainties. What is significant is not that people are unsure about what to do, or whether to trust the people in front of them, but that they find ways to overcome these hesitations.

The chapters in this volume demonstrate the multiple ways for what Tarabout calls the 'management of doubt', or what the editors also refer to in this volume as 'technologies of doubt'. The use of the language of technique and management is important here, as there is no necessary deep claim about truth in these methods for controlling doubt. Rather, there is a practical concern with making particular forms of social life possible. Doubt is not necessarily eradicated here, but put to one side, frozen in time and space, while people find ways to get on with life.

The dual focus of this volume on ritual and law, or even the rituals of law, is particularly appropriate, as both represent key devices for the practical management of doubt. Neither ritual nor law seek to destroy doubt. Indeed, as Berti points out in her contribution to this volume, rituals might even make doubt possible by inviting reflection on particular claims to truth. The same could be said of legal processes too. Judicial truth is famously distant from more everyday notions of 'what really happened'. As such, law and ritual can be understood as techniques for helping people to decide between their 'two minds'. In these processes doubts are controlled and channelled rather than eradicated. The British asylum process, for example, described here by Good, attempts to manage and control doubt, turning it ultimately into a form of narrow judicial truth. It does so through the deployment of technical legal categories of assessment, such as the burden and standard of proof. Rituals too can involve technical processes for the management of doubt. As Homola describes in this volume, for example, Taiwanese diviners can be keen to stress that their work is a scientific process, with standardized techniques and procedures.

Law though differs here from other forms of ritual, in that it is in a particularly strong position to have the final say on questions of doubt. Technical legal procedures may open up questions of doubt, but once a decision is made, the issue is closed, at least for the time being (see Tarabout, this volume). Whether people are convinced or not, they are forced, or able, to act 'as if' they are. A judicial or legal decision can put in place a chain of events that simply leaves behind previous scepticism. A judge or a jury may have been in two minds, but in the end only one of those minds counts. A convict is not a little bit guilty, a couple are not partially divorced, a forced migrant is not half a refugee. Legal processes come down on one side or the other, and have the institutional resources to make this stick. It matters little whether the general public, or even the lawyers and judges involved, are entirely convinced, or have had their doubts eradicated, reasonable or otherwise. What matters is that a decision has been reached. It is for this reason that the law is a particularly powerful technique for the management of doubt.

A Sense of Doubt

Let us return here to the picture with which this Afterword started. For Caravaggio's incredulous Thomas, seeing and feeling really was believing. Yet, the prioritization of touch and sight as paths to the truth is far from universal. Maurice Bloch (2008) has gone so far as to argue that the privileging of sight as a pathway to the truth can be generalized cross-culturally. The empirical tradition in philosophy and science has also emphasized the greater truthfulness of what is seen over what is reported through language. In contrast, though, Martin Jay

(1994) has claimed that twentieth-century French thought in particular has sought to challenge the privileged position of sight in giving access to the world. In a very different context Alfred Gell (1995) has argued that the Umeda of Papua New Guinea value hearing above vision. The important point to make is that in the assessment of evidence, the priority given to different senses and faculties will make different forms of evidence more or less persuasive, creating particular forms of doubt.

The chapters collected here show the different ways in which doubt, and attempts to manage that doubt, are materialized and made available to the senses. Inductive reason requires that otherwise ungraspable processes are given a material form, so that they can be assessed and evaluated. In her chapter comparing temple consultations and Indian criminal trials, for example, Berti shows how doubt is quite literarily inscribed into the court transcript. The judge can direct the recording of evidence by the stenographer, as it is translated into English, in such a way as to open up or close down questions about the veracity of the evidence being presented by a witness. The written text then becomes the formal basis for the judicial decision. In Bouillier's discussion of French criminal trials she shows how the formal presentation of physical evidence, on a table at the front of the court, is given particular judicial weight, even if this is ultimately overcome by other forms of testimony and documentation. In his chapter on the Danish asylum system, Whyte argues that documents are the most persuasive forms of evidence for someone seeking refugee status. Oral testimony is questioned and suspected, but birth certificates and arrest warrants, for example, can help overcome the doubts raised about particular claimants. Whyte goes so far as to call such documents 'fetishes', as they obscure the conditions of their own production and take on a uniquely authoritative force.

Ritual processes can also see doubt made manifest in material form in order to become persuasive. In the part of her chapter that concerns temple consultations, Berti shows, for example, how mediums use stones in order to make the possible causes of misfortune physically present. It is only once the stones have been associated with particular causes that the medium can choose between them. Similarly, in her chapter on Taiwanese horoscopes Homola shows how paper grids are a crucial part of the divinatory process. Tarabout also shows how Indian astrologers use particular objects, such as rice, betel leaves, coins and rings, in order to materialize the otherwise unknown will of the deity. The surfaces through which doubt takes shape though do not necessarily need to take on material form. As Budniok shows in his chapter, Ghanaian judges can seek to dispel or at least manage doubt through their mastery of the correct linguistic forms. Speaking well, formally and eloquently in court can go some way to putting to one side the question marks about judicial integrity. Whether it takes on verbal or physical forms though, doubt is often mediated through aesthetic forms and judgments.

The otherwise unseen processes about which we have doubts are given a material presence through words, documents or betel leaves, for example, allowing us to grasp the otherwise unperceivable and thereby come to judgment. Yet, at the same time, questions remain as to how and why these processes take the particular forms they do, and whether such forms are ultimately revealing or deceiving.

Doubt though is never entirely a rational issue. It is also, often, emotional. Doubt can nag and cause unease. Doubt can be as much physical as mental. We do not simply rationally engage with the evidence of our senses, but also have strong emotional feelings about them. The assessment of the fragments of evidence upon which we make judgments can be as much aesthetic as it is rational. The phrase used by Homola in her chapter, 'a sense of truth', has its twin in 'a sense of doubt'. The chapters here show how law may be technical and procedural, but it is also at the same time, perhaps necessarily so, an affective process. In her chapter in this volume, Kobelinsky shows how decisions about whether or not to grant refugee status are often justified through the language of emotional identification. Judges openly speak about how they admire or hold some applicants in high esteem. Similarly Bouillier describes in her contribution how French criminal juries are instructed to refer to their 'inner feelings' and 'most intimate convictions'.

The combination of the technical and the emotional points to what Elizabeth Povinelli (2002) has referred to as the split between moral sense and reason. On the one hand we have a way of knowing, and doubting, that privileges apparently rational critical discourse. On the other hand we have a way of knowing, and doubting, that prioritizes embodied moral intuition. Here let's return one last time to Caravaggio and his Doubting Thomas. As Glenn Most (2005) argues, in the end Thomas cannot simply rationally justify his renewed faith. Instead, it is a visceral experience, caught up not only in the physicality of flesh. Alongside the empirical demand to see for himself is an emotional response. What is more Thomas demanded empirical verification for a process that itself was supposed to be miraculous. What is important though is that Thomas did not collapse into scepticism, but was able to find a way to move through and overcome his doubt. We do not have to be Christians to recognize that between sense and sensibility, the management of doubt is central to our social and cultural lives. We do not know what other people are thinking, or what they might do in the future, but we continue to make friends and to place our trust in the good intentions of strangers. Doubt does not stop us from living, but is the very condition of the way we live.

References

Arendt, Hannah (1958) *The Human Condition*, Chicago: University of Chicago Press.

Bloch, Maurice (2008) 'Truth and sight: generalizing without universalizing', *Journal of the Royal Anthropological Institute* 14: S22–32.

Cavell, Stanley (1988) *In Quest of the Ordinary*, Chicago: University of Chicago Press.

Das, Veena (1998) 'Wittgenstein and anthropology', *Annual Review of Anthropology* 27: 171–95.

Dewey, John (1934) *A Common Faith*, New Haven, CT: Yale University Press.
Gell, Alfred (1995) 'The language of the forest: landscape and phonological iconism in Umeda', in *The Anthropology of Landscape: Perspectives on Place and Space*, ed. Eric Hirsch and Michael O'Hanlon, Oxford: Oxford University Press, pp. 232–54.
Guyer, Jane (2013) '"The quickening of the unknown": epistemologies of surprise in anthropology (The Munro Lecture, 2013)', *HAU: Journal of Ethnographic Theory* 3(3): 283–307.
Handelman, Don (1987) 'For an uncertain anthropology', in *Cultural Anthropology: A Perspective on the Human Condition*, ed. Emily Schultz and Robert Lavenda, St Paul, MN: West, pp. 310–11.
Jay, Martin (1994) *Downcast Eyes: The Denigration of Vision in Twentieth-Century French Thought*, Berkeley: University of California Press.
MacGregor, Geddes (1989) 'Doubt and belief', in *The Encyclopedia of Religion*, ed. Mircea Eliade, New York: Macmillan, pp. 1456–64.
Most, Glen W. (2005) *Doubting Thomas*, Cambridge, MA: Harvard University Press.
Pelkmans, Mathijs (2013) 'Outline for an ethnography of doubt', in *Ethnographies of Doubt: Faith and Uncertainty in Contemporary Societies*, ed. Mathijs Pelkmans, London: I.B. Tauris, 1–44.
Povinelli, Elizabeth A. (2002) *The Cunning of Recognition: Indigenous Alterities and the Making of Australian Multiculturalism*, Durham, NC: Duke University Press.
Segal, Lotte Buch (forthcoming) 'Disembodied conjugality', in *Wording the World: Veena Das and the Scenes of Inheritance*, ed. Roma Chatterji, New York. Fordham Press.
Weber, Max (2013 [1904–1905]) *The Protestant Ethic and the Spirit of Capitalism*, trans. Stephen Kalberg, Abingdon: Routledge.
Wittgenstein, Ludwig (1972) *On Certainty*, trans. Denis Paul and G.E.M. Anscombe, New York. Harper & Row.

Index